ALSO BY JEFFREY EISNER

The Step-by-Step Instant Pot Cookbook

*The Lighter Step-by-Step
Instant Pot Cookbook*

*The Simple Comforts Step-by-Step
Instant Pot Cookbook*

Super Shortcut Instant Pot

Simple, Speedy & Sensational Recipes with <u>Photos</u> of Every Step

PASTABILITIES

The Ultimate STEP-BY-STEP Pasta Cookbook

JEFFREY EISNER

Photography by Aleksey Zozulya

VORACIOUS

Little, Brown and Company
NEW YORK / BOSTON / LONDON

Voracious / Little, Brown and Company
Hachette Book Group
1290 Avenue of the Americas, New York, NY 10104
voraciousbooks.com

First Edition: September 2024

Voracious is an imprint of Little, Brown and Company, a division of Hachette Book Group, Inc. The Voracious name and logo are trademarks of Hachette Book Group, Inc.

The publisher is not responsible for websites (or their content) that are not owned by the publisher.

The Hachette Speakers Bureau provides a wide range of authors for speaking events. To find out more, go to hachettespeakersbureau.com or email hachettespeakers@hbgusa.com.

Little, Brown and Company books may be purchased in bulk for business, educational, or promotional use. For information, please contact your local bookseller or the Hachette Book Group Special Markets Department at special.markets@hbgusa.com.

Photographs by Aleksey Zozulya
Food styling by Andy Liang
Interior design by Laura Palese

ISBN 9780316572491
LCCN 2023949278

10 9 8 7 6 5 4 3 2 1

RRD-APS

Printed in China

I PROMISE THAT THE RECIPES IN THIS BOOK ARE:

1. Easy.

2. Quick.

3. Fun.

4. Accessible.

5. Affordable.

6. Loaded with clear instructions and pretty pictures to reassure you that you've got this.

7. Completely devoid of AI.

8. ABSO-FRICKIN-LUTELY DELICIOUS.

—JEFFREY

Contents

Sea 172

Stir-Fry 188

Al Forno 206

GF+ As the introduction states, while I use specific pastas for each recipe, you can use any form of pasta you choose—including gluten-free. And I often tell you how to make a recipe's sauce gluten-free. As such, I thought it would be redundant to show the logo on each recipe, but rather give you full control as needed.

DF Dairy-Free
V Vegetarian
VN Vegan
\+ Compliant with Modifications

One Pot 234

Souper Zuppa 258

Pasta Salads 284

INTRODUCTION

From One Amateur Cook to Another

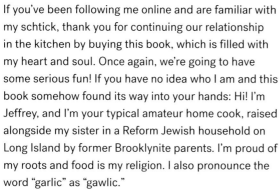

If you've been following me online and are familiar with my schtick, thank you for continuing our relationship in the kitchen by buying this book, which is filled with my heart and soul. Once again, we're going to have some serious fun! If you have no idea who I am and this book somehow found its way into your hands: Hi! I'm Jeffrey, and I'm your typical amateur home cook, raised alongside my sister in a Reform Jewish household on Long Island by former Brooklynite parents. I'm proud of my roots and food is my religion. I also pronounce the word "garlic" as "gawlic."

Now, I'm not kidding when I tell you I march to the beat of my own drum—especially in the kitchen. When I was somehow lucky enough to be chosen to appear on the Food Network in 2019, on their inaugural Hanukkah competition cooking show, I'm the guy who had the other contestants likely thinking, "So who's *this* yutz?" as I did my thing. I'm basically a MacGyver in the kitchen. I open the cupboards and pantry, do a quick inventory, and experiment. I happen to have a passion and knack for making serious flavors come to life with the simplest of ingredients. And, while I greatly respect and admire those who are formally trained in the culinary arts, I generally don't follow any rules. I make up my own techniques and when I find ways to achieve a lip-smackin' dish in the easiest way possible that works, I bang my gavel and toss my recipe out into the world.

Don't get me wrong, I am far from perfect. I cook in ill-fitting clothes, have messy hair when I do, and can be a huge klutz with many blunders along the way—something about being human. But when I fail, I learn and I grow and I get better. In short, failures pave the way for success, and, without some of my own, this book would not have been pasta-ble.

Everything Is Pasta-ble

The time has come for a new chapter (or, a new book) in my cooking journey and to take you along for the ride.

After devoting close to a decade of my life to obsessively and lovingly creating my orange, blue, yellow, and green Instant Pot cookbooks, now commonly referred to as "The Rainbow Collection," I'd been asking myself, "Where do I go from here?" While I'll forever love the Instant Pot for its versatility and convenience, I realized not everyone had the passion (or courage) to use one. Plus, I was ready for a bit of a cooking pivot to make more use of what's available to me. Nearly all of us have a stove and oven in our kitchens already, so why not make some simple use out of them?

If there's anything I've learned over the past seven years while holding this unexpected title of "food blogger," it's that people *want* to learn how to cook a meal. It makes them feel special, needed, and/or accomplished to put a meal on the table for family, friends, or just themselves. The problem is, too many cookbooks require lots of one's precious time and intimidating, "fancy" (aka pricey and/or hard-to-find) ingredients that often yield discouraging results. The cookbook user either spends a lot of time and money on something that ends up botched and/or disappointing, or they don't even bother with the recipe in the first place.

From getting to know you, my audience, both through social media engagements and in-person book signings (or being recognized in Costco or while walking my Norwich terrier, Banjo), I've found that it's critical to listen to what you all want and offer up what you're asking for. I've found my readers want easy, quick, and non-fancy recipes to make restaurant-quality meals that won't break the bank or cause a breakdown, regardless of the cooking method. And ease and satisfaction are my game, and exactly what I'm taking with me into this next chapter of my recipe writing career.

This fifth book of mine is entirely focused on a genre of food that is universally loved. Recipes that are loaded with meat, chicken, seafood, or that are simply vegetarian or vegan. Dishes that range from comforting and decadent to light and bright. A book where there's something for everyone. In case you hadn't guessed by now (I mean, come on, the cover gave it away), **this book is about all things PASTA!**

Now, there's more pasta cookbooks out there than there are ways to make meatballs. What sets this one apart from the rest?

Pastabilities, the fun-with-a-pun title of this book, doesn't lie. You'll be quickly making some of the most magnificent pasta dishes you've ever eaten, and, folks, it just doesn't get any easier than these recipes, both to follow *and* to make. There are absolutely zero fancy techniques, the recipes are completely foolproof, and no previous cooking skills are required to make any of these noodly gems.

Before I go on, **I know what you may already be thinking: "Oh, cute. This Jewish guy from *Lawng Eyelund* thinks he's going to try and teach me about pasta."** And I totally get it and don't blame you a bit if your brow is raised. But it's like the phrase I coined about Jews and Italians: "Same behavior, different savior." Besides, this Jewish guy from Long Island is *obsessed* with and *passionate* about pasta. I have just one favor to ask of you: Start with my Cacio e Pepe Americano (page 122). From there, I think I'll gain your trust and you'll be excited to try another recipe and then another and another, ultimately convincing you that this book will earn a spot on your kitchen counter only to eventually be covered in splatters of oil and dried particles of food from many a meal ago.

Here are a few key reasons why this book is a perfect fit for the no-fuss, sometimes intimidated, and possibly even lazy home cook, and for those who just love easy cooking in general.

Mission: It's Pasta-ble

In a world where prices always seem to be on the rise, one thing at the market that consistently remains budget-friendly is pasta. Tomato products and jarred sauces can also often be found on the cheap and are often on sale.

So, in keeping with my signature, user-friendly cooking instructions, the mission of this book is to show folks how to create the easiest, quickest, and tastiest of pasta dishes with no more than **ONE pot** (to boil the pasta) **and ONE pan** (to cook the sauce), featuring affordable and accessible ingredients, on any stovetop. Some recipes may also call for a casserole dish or lasagna tray if they're baked (i.e., al forno style), but that's as far as we go here.

It really pleases me to say that the recipes in this book aren't only respectful of your time and light on your wallet but are also abundant on your plate and palate.

Classic & Inventive Recipes

While I can devour Italian pasta dishes three times a day, every day, this book is going to diversify pasta. That means I'm going to focus on various cultures that feature noodles, or however I'm inspired to create a pasta that I feel works.

Of course, I'll be taking you on a journey focusing on the Italian classics we all know and love such as Spaghetti & Meatballs (page 54), Penne alla Vodka (page 47), Bucatini Carbonara (page 72), and a ton more. But I'll also be taking you on a trip to other regions where we'll make noodly treasures such as Asian stir-fry dishes (page 188), Jewish Kasha Varnishkes (page 165), and a Polish Haluski (page 70). Then, I'll take it a step further with new creations from my wild mind like Sour Cream & Cheddar Chicken Twists (page 104), Croque Monsieur (or Madame) Macaroni (page 61), and a one-pot Philly Cheesesteak Pasta (page 236), to name a few.

And if *that* wasn't enough, I'm also giving you chapters on soup (because pasta is present in many of them), one-pot recipes (if you really want things one-and-done), and pasta salads (because salads are more fun with carbs). Spanning inspiration from Italian, North and South American, Western and Eastern European, and Asian fare, this book literally has it all and the pastabilities are boundless.

What You See Is What You Get

Within these pages, I provide **color step-by-step photos as well as a final shot of what each and every dish should look like alongside very simple instructions on how to get there**—a rarity in most cookbooks. Most cookbooks don't show a finished shot of every dish. Would you make a recipe where you don't see a picture of the final product? (I won't.) How would you know if your final dish turned out the way it should if you have nothing to compare it to? (You wouldn't.) Breathe a sigh of relief here because not only will you see the final product of every recipe, you'll also be able to make sure that what you're doing along the way is correct by comparing it to the photos accompanying every step.

By the way, those photos are the real deal. Every step-by-step photo shows me genuinely cooking each recipe in my own home (those are my hands in the photos—so I guess that now makes me a professional hand model, joining the ranks of fine upstanding citizens like George Costanza). And the final shots for every recipe (also known as "hero shots") were quickly plated and styled by my genius and super-fun food stylist, Andy, and captured by my brilliant and experimental photographer, Aleksey, minutes after each dish was finished. There is no trickery in these pictures where the pasta is actually Play-Doh and/or sprayed with weird chemicals to enhance the look. **What you see in these photos is exactly what was cooked by a sloppy yours truly.**

Cutting Down Time, Work, and Stress

Now, unlike many other pasta cookbooks, this book ensures one thing: **There is no homemade pasta required in any of the recipes.** In fact, I never have you make your own pasta at all! Sure, it could be a fun activity for a rainy day or a date night, but the truth is making your own pasta is super messy and time-consuming, requires special flour and often a pasta maker, yields a dough with little room for error, and is just not as budget-friendly and convenient as what you can just get at the market. It's a huge learning curve and something I recommend for more skilled home cooks rather than the busy person who wants to put a quick and delicious dinner on the table. I'm not saying you *can't* make your own pasta, be it from your own recipe or another one you enjoy, but, remember, this is a book focused on two things: simplicity and speed.

Therefore, **every recipe in this book requires only a simple, accessible boxed or refrigerated (or even frozen) pasta** and features a universal stovetop method for cooking, making the recipes remarkably easy to follow.

Just one thing to bear in mind: There are a zillion and one ways to achieve many recipes by the same name. Sure, Bolognese (page 44) is a hugely popular pasta dish, but iterations of it run the gamut. I've had many a Bolognese and no two have ever tasted identical. In a nutshell, the recipes in this book are strictly my takes on them all. So, if you read a recipe and find it's not how your grandparents personally make it, I kindly ask that you refrain from chasing me with your rolling pins. As I said before, give one a shot and you just may be hooked. At the end of the day, the purpose of this book is to show you that making a satisfying pasta dish isn't a bore or a chore.

Pastabilities & Principles

I want to be crystal clear in case I haven't been already: **Cooking from this book should not only yield gourmet results without being fancy to get there, but it should also be STRESS-FREE and even FUN!** Remember, in the end you're just working with various forms of pasta, vegetables, proteins, and dairy where you boil the pasta, make a sauce, and then marry the two. It's not the end of the world if something should slip up. And to give you even more confidence, making a sauce is usually foolproof. You can always add a little more of this or a little less of that. And, although stranger things have happened, if you mess up the boiling of the pasta for whatever reason, luckily, it's one of the most affordable things you can get at the market. Just boil more!

Before we dive into the recipes, I want to briefly explain a few things that will help you immensely in your pasta-cooking journey.

Breaking Down a Recipe

Before starting a recipe, I strongly suggest reading it through so everything is crystal clear to you. The following information will help.

Dietary Lifestyles: In the heading of each recipe, the circular icons indicate which dietary lifestyle the recipe is compliant with (Dairy-Free, Vegetarian, and/or Vegan).

Timing: Since practically every recipe in this book celebrates the holy matrimony of pasta and sauce, timing the cooking so both are done at around the same time is the ideal way to put a quick and easy pasta meal on the table. Those cook time numbers will help you do that, especially if you choose to use a different pasta than I suggest.

Additionally, the timing bar includes the general prep time, suggested pasta cook time, and sauce cook time, as well as timing for any other steps, be it baking or cooking a protein. All close approximations, of course.

Steps: Every step indicates when a certain action happens, be it heating the water for the pasta, starting the sauce, cooking the pasta, or that final step of marrying the pasta to the sauce.

 JEFF'S TIPS When you see the Jeff's Tips icon within each recipe, read them. They will come in very handy.

Mise en Place

Every recipe in this book lists the ingredients in the order they're used. To cut down on any chaos or stress, I cannot recommend strongly enough to do what the French call "mise en place." This means prepping all your ingredients and lining them up in the order they'll be used *before* beginning a recipe's cooking process. Do veggies need to be peeled and chopped? Do it. Measure out all your liquids and seasonings with the proper measuring utensils. Having everything ready to roll before you turn on the stove is truly the way to the most successful and worry-free cooking experience.

You've Got Pastabilities

You'll notice that whenever a pasta is called for in a recipe, I list and show the pasta I used when I made the dish. While these are my suggested pastas to accentuate the recipe's sauce, they are just that: *suggestions.*

Let's say the recipe calls for orecchiette but you don't have any and don't feel like running out to buy a box. Yet you have a box of medium shells. Problem solved—use the shells! Just cook them for the time the box suggests for al dente (which is Italian and means "to the tooth").

See page 18 for a detailed explanation of sauce-to-pasta timing ratios when subbing a different pasta for the one suggested. And, for a more in-depth look at a multitude of pastas, check out the handy Pasta Glossary on page 30.

The Evolution of Pasta

The most common dried pastas on the market are made from semolina (aka durum wheat) flour and are what I use in these recipes, but you are most definitely not limited to using that type. While it once may have been considered "im-pasta-ble," pasta has come a long way in recent years with so many more varieties offered than the standard semolina. Pasta has evolved into whole wheat, chickpea, lentil, gluten-free, and other types of nontraditional varieties. I realize that everyone makes/has different lifestyle choices and/or restrictions, or simply may want to eat lighter. As such, most every recipe in this book is designed for you to use with any pasta you wish (see Note). Again, just follow the box's cooking instructions and make sure you account for the pasta cook time when figuring out when to start cooking the pasta, since each recipe's suggested pasta is timed to be done with the sauce. From there, you're good to go.

NOTE: The only chapter where alternate pastas, other than the gluten-free and whole wheat varieties, may have issues is the One Pot chapter (page 234). This is because you don't drain the pasta of the cooking liquid so it could become mush. And if using gluten-free options in those chapters, cook the pasta for 2 minutes less than the al dente time the box specifies.

Boiling Pasta

Pasta is cooked using (usually) two things: water and salt. As each recipe states, I strongly suggest using an 8-quart pot and filling it only halfway with hot tap water to boil your pasta (so 4 quarts). While using hot water from the faucet is by no means critical, it will significantly speed up the time it takes to bring the pot to a boil. Once you bring the water to a rolling boil over high heat and add your pasta, reduce the heat to medium and keep the pot uncovered. Not only will your pasta still cook perfectly, it will also avoid any starchy, salty overbubbling onto your stovetop (I find this is much more trusty than the wooden-spoon-over-the-pot method). While your pasta cooks and you're working on the sauce, take a moment to stir the pasta every so often, making sure no pieces are stuck to the bottom of the pot or to each other and everything is nice and liberated as the pasta cooks in the hot water. Also, unless instructed otherwise (don't worry, I'll let you know—like in the One Pot chapter, page 234), always keep the pot uncovered while boiling your pasta.

And as for giving that naked pasta a bit of flavor? My general rule is to add 1 tablespoon of any salt you enjoy per 4 quarts of water (I use iodized salt, but kosher, garlic salt, or seasoned salt will work nicely). For recipes that call for reserving some pasta water, and to enhance your dish with even more hints of flavor, you can also absolutely use a bouillon base to season the pasta water, such as 1 to 2 teaspoons of any variety of Better Than Bouillon (see page 25). However, **avoid adding olive oil to the boiling water**. Not only is it expensive and should only be used when the pasta is done cooking, but it is prone to preventing the sauce from sticking to the pasta. And Sophia Petrillo would never approve.

Again, as each recipe states, when boiling your pasta I suggest using the al dente cook time on the package since the final step of marrying the pasta with the sauce continues to cook the pasta, so we don't want it to be overcooked. Setting a timer the moment the pasta hits the water will ensure smooth sailing.

Draining Pasta and the Magic of Pasta Water

Hold on there, pardnuh. **Before draining your pasta in a colander in the sink, check to see if the recipe calls for you to reserve the pasta water!** The reason for this is that while the pasta is boiling in the water, it releases a good amount of its starch into it. When you reserve some water to add to a sauce in the final steps *if and when instructed to do so*, you're reserving a flavorful thickening agent that really brings the pasta and sauce together nicely as they rest. It also ensures that the sauce will cling to the pasta. In fact, even if a recipe *doesn't* call for you to reserve pasta water, feel free to reserve a cup or two just in case you want to use some to thin a sauce out if it's a tad too thick for your liking.

Now while I always drain my pasta in a colander after reserving any pasta water, some other cooks would argue to not drain it, but rather transfer the pasta directly from the pot to the sauce using tongs or a slotted spoon. You can do this, but it takes more time, work, and will likely guarantee splatters of super hot water dripping off the pasta and onto the stove or counter and possibly yourself. I personally don't find it necessary at all and much prefer reserving some pasta water and then draining the pasta in a colander.

And while it may seem like the natural thing to do, unless otherwise instructed, try not to run water over your pasta in the colander. Doing so removes the starch from the pasta, which helps the sauce cling to the pasta and thickens the sauce a bit. The big exceptions to this rule are pastas cooked for cold pasta salads, as rinsing cools down the pasta, and rice noodles, as they are starch-free and should be kept wet in a colander to avoid drying out (which happens much quicker than with common semolina-based pasta).

What Saucery Is This?

When it comes to classic Italian sauces, there are three types of bases: herb-seasoned oil, broth, and/or wine (clear to green); cream (white); and tomato (red). These also happen to be the same colors of the Italian flag. Coincidence? You decide. But make no mistake, the sky is the limit when it comes to how they can be built upon and doctored up, creating a countless number of sauce options, from meat-filled carnivorous favorites to vegetable purees for vegan/vegetarian treatments. In fact, all three types of sauces can be

TO LID OR NOT TO LID

My general rule is to rarely cover the pot while a sauce is cooking, especially if it needs to reduce. For that to happen, the steam needs to escape, leading to evaporation so the sauce can thicken properly and become more flavorful in the process. (That said, it's always wise to keep a lid on your pan when the heat is turned to low or turned off if the sauce is done and you're waiting for the pasta to finish cooking before marrying the two.) However, the recipe will be clear whenever you need to add a lid to the pan during the cooking process (such as while simmering the meat in my Sunday Sauce, page 56, while steaming the mussels and clams in Frutti di Mare, page 176, or the One Pot chapter, page 234).

married into one, like in my Pasta Italia recipe (page 68)!

The main thing I love about sauces (other than how they taste) is that while they're super varied and simple to make, the attributes don't stop there. Here are just a couple other key reasons making a sauce makes you feel more confident and accomplished in the kitchen.

THEY'RE FORGIVING

While the recipes in this book are designed to be foolproof, we're only human and some people can get side-tracked and scramble a recipe's instructions. But fret not! A sauce can almost always be saved if you make an error. Did you add too much cream or wine, making it a bit thinner than you'd like? Just let it simmer until it reduces. Or for a quick fix, stir or whisk in some grated/shredded cheese, flour, or a cornstarch slurry (equal parts cornstarch and cold water that are mixed together in a separate bowl, usually 1 to 2 tablespoons each). Or did you overseason the sauce? Simply add more dairy, pasta water, or broth to thin it out some and dilute the seasoning.

THEY GO BEYOND PASTAS

The sauces within each recipe of this book aren't limited to pasta! They can be for *anything* that requires a sauce. Just skip the pasta steps and serve the sauce over chicken, meat, seafood, rice, grains and/or veggies!

Speaking of sauces, let's discuss your key basics.

Red Sauces

Generally, a red sauce's base is achieved by sautéing some onion and garlic in olive oil, then adding tomatoes (usually a variety of canned ones or whole or halved cherry/grape ones). The tomatoes you use will have an impact on the sauce's flavor, so if you want it to be the best it can be, use the San Marzano varieties.

Making a red sauce (or "gravy" as many of my Italian friends refer to it) is practically the equivalent of establishing a family's crest—they're all unique with their own character. But for the sake of simplicity, we'll focus on the two most common types of tomato-based sauces.

MARINARA (page 40)

A marinara is the most common tomato-based sauce and usually made with canned crushed or whole peeled tomatoes (again, San Marzano tomatoes will give you the most premium results). While the sauce is generally medium-thick in consistency, the texture is on the smoother side and seasoned with basics like (but not limited to) Italian seasoning and salt and pepper, or a mix of goodies such as fresh basil leaves (or dried basil), oregano, sugar, garlic powder, onion powder, and/or grated Parmesan or Pecorino Romano cheeses. It is, simply put, to die for.

POMODORO (page 130)

A pomodoro is more of a whole tomato situation (I use cherry or grape tomatoes of any color, although red is the most common), with the tomatoes sautéed in olive oil with garlic until they burst and their juices seep into the mixture to form a sauce, making it slightly chunky and textured with the skins of the burst tomatoes. This isn't a super saucy situation like a deep marinara, but rather refreshingly light, sweet, and savory instead. It can also be doctored up with any spices and seasonings you enjoy.

Whichever red sauce you go for, it is perfectly acceptable to add chicken, pork, beef, or seafood.

Since tomatoes are acidic, which can lead some people to a bitter and heartburn-prone experience, you can always temper the acidity by adding a few sprinkles of baking soda. To get a little scientific, this is because it's alkaline and helps balance out the acid.

The best way to thicken a tomato-based red sauce is with some tomato paste (a few tablespoons or up to a 6-ounce can should do the trick, depending on how many tomatoes you're using). Once added to a simmering red sauce, it will meld into the sauce as it simmers down, thickening it significantly.

Cream Sauces

While simple to make, cream sauces are a bit more of a learning curve than red sauces because you need to find the proper consistency and thickness for the type of the cream sauce desired.

Some of my recipes that feature cream sauces have flour incorporated into the fat (butter or oil), forming what the French call a "roux" (pronounced "roo"), before adding a generous amount of milk, half-and-half, or heavy cream for extra rich and thick creaminess—which makes a French sauce called "béchamel" (pronounced "BAY-shuh-mel"). Some other cream sauces leave the flour out and favor broth, wine, or tomatoes for a more complex, yet thinner sauce.

Because I always find it helpful, I want to share the differences between **three classic creamy sauces:** Alfredo, Carbonara, and Cacio e Pepe.

ALFREDO (page 42)

This may well be the holy grail of cream sauces. In Italy, this sauce generally consists of Italian butter, Parmesan cheese, and pasta water. But in America, many cooks swap the pasta water for cream (as I do).

CARBONARA (page 72)

By most standards, this sauce doesn't use cream and, although I add it in my Instant Pot version, I don't in this book's. Carbonara's main ingredients are eggs, Parmesan and/or Pecorino Romano, pasta water, and either diced pancetta, guanciale, or bacon (and its oils). However, like Alfredo, it is quite a creamy sauce due to the fusing of these four key ingredients.

CACIO E PEPE

Classically, this Roman dish combines no more than pasta water, Pecorino Romano, and pepper. No cream or butter, but the mix of the cheese and water gives it a creamy consistency. However, to give it my own spin, I took advantage of the word *cacio* (it means "cheese" in Italian) and used an enticing combo of sharp white Cheddar and white American cheese for my Cacio e Pepe Americano (page 122).

Should you wish to experiment on your own, **I offer up two recipes (pages 16 and 17) for three different varieties of cream sauce.** Of course, feel free to adjust them as you see fit!

A FEW FINAL NOTES ON CREAM SAUCES:

- Half-and-half or even whole milk are acceptable substitutes for heavy cream, but only if you are using flour in the sauce as well as an equal amount of fat (butter or olive oil). If there's no flour in the sauce, you should use heavy cream for it to thicken properly.

- **To make it extra creamy,** add reserved pasta water or cream in ¼-cup increments (until you're happy) and stir until combined into the pasta before serving.

- If you have leftovers, chances are your sauce is going to get super thick or even get absorbed into the pasta—especially when cooled in the fridge. To reheat a cream sauce and keep it creamy, add some additional cream, half-and-half, or milk when microwaving, stirring every 30 seconds or so, to reconstitute it.

- And if you're gluten-free and cannot tolerate all-purpose flour, check out The More You Know (page 18).

Jarred Sauces

Obviously, every recipe in this book instructs you how to make your own sauce, or refers you to another recipe's sauce. However, if you'd rather use a jarred sauce to cut down on time or for convenience, be my guest! As much as I adore my marinara sauce (page 40) and keep a few batches on hand (frozen or otherwise), I do this more often than not as it saves time and money, and adds major convenience. My absolute personal favorite brands are Rao's and Victoria for Alfredo, marinara, and vodka sauces, and Costco's Kirkland Signature brand or Rana for pesto—just get a refrigerated pesto sauce versus a shelved one. There is a big difference in quality.

Classic Béchamel
(with Mornay Option)

This simple French-style cream sauce is made only of butter, flour, milk, and a few basic seasonings. Adding cheese turns the béchamel into a Mornay sauce, which is the common base for many a mac & cheese. This recipe is perfect for 1 pound of pasta.

8 tablespoons (1 stick) salted butter

¼ cup all-purpose flour (see Jeff's Tip)

4 cups whole milk or half-and-half

1 teaspoon salt, plus more to taste

½ teaspoon pepper, plus more to taste

¼ teaspoon nutmeg

OPTIONAL MORNAY SAUCE

1–4 cups (4–16 ounces) shredded melty cheese of your choice (like Cheddar, American, Monterey Jack, pepper Jack, mozzarella, Swiss, or a Mexican blend)

¼–½ cup grated Parmesan cheese

1. Melt the butter in a 4.5- to 5-quart sauté pan over medium heat. Add the flour and whisk until the color is a light and toasty brown (about the color of peanut butter), 1–2 minutes. Ooh! You've just made what's called a roux!

2. While whisking, slowly add the milk or half-and-half to the pan. Increase the heat to medium-high and bring to a light boil. Once bubbling, reduce the heat to medium-low and simmer and whisk for 3–5 minutes, until the sauce thickens and coats the back of a spoon.

3. Stir the salt, pepper, and nutmeg into the sauce. Taste and adjust seasonings to taste. Congrats! You just made a béchamel sauce!

BÉCHAMEL

MORNAY

4. If making a Mornay sauce, add the cheeses and stir until combined into the sauce. Start with 1 cup (4 ounces) shredded cheese and ¼ cup Parmesan. You can always add more to your liking while stirring. This will adjust both the taste and thickness of the sauce.

5. Turn the heat off. Add 1 pound of any pre-cooked pasta to the sauté pan with the sauce and toss until combined.

JEFF'S TIP

I personally feel this is the perfect béchamel consistency, but for a thicker one, whisk up to an additional ¼ cup flour (1 tablespoon at a time) into the milk or half-and-half in Step 2 until thickened to your liking. Everything else remains the same. And if you decide it's too thick, simply whisk in more milk until thinned out to your heart's content.

Non-Béchamel Garlic Cream Sauce

2 tablespoons (¼ stick) salted butter

3 cloves garlic, minced or pressed

½ cup liquid of choice (any combo of broth, dry wine, and reserved pasta water)

2 cups heavy cream

Seasonings according to taste (see Jeff's Tip)

If you want a thinner cream base sauce that doesn't employ a roux for thickening, and would like an element of additional flavor tones, I have found a most foolproof and incredibly easy method.

This recipe will work perfectly for 1 pound of pasta, cooked separately, reserving 1 cup of pasta water (see Step 5).

1. Melt the butter in a 4.5- to 5-quart sauté pan over medium heat. Add the garlic and sauté for about 2 minutes, until lightly browned.

2. Add the liquid of choice and bring to a bubble for 1 minute.

3. Add the cream and any seasonings (**see Jeff's Tip**), increase the heat to medium-high, and bring to a light boil.

4. Reduce the heat to medium and simmer for 5–8 minutes, stirring or whisking frequently, until the sauce is thickened up a bit and decently coats the back of a spoon. (**NOTE:** The longer the sauce simmers, the thicker it will get.)

5. Turn the heat off. Add 1 pound of any cooked pasta and toss until combined. (**NOTE:** Feel free to add reserved pasta water in ¼-cup increments for an even creamier sauce or double the sauce ingredients if you want it super saucy.)

JEFF'S TIP For the seasonings, I suggest starting with ½ teaspoon each of salt, pepper, oregano, Italian seasoning, garlic powder, and/or onion powder. You can always add more to taste as well as any other seasonings you wish.

The More You Know

This is the book's little FAQ section, where I address the most common of queries (or at least do my best to anticipate them).

What do I start with first, the pasta or the sauce?

Like the chicken or the egg, there is always the question of what comes first: cooking the pasta or the sauce. And it's an excellent question. Ideally, the goal is for the sauce and pasta to be timed so they are done at the same time, or as close to each other as possible, and that's how the recipes in this book are designed. Therefore, within the recipe steps, where appropriate, I let you know precisely when you should heat the water, start the sauce, and cook the pasta. This way, their completed cook times will be as close as possible.

Often, the first step is to heat the water for the pasta, then add the pasta a few steps later; or to cook the pasta in the first step as soon as the water is boiling. If cooking the pasta a few steps later, you can begin the sauce (or sauté the protein) while the pasta water is coming to a boil to save time. If you reach the pasta cooking step before the water is boiling, simply pause your sauce process by turning off the heat and covering the sauté pan with a lid. Then, once the water is boiling, add the pasta and resume the recipe as written.

As a general rule, it's better for the sauce to be done before the pasta. It's fine if a pasta sits in a colander undisturbed for 3 minutes or so after it's done. But if it sits too long it can begin to dry out and harden. While you can rinse the pasta with cold water while shaking it in the colander to revive it and keep it fresh, that's frowned upon because it removes the starch, which is a great agent for helping the sauce cling to the pasta when tossed together. (But if the pasta is done way ahead of the sauce, rinsing it under cold water and shaking it so it doesn't stick and dry out is your best bet.) But it is better if the sauce is done first, because you can turn the heat down to low (or turn it off completely) and cover the pan to keep the sauce warm until the pasta is ready to be married to it.

I really want to make that recipe, but either I can't find the pasta you're suggesting or I feel like using what I already have in the house. Can I still make it?

In short, *of course*! So here's the scoop. Although each recipe is tailored to the type of pasta I suggest, you can absolutely use a different one. If I call for penne, which takes 10-ish minutes to cook, but you want to use a refrigerated tortellini that takes 4-ish minutes, go ahead! But keep in mind that it might change when you should start cooking the pasta. The simple solution is to take a look at how long the sauce takes in the timing bar, and start cooking the pasta 4 minutes before the sauce is set to be done. To make things even simpler, refer to the Pasta Glossary (page 30) and see what other pastas cook around the same time as the one I suggest and the timing will still be spot-on as written! So if you can't find mafaldine, try spaghetti or fettuccine as their cook times (and pasta genre) are very similar.

What does cooking pasta "al dente" mean?

"Al dente" is Italian for "to the tooth." This means the pasta will have a firmer bite when removed from the water but will be practically fully cooked. It should still have some bite to it because it will continue to cook once married to a heated sauce. This ensures the pasta will be *perfectly* cooked once served, instead of potentially mushy and overdone.

That said, it's always suggested you taste the pasta before draining it to make sure it's not too underdone. But just make sure you don't forget about it and let it go past the suggested cooking time on the box. Otherwise, you'll end up with overdone, mushy pasta and that's no fun at all. Setting a timer the moment the pasta hits the water will prevent this.

Every pasta brand will give you different times for cooking any type of pasta (so Ronzoni penne may have a different cooking time than De Cecco penne). Just be sure to follow the box's instructions for the al dente cook time. It's that simple!

Does it matter which pasta brand I use?

No. Just use any brand you prefer—and that can mean a fancy brand imported from Italy (Colavita, Anna, Garofalo, and Rummo are typical), a common brand sold in your country (Ronzoni, Barilla, De Cecco, San Giorgio, and Rana are typical in the U.S.), or a store's value brand. It can also mean using fresh (instead of dried) pasta from your supermarket, local Italian market, or right from your own kitchen if you made it yourself from a trusted recipe. No matter what brand, or if boxed, bagged, frozen, or fresh, just follow the package's al dente instructions for cooking success.

I see some of your sauce recipes call for all-purpose flour. That won't work with my gluten-free lifestyle. What can I use instead so it's just as good as you intend it to be?

I totally hear you and, thankfully, the solution is very simple and lies in a basic, everyday ingredient: **cornstarch**. Not only is it gluten-free, but it has twice the thickening power as all-purpose flour. Therefore, whenever a recipe calls for all-purpose flour to be added, use half the amount in cornstarch. For example, if I call for 2 tablespoons all-purpose flour, measure out 1 tablespoon cornstarch. Then, in a small bowl whisk the cornstarch with an equal amount of water (so 1 tablespoon cornstarch + 1 tablespoon cold water). Once mixed together, after it goes from a thick consistency to a smooth one, you have what is called a cornstarch slurry (which thickens in a hurry)! Unless otherwise instructed in the recipe, we generally don't add the slurry when we add the flour. Rather, we usually add it in the final moments, when the sauce is just ready for the pasta. Bring the sauce to a simmer, stir in the slurry, and watch the magic happen as it thickens. Once it does, turn off the heat, add your gluten-free pasta, toss, and enjoy your 100% gluten-free meal!

As for gluten-free flours, I find that they can be a bit finicky when it comes to thickening sauces, depending on the brand used, and that the cornstarch slurry option is the most reliable. But if you wish to use a GF flour (King Arthur brand is what I'd suggest), just sub it in place of the all-purpose flour when called for in a recipe.

You often call for "salt" but don't specify which kind. Which do you suggest?

A great question! If you see just the word "salt," assume it's your basic iodized salt. If I specify other types of salt, such as kosher or sea, those are suggestions, but if you only have iodized or even something like pink Himalayan salt, those are also perfectly adequate. Basically, any salt you have on hand will do the trick.

The exception here is seasoned salt. That is salt that is blended with other seasonings, so when called for in a recipe, use seasoned salt specifically (I use Lawry's). You can salt pasta water with it, but one of the salts mentioned above will work better there.

What does "simmer" mean?

Well, if I'm talking to my Jewish mother from Brooklyn, it means to calm down. But seeing as I refer to this often throughout the book's recipes (the sauces in particular), in cooking it means a low, contained boil—more like a gentle bubble, in fact. Picture a steamy, yet relaxed volcano filled with bubbling lava. It's not quite erupting yet, but instead it's just keeping the lava at a happy, steamy, bubbly level—it's simmering.

What does "shimmering" mean?

At first glance, this word can make you think of Charo saying "Cuchi Cuchi!" while shimmying on by. But *shimmering* is a different game than shimmying, and the above simmering! (Picture me saying these words in a Long Island accent, by the way: "Shimma! Simma!") Anyway, you'll often see the word *shimmering* in a recipe's steps when heating oil. That's because once the oil is hot (which takes 2 to 3 minutes given the amounts I use), it begins to shine and give off a bit of a wavy distortion, which is known as shimmering. That means it's hot and your veggie and/or protein is ready to shimmy in the shimmer.

Parmesan or Pecorino Romano cheese? What's the difference?

As is the case with much Italian cooking, the two main cheeses you'll find in many recipes are Parmesan (more formally known as Parmigiano Reggiano) and Pecorino Romano. And seeing this is a pasta book with many Italian and Italian-inspired recipes, they will often be present here. Both are Grana cheeses, meaning they are hard and usually shredded or grated (see next question) due to their firm, crumbly texture. They're also both melty cheeses that blend well into a sauce, but they come from different regions of Italy with slightly different flavor profiles.

Parmesan, from the Parma, Reggio Emilia, and Modena regions of Italy, is made with milk produced by cows whereas Pecorino Romano, from the Sardinia, Lazio, and Tuscan regions, is made with sheep's milk. As such, while the tastes are comparable, Parmesan is milder and nuttier in flavor while Pecorino Romano is saltier and has a slightly richer and more intense flavor. So, while they're not quite the same, you can use either/or in any recipe. They are interchangeable cheeses and if you see a recipe call for Parmesan (as most will), you can absolutely use Pecorino Romano in its place and vice versa—just know it may increase or decrease the sauce's salt factor.

Do I need to grate or shred my own cheese?

While some traditionalists would answer this question by simply glaring you down as intensely as Dorothy Zbornak shoots daggers to Rose Nylund after she tells a story about St. Olaf, my response is far more lenient. "No!" I say. Feel free to use any cheese that has been grated and shredded for you (Costco usually sells big bags of grated Parmesan and Pecorino Romano). Since I'm the writer of this book, I'm telling you that packaged grated cheese (snow-like in texture) and bagged shredded cheese (little matchsticks in shape) are perfectly acceptable for use in these recipes. In fact, that's what I used in most of them myself! To make things even easier on your wallet, even the value brand is totally fine if that better suits your budget. You have my full permission. The exception to this rule is in my recipe for Carbonara (page 72), where the cheese is the sauce's main ingredient. There, I'd suggest using freshly grated Parmesan and Pecorino Romano as they have no additives and won't clump while mixing.

Now this isn't to say that you *can't* grate and shred your own cheese from a block or wedge. And yes—the quality of the cheese will likely be better, which can lead to even more decadent results, but there is no obligation to do so. The recipes are already plentifully flavorful if using pre-grated and pre-shredded varieties.

How should cheese be measured?

When it comes to measuring shredded or grated cheese, I find there is a difference depending on the type of cheese. Store-bought shredded cheeses, such as mozzarella, Cheddar, Swiss, Mexican blends, etc., are usually sold in bags of 8 ounces/½ pound (approximately 2 cups) or 16 ounces/1 pound (approximately 4 cups).

But you'll notice that while pre-shredded cheeses are equivalent in *weight,* they can vary in *volume* depending on how thickly or finely the cheese is shredded. That means the thicker the shred, the less volume it'll take up in a measuring cup. The finer the shred, the more volume. As such, I suggest using store-bought *regular-cut* shredded cheese. But if you *do* use fine or thick, just go by the same measurements as it honestly won't have a noticeable impact in these recipes. (Or you can just eyeball an 8-ounce bag knowing that half of it is 1 cup and the whole thing is 2 cups.)

Whether you're shopping for pre-shredded bags or hunks of cheese to shred yourself, the simple chart below is super handy to bear in mind.

If using grated Parmesan or Pecorino Romano (which you'll find often in this book), I find it wiser to scoop it out in measuring cups or spoons rather than consulting the weight. The reason is that although finely grated cheese will weigh the same as shredded, it isn't quite the same ratio when added to a dish, as the *volume* of finely grated is denser and tends to go further. So 1 cup of finely grated Parmesan will have more of a cheesy impact than 1 cup of shredded Cheddar.

In a nutshell: Gauge shredded cheese by weight *or* measuring cups and gauge grated cheese by measuring cups and spoons only. I make this very clear in all the recipes by stating the shredded cheeses in both cups and either ounces (if under 4 cups/1 pound) or pounds (if 4 cups/1 pound or more). (**NOTE:** In addition to grated Parmesan and Pecorino Romano, I consider crumbled varieties of feta, cotija, and blue cheese to be counted as grated as well.)

Approximate Weights and Volumes of Regular-Cut Shredded Cheeses		
Ounces	Pound(s)	Cup(s)
2	1/8	1/2
4	1/4	1
8	1/2	2
16	1	4
32	2	8

My sauce looks like it separated! Can it be fixed?

Sometimes, in a cream sauce, if the ratio of fat (meaning butter or oil) to the cream or milk itself is high, the sauce can begin to separate, leaving you with a watery sauce and an oily layer on top. This means that the sauce has broken. But don't flip out, it can be easily fixed! To mend a broken sauce, add more cream or pasta water and whisk well until the sauce resets itself. Crisis averted.

I don't cook with alcohol, but I want to try that recipe! What can I use in its place?

I got you. Since not everyone is keen on cooking with wine, booze, and/or beer, simply sub the same amount of a broth of your choice in its place. It's as simple as that!

This recipe looks great! But I don't like an ingredient in it. Can I still make it?

Of course you can! If a recipe calls for mushrooms or peas and you aren't into them, leave them out! Or simply sub a different veggie you enjoy in its place. As I've said many times before to my readers—through my books and at live appearances—use my recipe as a blueprint and tailor it to your tastes and liking. You don't need my permission. Your food, your rules!

Most of your recipes call for 1 pound (16 ounces) of pasta, which is usually a box. But some brands only sell 12- or even 8-ounce packages. What's up with that?

I know. It's annoying. While most pastas do come in 1-pound boxes, some brands choose to sell more "premium" pastas in smaller-size packages. In cases like that, I just get enough to total 1 pound. Then I save the leftover pasta from the second box for something in the future. Luckily it stores well in the pantry for years!

The exceptions to needing a full pound of pasta are jumbo shells and manicotti, which are perfectly fine at 12-ounce and 8-ounce boxes, respectively. And if using fresh pastas found in the deli or refrigerated section of your market (pappardelle, tagliatelle, ravioli, and tortellini, for example), you should generally use 1½ to 2 pounds since they're fresh and there will be less once boiled compared to dry pasta. Same for udon noodles. All measurements are accurate within the recipes themselves.

You call for a 12-ounce jar, can, or bag of something, but I can only find a 10-ounce. Can I use that instead?

Of course! I try to do my best to use the most common sizes of jars, canned goods, and frozen items available. But I also realize not every region and market carry the same size as the stores I shop at. So if you're a few ounces off on a jar of roasted red peppers, a can of artichoke hearts, or a box of frozen peas, just get whatever's closest in size and you'll be fine. It will have practically no bearing on the recipe's end result.

Why isn't nutrition info included in your recipes?

Because this is a pasta book. Do you *really* want to know?

But in all seriousness, I have determined that nutrition information is too ambiguous and broad to permanently print in a book. This is because different brands of ingredients can vary greatly in nutrition numbers, and there are many variations and variables to factor in (especially in this ever-changing food product landscape where trends run rampant). If you wish to know the nutrition info of a recipe, my advice is to plug the exact brands of ingredients you use into a reputable nutrition calculator app for the most accurate information.

I notice that most recipes are family-style (feeding 4 to 6). I live alone or with one other person and/or I'm not into leftovers. How can I halve them?

You're in luck! While it's true that all my recipes default to a family-style meal for which one pound box of pasta will feed 4 to 6 people, in my green *Super Shortcut Instant Pot* cookbook, I explained how to halve every recipe to feed smaller households, which is ideal if you don't want leftovers for the week. Since readers gave very positive feedback, I'm doing it again. You'll find how to do this within each recipe.

Can leftovers be frozen?

They sure can! Place them in an airtight container and freeze for up to 2 months. To reheat, let thaw and then microwave or sauté in a saucepan over medium heat until warmed through. While reheating, feel free to add more cream/milk or marinara sauce, if desired.

The School of Stovetops

As of this writing, there are three types of stoves available for home kitchens: electric, gas, and induction. While each will work beautifully with the recipes in this book, they differ from one another. Here's how:

Electric

 Generally heated by a coiled heating element that's either directly exposed to rest your cooking vessel on or recessed under a sheet of darkened glass, an electric stovetop will accommodate any type of pot or pan. While electric stoves take the longest to heat pots and pans (meaning they take the longest to boil water), the trade-off here is that the heat is usually distributed evenly, especially on a glass surface.

Glass tops are also very easy to clean if any salty, starchy water or sauce spills onto them. Using a razor scraper and Cerama Bryte works wonders for this. Just be careful and treat it lovingly as the surface can be easily scratched. Be especially careful when using a cast-iron skillet—don't slide it on the glass, but rather place it there. A pot, pan, or Dutch oven with a smooth bottom is preferred.

Gas

 Throwing it back a few million years ago, fire was the way humans first cooked, so this seems to be the most natural method of cooking. A gas stove will heat up faster than an electric one because you're dealing with an open flame (the bluer the flame, the hotter the fire). The flame is typically recessed under cast-iron grates, making the cooking surface incredibly durable and much less problematic if sliding a pan back and forth over it, as you won't scratch it.

The cons to a gas stove are that it doesn't distribute the heat as evenly as an electric or induction stove at lower temperatures. This is because the more intense the flame, the larger it grows and so will hit more of the bottom of the cooking vessel. But lower temperatures, which have more centered heat, can be prone to uneven heating. The solution here is to make sure you invest in good pots and pans that can evenly distribute the heat. Gas stoves can also be a pain to clean as you need to remove the heavy grates and use something such as Easy-Off to clean any stubbornly caked-on remnants from your pots and pans. A good solution to cut down on cleanup is to lay aluminum foil on top of the surface surrounding the burners.

Induction

 Most recently introduced to home kitchens, this marvel of a stovetop looks like a glass top electric stove and shares the same warnings to be careful with your cooking vessels so as not to scratch the glass. It also distributes heat evenly and is cleaned in the same way as an electric stovetop, but that's where the similarities end.

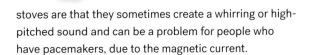

First off, an induction stovetop uses touch-sensitive controls in a few ways to select your heat: either with numbers (usually from 1 to 10, with 10 being the highest), low to high markers (like electric and gas stoves), and/or in degrees (either Fahrenheit or Celsius), making it incredibly precise. In a nutshell, you have lots of options with this stovetop!

But the revolutionary thing with induction is that it will heat up your pots and pans and boil water the fastest of the three types of stoves. This is because the heat is generated by magnetic currents between the stove and the bottom of your cooking vessel, creating minimal heat on the surface other than the heat from the cooking vessel itself. This means once the pot or pan is removed, the glass surface will cool in a fraction of the time an electric stove takes. No doubt, it will keep your kitchen much cooler than an electric or gas stove.

But there is a catch. In order for your pots and pans to heat up, you must use induction-ready cookware, which means they are magnetic. If your pot or pan doesn't have the squiggly-lined induction icon or say it's induction-ready on the bottom, try testing with a magnet on the bottom. If it sticks, it should work on an induction stovetop.

Now as amazing as it is to have rapid heat generated between vessel and stovetop using synthetic heat, that can also work against you as sometimes high heat on an induction cooktop is more like nuclear-hot high heat! As with a gas stove, make sure you're employing your common sense and if the recipe says to simmer, adjust the heat to the proper temperature (often lower than normal in the case of induction tops, but all brands vary). A couple other cons with today's induction stoves are that they sometimes create a whirring or high-pitched sound and can be a problem for people who have pacemakers, due to the magnetic current.

Based on this information, the grass is always greener no matter which type of stovetop you have. But, again, all three types of stoves are practical in their own right and will work great with these recipes. **It's just worth noting that every type and brand vary from the next and temperatures may be more intense or weaker. When a recipe has you setting and adjusting the heat at certain temperatures during the course of its instructions, just use your best judgment so that it isn't too hot or too weak.** If the recipes say the pot should be simmering, adjust the temperature so it's doing just that. **A general rule is that the heat will almost always start at a higher temperature when making a sauce and then you'll reduce it to a lower temperature as you cook and mature the sauce.** For a more in-depth discussion of the types of pots and pans I suggest, see page 24.

In the meantime, here's a general chart comparing the three stoves' temperature settings and ranges. Due to its versatility with control options, induction will have much more of a range than electric and gas. Keep in mind that covering the pan will increase the simmer action, as it's trapping steam from escaping.

Target Simmer/Cook Level	Electric or Gas Setting	Induction Temperature Settings
Very minimal simmer (almost just keeping the contents heated enough)	Low	Low, 1–2, or 150°F/65°C
Mild simmer	Medium-low	Medium-low, 2–3, or 180–200°F/82–93°C
Regular simmer, or for sautéing most proteins and veggies slowly but surely	Medium	Medium, 4–5, or 210–270°F/99–132°C
Aggressive simmer to a gentle boil, or for sautéing most proteins and veggies aggressively without overdoing it	Medium-high	Medium-high, 6–8, or 280–360°F/138–182°C
Rolling boil or for a roasted, charred sauté	High	High, 9–10, or 370–450°F/187–232°C

The Practical, Well-Stocked Kitchen

This section is helpful for not only detailing the cooking vessels I find the most practical (and that I used while developing every recipe in this book), but also includes some key cooking accessories and fridge and pantry staples I recommend you have on hand as well.

Cooking Vessels

Since virtually every recipe was cooked in a pot (soup and/or pasta), a pan (proteins and sauces), and/or a casserole dish (for recipes in the Al Forno chapter, page 206, and other finishing touches), let me begin with exactly what I suggest for this avenue.

SAUTÉ PAN

While there are many varieties of pans out there, the one that I find the absolute best to cook sauces in, and then marry the pasta with, is a sauté pan that's within the 4.5- to 5-quart range. (Speaking of which, **do not go any lower than a 4.5-quart sauté pan for the recipes in this book** because you'll need all the space—especially when marrying the pasta with the sauce.) These are pans that have a wider bottom and higher sides, which provide two major benefits:

1. If sautéing proteins or veggies in oil, the high sides help keep splatter more in your pan and less on your stove (although I don't use one, a splatter guard can help with this as well).

2. This is the perfect size pan to toss the sauce with the pasta without it falling out of the pan and onto the stove (again, thanks to the high sides).

As for which sauté pan to get? Let me make this very clear: **Not all pans are created equal.** Since you will become very close friends with your pan, I strongly suggest you get a good-quality one that will distribute the heat across the bottom as evenly as possible.

The sauté pan I use for the recipes throughout this book is a nonstick with a 4.5-quart capacity. Solid brands I suggest are All-Clad, Calphalon, Caraway, Circulon, Cuisinart, GreenPan, Ninja, Misen, Scanpan, and T-fal. They will range in price, but even heat distribution is super important and, like knives, you definitely get what you pay for. A quality pan can last for a lifetime and is a worthwhile investment. And remember, it must be induction-ready (magnetic on the bottom) to cook on an induction cooktop (and will also work on electric and gas tops).

As for stainless-steel versus a nonstick interior, I'd say to go with nonstick (which is what I use for all the pots and pans for this book). This way, you won't have to worry about food sticking to the bottom and it will be very easy to clean.

SOUP POT OR STOCKPOT

While I'm a stickler for having a good-quality sauté pan (see above), you can basically get away with any type of soup pot because it will mostly be used for boiling the pasta water. However, I also use this very pot for the Souper Zuppa chapter (page 258) and One Pot chapter (page 234).

As for the size, you'll want an 8-quart pot and, like the sauté pan, I find that nonstick will work *much* more in your favor since the pasta is far less prone to stick to the bottom while boiling and being used in pasta soups and one-pot meals.

CASSEROLE DISH

Pretty self-explanatory, you use a casserole dish to give a dish a baked (al forno) finish. They are generally 9x13 inches and come in many varieties: metal, ceramic, glass, and cast iron coated with enamel. You can also use disposable aluminum tins if you wish. Because my al forno pastas are pretty loaded, I strongly suggest any dish or tin be about 9x13 inches in size and about 3 inches deep (just make sure it's oven-safe).

Suggested Cooking Vessels	
Boiling and cooking pasta	8-quart nonstick soup pot
Making sauce	4.5- to 5-quart nonstick sauté pan
Soups and one-pot pastas	8-quart nonstick soup pot
Baking in the oven	9x13-inch casserole dish (ceramic, glass, enamel) or disposable tin

HOW TO CARE FOR YOUR POTS AND PANS

The obvious answer? Read the label that comes with it. But the general rule is that while stainless-steel pots and pans are perfectly safe (and convenient) to run through the dishwasher, a nonstick or enamel cooking vessel should *always* be gently hand-washed with warm water, dish soap, and a sponge and *never* put in the dishwasher. The reason being that the cycle and detergent can wipe off the nonstick and enamel surfaces, damaging the pot.

If your nonstick or enameled vessel has food caked onto it, just add some dish soap and hot water and let it rest for a few hours or overnight, then gently scrub with a nonabrasive sponge or scrub pad to free up any remnants, which should come right off.

And although I don't call for a cast-iron skillet in this book, the rule there is to avoid the dishwasher at all costs. In fact, a cast-iron skillet should never be fully "cleaned" because with each use it becomes more and more seasoned. Think of it as a family heirloom being passed down from generation to generation (which your cast iron may well be), gaining history, respect, and admiration with time. Cleaning it with TLC ensures meals cooked in it get more flavorful with each use.

To clean, after the cast-iron skillet cools down, take some paper towels and wipe out any excess oils. Then wash by hand with some running hot water (just a little soap is okay to use here) with a nonabrasive sponge or scrub pad to remove any food remnants. Once gently cleaned, dry it with paper towels or a dish rag and heat over medium-low heat until totally dried. Then, depending on the size of your pan, add ½ to 1 teaspoon vegetable or olive oil to the skillet and (wearing oven mitts) rub with more paper towels until the surface is smooth and dry. Let cool before storing for its next use.

Oils, Vinegars, Sauces, and Other Pantry Staples

Broth (broths made from all varieties of Better Than Bouillon base are my favorites, with low-sodium options if you're watching your sodium intake; generally, 1 teaspoon of Better Than Bouillon + 1 cup water = 1 cup broth)

Chili-garlic sauce (my favorite comes from Huy Fong Foods, the same company that makes sriracha)

Coconut milk, unsweetened (when you shake the can, it should sound like water)

Cornstarch

Fish sauce

Flour, all-purpose or gluten-free (I use King Arthur brand for both)

Ginger, squeeze (get this at Costco or many markets; it looks like applesauce and is the easiest sub for minced or grated ginger)

Hoisin sauce (check label to ensure brand is gluten-free if necessary)

Honey

Hot sauce (I like Frank's RedHot)

Liquid smoke (I prefer hickory flavor, but any will do)

Maple syrup, pure

Mayonnaise

Mustard (Dijon in particular, like Grey Poupon)

Oil, chili (Lao Gan Ma and Lee Kum Kee are my favorite brands, especially for the spicy chili crisp in my Dan Dan Noodles, page 202)

Oil, extra-virgin olive

Oil, sesame (either toasted or untoasted is fine)

Oil, vegetable

Oyster sauce (check label to ensure brand is gluten-free if necessary)

Pasta (of course, any boxed variety you enjoy)

Pasta sauces, jarred (marinara, vodka, Alfredo, and pesto; Rao's, Victoria, and Costco's Kirkland Signature are my favorite brands)

Soy sauce, regular or low-sodium (you can also use tamari [which is gluten-free] or coconut aminos [gluten-free and soy-free])

Sriracha

Sweet and sour sauce

Tomatoes, canned (crushed, diced, paste, and sauce; use either plain, seasoned, or no-salt-added varieties for low-sodium intake)

Vinegar (apple cider, balsamic, red wine, rice, and white)

Wine (dry white like sauvignon blanc, dry red like cabernet sauvignon, dry and/or sweet Marsala, sherry, and Shaoxing [Chinese rice wine])

Worcestershire sauce

Dried Herbs, Spices, and Seasonings

Basil, dried

Cajun/Creole/Louisiana seasoning (I love Tony Chachere's—it's like a spicy seasoned salt)

Cinnamon, ground

Cumin, both ground and seeds

Garam masala (I like Rani or Swad—easily found online)

Garlic powder (or granulated garlic)

Italian seasoning

Old Bay seasoning

Onion powder

Oregano, dried

Paprika (smoked and regular)

Parsley, dried

Pepper (black, white, and cayenne)

Pepper flakes, crushed red

Sage, dried/ground

Salt (iodized or kosher, garlic, and seasoned [I use Lawry's for the garlic and seasoned])

Sugars (white/granulated, light brown, and dark brown)

Thyme, dried

Dairy

Butter, salted or unsalted (I only use salted in my recipes)

Cheese
• Cream cheese (by the 8-ounce brick)
• Crumbled (blue/gorgonzola, cotija, feta, or any other varieties you like)
• Grated (Parmesan and Pecorino Romano—see The More You Know, page 18)
• Herb cheese (Boursin, Alouette, Rondelé, or save money and make mine, page 28)

• Ricotta (whole or part-skim is fine—but don't use a store brand on this one, Polly-O is where it's at)

• Shredded (Cheddar, Mexican blend, Monterey Jack, mozzarella, or any other varieties you like)

Half-and-half

Heavy cream

Milk, whole, or unsweetened nondairy milks (such as almond, cashew, oat, or soy)

Sour cream

Produce

Basil, fresh

Carrots

Garlic (pre-peeled cloves or jars of minced garlic are always time savers; also, I often call for 3 cloves of crushed or minced garlic—1 tablespoon of jarred minced or crushed garlic is about the equivalent of 3 cloves)

Ginger (see also squeeze ginger, page 25)

Lemons

Limes

Onions (any kind can be used, but I suggest the type I prefer in each recipe)

Oregano, fresh

Parsley, Italian (flat style), fresh

Peppers, bell—any color (jalapeños and any spicier varieties are also good to have on hand for heat lovers)

Spinach (regular or baby)

Tarragon, fresh

Tomatoes, fresh (cherry, grape, and Roma are best)

Essential Accessories

1. Aluminum foil (preferably nonstick)

2. Cheese grater (both a classic one for shredding and a handheld with a crank for garnishing)

3. Colander (plastic or silicone is best as metal will continue to cook your pasta when resting—plus it gets hot!)

4. Food processor or blender

5. Fine-mesh strainer (for draining tiny pastas like orzo, pastina, and acini di pepe)

6. Hand or stand mixer

7. Immersion blender (this is heaven-sent for soups as it eliminates messy batched trips to the blender)

8. Juicer (handheld is fine)

9. Knives (an 8-inch chef's knife for chopping, slicing, and dicing; a paring knife for finely slicing small veggies and getting ribs out of peppers)

10. Ladle (not only great for soups, but for reserving pasta water as well)

11. Measuring cups and spoons (Pyrex will come in handy for reserving hot pasta water!)

12. Microplane (amazing for zesting lemons and limes or for topping a dish with some freshly grated Parmesan or Pecorino Romano)

13. Mixing bowls

14. Mixing spoons and spatulas (both regular and slotted for when needed; wooden and silicone are best)

15. Oven mitts/dish towels (to handle hot pots, pans, casserole dishes, and oven trays)

16. Parchment paper

17. Pasta fork/spaghetti server

18. Peeler

19. Slotted spoon

20. Tongs

21. Whisk (silicone is best)

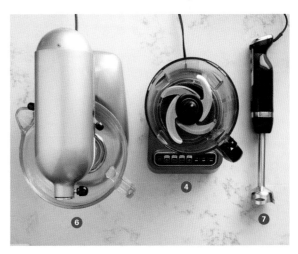

HERB CHEESE

Throughout this book, you'll notice quite a few of the recipes feature a cream-based sauce that calls for herb cheese. But what exactly *is* this herb cheese I speak of?

When I was developing my world-famous Sausage & Shells for the Instant Pot (there's also a new stovetop version on page 75), I noticed I had a package of Boursin in my fridge left over from a party. This is the stuff that you normally find on a charcuterie board and spread over crackers and that tastes like an elevated cream cheese. Well, seeing as it was about to expire and since I'm a fervent believer in not letting food go to waste, I decided to toss it into the pan while combining the pasta with the sauce. The result was nothing short of jaw-dropping and a huge cooking trend was born. (And copied by many other bloggers. Well, they do say imitation is the best form of flattery!)

You can find herb cheese made by brands such as Boursin Gournay cheese (in 5.2-ounce packages) or Alouette soft spreadable cheese or Rondelé (both in 6.5-ounce tubs and less dense and more whipped than Boursin) in your markets, usually near the deli meats and fancy cheeses. (Boursin can also be found in Costco in packs of three at a great price—and frequently on sale.) They often come in various flavors so choose the one you like best, as any will work. Or make your legitimate own for a fraction of the cost with the recipe here.

Since the fancy cream cheeses aren't available everywhere and because I want you to get that true flavor experience I've intended in these recipes, I'm sharing how to make your own garlic herb cheese! Not only is this more budget conscious, but it tastes just as great as the fancy stuff in the market (if not better since it's homemade).

This will yield the equivalent of about *five* 5.2-ounce packages of Boursin! You can also use it as a spread for crackers on your charcuterie board. It will last up to 3 weeks in your fridge and can be frozen for future use. All it takes are the following:

2 (8-ounce) bricks cream cheese, softened for 2 hours at room temperature (don't microwave)

8 ounces (2 sticks) salted butter, softened for 2 hours at room temperature (don't microwave)

¼ cup grated Parmesan cheese

3 cloves garlic, minced or pressed

1 teaspoon dried parsley

1 teaspoon dried dill

½ teaspoon garlic powder

½ teaspoon dried thyme

½ teaspoon dried basil

½ teaspoon black pepper

½ teaspoon Italian seasoning

Simply add all the ingredients to a large mixing bowl. Take a silicone, rubber, or wooden mixing spoon and mix it all together, folding it over until well combined with even seasoning distribution. (**NOTE: You can also use a hand mixer if that's easier, but I find that the familiar consistency is best achieved when mixed by hand.**)

Macaroni & Ease

So, yeah. I just threw a lot of info your way. I promise it's all to your benefit as it should about cover literally all you need to know to get going! But before you do, a few final thoughts:

I'm not going to sit here and pretend to be an expert on pasta origins and how to make them from scratch, because I'm not your fella for that. And I'm certainly not going to be like my Jewish mother with no traces of Italian in our blood who attempts to pronounce "ricotta" as "ree-GUT," because who am I (and she) kidding? Rather, I'm going to teach you the best way I know how: with the extremely helpful, yet bare-minimum basics and knowledge needed to put a spectacular meal on the table. From there, it's my hope you'll learn a thing or two and use my recipes as blueprints for when you wish to experiment with your own sauces.

This also isn't going to be one of those cookbooks where I'm in a ton of photos, laughing with the food I just made and acting like I just won big playing Plinko. You know, similar to advertisements of people having overly and bizarrely happy moments with salad. This book is about the food and about you feeling confident enough to make it.

Oh, and one more thing: I don't believe in cooking a meal that's stressful or full of hassles. This book is designed for you to have fun, feel accomplished, perhaps step out of your comfort zone just a little, and make your life easier in the kitchen and tastier than ever. It's as simple as making macaroni and cheese, or perhaps I should say macaroni and *ease*.

At the forefront of it all, pasta is fun and, dare I say it, cooking it can be too. Well, at least I've designed this book so it is. I casually invite you to put on some comfy clothes, roll up your sleeves, perhaps pour a glass of wine or your favorite beverage, and *have a blast* while making any tasty creations that call out to you. And if, for whatever reason, it all ends in a slapstick scene à la *I Love Lucy*, remember these words of wisdom: There's always pizza (or Pepperoni Pizza Pasta, page 222).

No pasta's too big or roTINI

You wish to cook well? I'm your genie.

Let's get all fuSILLI

From gnocchi to ziti

SpaGHETti ready, it starts with linguine.

—Love, Jeffrey

The Pasta Glossary

While a pasta shape may be identical from two brands, sometimes each brand names it differently (and may give different cook times). A classic example of this is cavatappi/cellentani and bucatini/perciatelli. To make matters even more confusing, some brands call a pasta by the same name, but they're totally different shapes. For example, depending on the brand, rotelle can either look like rotini *or* wagon wheels!

Did you ever notice how most pasta boxes assign the pasta a number? You really don't need to worry about that (I certainly don't), but the numbers are specific to the brand's labeling for each pasta (they differ by brand). But the general rule for the numbering system is the higher the number, the thicker the pasta. The number system is just a way for one to alternatively associate a pasta shape by number instead of the pasta by name. (It's sort of like if you order, say, the #3 lunch special from Chinese restaurant A, instead of specifying the sesame chicken lunch combo—but the #3 lunch special at Chinese restaurant B may be beef with broccoli).

As for brand, use whatever you like the most or whatever's on sale—they'll all work well.

So, to avoid all confusion, and because you'll soon learn this book is all about the visuals, I'm pleased to share this super fun pasta glossary, which lists all the pastas this book touches upon, categorizing them by genre, and listing alternative names, a description, and the cook time range to achieve an al dente result (the range reflects the most popular brands' varying cook times). Not every pasta shape ever created is represented, as that list would be longer than Santa's, but it covers the most popular ones, as well as some you may have never heard of, but that you might find at many markets and online.

> The box or bag of the selected pasta you use will tell you just how long to cook it al dente, so always be sure to use that as the guideline.

Al Forno Pastas

These are the largest pastas we'll deal with. Once they're boiled, they're usually stuffed with a cheese, meat, and/or veggie filling, covered with sauce and more cheese, and then baked. Some lasagna noodles offer a no-boil variety for which you can skip the boiling step altogether.

Pasta	Description	Al Dente Cook Time
Cannelloni	Long smooth tubes that resemble giant ziti and are meant to be stuffed. Essentially manicotti without ridges.	9 minutes
Jumbo Shells	Massive, ridged hollow shells that are meant to be stuffed. A creamy cheese mixture is the common stuffing, but the rich and loaded meat sauce for my Baked Ziti (page 211) also works nicely.	9 minutes
Lasagna/Lasagne	The broadest of all noodles, these sheets of pasta with ruffled edges are meant for layering with sauce and cheese, making it the cake of the pasta world.	8–12 minutes
Manicotti	Long ridged tubes that resemble a giant ziti rigate and are meant to be stuffed. Essentially cannelloni with ridges.	7–9 minutes

Short-Form Pastas

These bite-size pastas come in a variety of fun shapes and textures—from rigid and chewy to hollowed to thin and bendy.

Pasta	Description	Al Dente Cook Time
Farfalle	Also known as "bow ties" because that's how they're shaped, with frayed edges. They work really nicely with meaty and oil-based sauces alike due to the pinched center's folds lapping up plenty of goodness.	10–11 minutes
Gemelli	Braid-like in shape, similar to a twisted pretzel stick.	12 minutes
Gnocchi, at room temperature in an airtight package	Fluffy yet slightly dense little pillow-shaped pasta. They're usually made from potatoes but there are other varieties as well. Some also consider them dumplings although they generally aren't stuffed. I prefer the DeLallo brand.	2–3 minutes
Mafalda	Resembles a mini lasagna noodle with ruffled edges. It's essentially just a strand of mafaldine divided into bite-size rectangular pieces.	8 minutes
Racchette	Shaped like mini racquets. This shape is exclusive to the De Cecco brand under this name (but may be made by smaller brands under a different name). Too fun not to include, it inspired my Pickleball Pasta Salad (page 290).	9 minutes
Radiatori/ Radiatore	A cylindrical pasta with ruffled edges, these look like mini car engines or radiators, as the name suggests. The tiny grooves make this pasta ideal for super cheesy dishes like my White Pizza Pasta (page 154).	5–8 minutes
Rotini	Sometimes known as short fusilli or rotelle (which is sometimes a slightly larger rotini), this pasta has curly ridges and resembles a spinning barbershop pole.	7–10 minutes
Wheels, regular and mini	Shaped like wagon wheels or a tiny sliced pizza pie. Sometimes also called rotelle, though that may confuse some as rotelle can also have a near identical shape to rotini, which is totally different from a wheel.	6–7 minutes

Tubular Pastas

These pastas all have a hollow center, making them ideal for a sauce to flow through so you get a nice burst with each bite. They all vary in how long, wide, and thick they are, but are terrific with sauces featuring smooth or chunky textures.

	Pasta	Description	Al Dente Cook Time
	Cavatappi/Cellentani	A hollow pasta that's shaped like a corkscrew or pigtail. This is my go-to pasta for Macaroni & Cheese, page 138.	6–11 minutes
	Macaroni/Elbows, regular and large	Tube-like pasta with a crescent curve. Some have ridges and some don't.	6–8 minutes
	Macarrones	Essentially a shorter, wider ziti or a short rigatoni without ridges. While I've seen the Ronzoni brand in some stores, it's more common to find in larger supermarkets. I always grab a few boxes when I spot it because I just find this pasta so satisfying with any sauce.	11–15 minutes
	Mezze Penne/Mini Penne	Since "mezze" means "half," this is a smaller-sized version of standard penne.	9 minutes
	Mezzi Rigatoni/Short Rigatoni	A shorter version of a longer rigatoni. Although some brands cut their rigatoni short and still call it rigatoni, others differentiate this from a classic rigatoni by adding "mezzi" to the name.	10–14 minutes
	Paccheri/Schiaffoni	Perhaps the widest of all tubular pastas, it is smooth on the edges and loves to collapse on itself due to its girth, making for a beautiful, yet sloppy, pasta shape that's great for swirling through hearty sauces. There are also shorter versions called mezzi paccheri and calamarata.	14–15 minutes
	Penne Lisce/Mostaccioli	A smooth, tubular pasta with angled ends.	9–11 minutes
	Penne and Penne Rigate/Mostaccioli Rigati	A tubular pasta that is similar to penne lisce and mostaccioli, except it has a ridged surface instead of a smooth one.	10–11 minutes
	Pipette	Also known as "shellbows" due to their hybrid shape of a shell and elbow macaroni, this is a hollowed pasta with one end open and the other pinched shut.	8 minutes
	Rigatoni	A thicker pasta tube that is ridged. Generally longer in size, it comes in various lengths sharing the same name. Depending on the brand, shorter ones can also go by mezzi rigatoni and thinner ones can go by small rigatoni.	12–14 minutes
	Ziti	A smooth, tubular pasta. Similar to penne lisce and mostaccioli, but slightly wider and with straight ends.	10–11 minutes
	Ziti Rigati	Ziti with ridges. Very similar to longer varieties of rigatoni, but not quite as thick.	7–8 minutes

Scoopy Pastas

If you have a sauce that's loaded with goodies, a scoopy pasta is going to give you the maximum experience. This is because the nooks and crannies will be filled with every aspect of the sauce it's paired with.

Pasta	Description	Al Dente Cook Time
Campanelle	Some see them as trumpets and others as bellflowers, but this pretty-shaped pasta with a ruffled edge has a serious scoop factor.	10 minutes
Casarecce	A cross between gemelli, in that it has a very slight twist, and cavatelli, in that it has a slit down the center. As of this writing, the big box brands don't make it, so look for imports from Italy.	8–12 minutes
Cascatelli	One of the newest pasta shapes by Sporkful, this playful and practical pasta is hook-shaped. A trench lined with ruffled edges spans the length to trap sauce and meat.	13–15 minutes
Cavatelli	A hot dog bun–shaped pasta with a scoopy center. If you can't find it in the pasta aisle (since the big box brands don't make it), check the frozen section of your market.	3–10 minutes
Creste di Gallo	It means "cock's combs" and refers to the texture of a rooster's crest. It features a solo ruffle affixed to a curved, ridged tube, making it ideal for scooping meaty and creamy sauces. It's basically pasta with an edible mohawk.	8–10 minutes
Orecchiette	Shaped like little ears or mini Frisbees, this disked pasta has a divot for sauce to pool into. They also remind me of those little pushy-popper toys you'd lay on a flat surface, press the center of, and then watch pop into the air. (Are these still a thing? I'm old).	9 minutes
Shells, medium and large	A hollow shell and usually ridged. Some brands call them medium shells and others call them large shells when they're actually the same size. They shouldn't be confused with jumbo shells you'd stuff, though.	8–14 minutes
Zucca/Zucchette	Shaped like a hollowed-out pumpkin, making it super scoopy. This is the perfect pasta for any fall dish, like my Pumpkin & Sausage Pasta (page 80) or even in place of the ravioli in my Ravioli in Roasted Carrot Sauce (page 162).	10 minutes

Long Pasta

It you prefer a noodle long enough that you'll need to twirl it around a fork (or eat it with chopsticks), these varieties will undoubtedly be your favorite pastas. They work well with all sauces.

Pasta	Description	Al Dente Cook Time
Angel Hair and Capellini	Very thin, delicate noodles that cook very quickly. Try using them instead of penne in my Penne alla Vodka (page 47) or the shells in Pasta Pomodoro (page 130).	2–4 minutes
Bucatini/Perciatelli	A thick, hollowed noodle, ideal for scooping up thinner sauces or using in place of udon noodles. Think of it as fat, hollow spaghetti that you can slurp sauce through like a limber straw.	7–11 minutes
Fettuccine	A flat, medium-broad noodle that's between the width of linguine and pappardelle.	10–12 minutes
Fusilli col Buco	Although it can also refer to a shorter, spiralized noodle that shares the name with rotini, in the long noodle department it goes by fusilli col buco, and it's like a squiggly bucatini or perciatelli.	13 minutes
Linguine	A flat, slightly broad noodle that's between the width of spaghetti and fettuccine.	10 minutes
Linguine Fini/Thin Linguine	A slightly thinner variation of linguine (or what I call "thinguine").	6–8 minutes
Pappardelle	A flat, wide broad noodle—even wider than fettuccine. It's often found fresh in the deli section of your market but can also be found on shelves, sometimes formed as nests.	5–8 minutes
Mafaldine	A longer version of mafalda, this broad, long noodle with ruffled edges bears a close resemblance to a lasagna noodle, but about a quarter of the width.	8–9 minutes
Spaghetti	The most classic of long noodles with a Goldilocks "just right" width for many.	9–10 minutes
Thin Spaghetti/Spaghettini	A slightly thinner version of a spaghetti noodle, but not quite as thin as angel hair or capellini.	6–9 minutes
Thick Spaghetti/Spaghettoni	A slightly thicker version of a spaghetti noodle, but not quite as thick as bucatini or perciatelli.	11 minutes
Spaghetti Rigati	Spaghetti with ridges.	6 minutes
Vermicelli	Similar to spaghetti, but in Italy, vermicelli is thicker (like a spaghettoni), whereas in most English-speaking countries, it's thinner (like a spaghettini). It's also commonly used in Asian dishes in a rice noodle format.	5–6 minutes

Tiny Pastas

These pastas are itty-bitty and while they work nicely in a sauce, they are perfect in soups (see page 258).

Pasta	Description	Al Dente Cook Time
Acini di Pepe	Italian for "peppercorns," due to its shape and size. It's not spicy on its own. They also resemble little pearls, and you'll often find them swimming in Italian & Jewish Wedding Soup (page 262).	8 minutes
Ditalini and Tubetti	Tiny, short tubes of pasta. Not much more to it than that, but oh-so-satisfying to sink your teeth into in vegetable soups and cold pasta salads like my La Scala Pasta Salad (page 292).	8–10 minutes
Mini Farfalle/Farfalline	Just a mini version of farfalle that resemble mini bow ties. Think of them as the ring bearer at a wedding.	7 minutes
Orzo	Rice-shaped pasta. They differ from rice in flavor and texture, though. These comforting shapes are buttery, melt-in-your-mouth fun, especially in my Red Beans & Orzo (page 246).	9 minutes
Pastina	Tiny star-shaped pasta. Perfect for soups or for making your own bowl of porridge-like Parmesan stars. Try it in my Cacio e Pepe Americano (page 122).	6 minutes
Pennettine	Miniature version of penne pasta, which is a ridged, tube-like pasta with angled ends.	7 minutes
Rings	Pretty self-explanatory, they look like SpaghettiOs.	9 minutes
Shells, small and mini	A mini version of pasta shells, which are shaped like a hollow shell.	8–10 minutes
Stars/Stelline	A star-shaped pasta that's about double the size of pastina, with more pointed ends. There's also usually a hole in the center.	6–8 minutes

Refrigerated and Frozen Pastas

Fresh or frozen pasta will not only cook more quickly than dried pasta, but may also give you a more premium experience in taste and texture. I've listed the most common refrigerated and frozen pastas here, but if you find others that catch your eye in the deli department or in an Italian market feel free to use them as your pasta in any recipe in this book. Just follow the cooking instructions on the package.

Pasta	Description	Al Dente Cook Time
Fresh Fettuccine, Tagliatelle, and Pappardelle	Long, flat noodles of varied widths. Their width increases depending on how they're listed. That said, there is a very fine line between fettuccine and tagliatelle, where the latter is typically just slightly broader than fettuccine but also thinner, making it more delicate. As for pappardelle, I suggest using fresh when possible.	2–4 minutes
Gnocchi	Fluffy little pillow-shaped pasta that's chewy in texture. They're usually made from potatoes but there are other varieties as well. I prefer the ones that are in an airtight package on the shelf because the frozen and refrigerated ones can sometimes be too delicate and become mush while boiling.	2–3 minutes
Ravioli	Italian ravioli is made with a pasta sheet laid out on a flat surface where dollops of a cheese, meat, and/or veggie filling are spooned onto it and then topped with another pasta sheet. It is then cut into square, round, or crescent shapes of various sizes, where the edges (sometimes fluted) are pinched shut, sealing the filling in. Costco sells their own refrigerated and frozen brand with solid quality at a great value.	4–5 minutes
Tortellini	Pasta that is filled with cheese, meat, and/or veggies and rolled into small stuffed ring-like shapes with the ends pinched together. Sometimes this variety of pasta can be found in the dried pasta section as well, but those will take longer to cook and won't be filled with fresh ingredients. Costco sells their own refrigerated brand with solid quality at a great value.	2–4 minutes

Udon and Other Asian Noodles

Commonly found in both Japanese and Shanghai cuisines, udon are long noodles that range from a medium width like spaghetti (hokkien-style) to thick like bucatini (sanuki-style, but even denser than bucatini as they aren't hollow). Udon noodles are usually made of flour and water, making them soft and chewy. Their darker counterparts, soba noodles, are usually made with powdered buckwheat, making them more textured to the bite, and also gluten-free. Any of these noodle varieties work great in my Asian Fusion Noodles (page 190) and Dan Dan Noodles (page 202).

Like rice noodles, they can be found either frozen, refrigerated, or on the shelf in the Asian section of most markets, at any Asian market, and online. Cook times will vary by the brand, so just follow the package instructions. I prefer frozen udon noodles, as they usually take just 1 minute to cook in boiling water and taste super fresh. It is, however, worth mentioning that the more easily found Ka-Me brand is very common in many supermarkets. They are usually located in the Asian section on the shelf and are already softened.

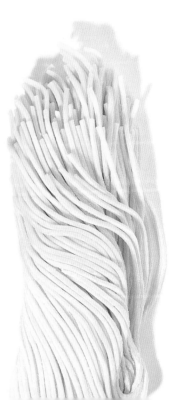

Egg Noodles

Egg noodles are a bit different from classic semolina Italian pasta because, as the name suggests, they're always made with eggs. While many Italian-style pastas are also made with eggs, most of the dried store-bought pasta brands (that I used when developing most of the recipes in this book) are not. Egg noodles are common among Eastern European and American cuisine and taste great in casseroles, goulash, stroganoff, noodle puddings, and chicken soups.

Their usual shape resembles ribbons of varied sizes, wide or short, straight, thinner noodles. They are available in versions made both with and without the egg yolks.

Pasta	Description	Al Dente Cook Time
Flakes	They look like tiny squares and are most practical in soups, such as matzo ball and vegetable.	5–8 minutes
Thin/Fine Noodles	These look like cut spaghetti and are most practical in soups, especially chicken noodle.	2–4 minutes
Wide Noodles	This is what I use when I call for any egg noodle in this book. They look exactly as they sound: like wide ribbons. They also come in the extra-wide variety.	6–11 minutes

Rice Noodles

Generally used for Asian dishes, rice noodles are not made with all-purpose flour and eggs, but rather with rice flour and water. They go by a few names, such as rice noodles, rice sticks, and banh pho, and can be found in the Asian section of most markets, at any Asian market, and online.

Rice noodles range in size and shape similar to Italian vermicelli (thin), linguine (slightly broad), fettuccine (medium broad), and pappardelle (quite broad). Therefore, the cook time will depend on both the size of the selected noodle and the brand.

As for how long to cook them, you'll find that some recipes will require a cook time of 8 minutes with the noodles soaking in hot (but not boiling) water. Others will require the noodles to soak for up to an hour in room-temperature water before tossing with a sauce in a heated pan. And others won't specify a time at all! However, I've found that regardless of the instructions, a universal and quick way to cook rice noodles is to fill an 8-quart pot halfway with tap water, bring to a rolling boil over high heat, then reduce the heat to medium. Once it's at a very gentle simmer-boil, add the rice noodles and cook, stirring often, not leaving the pot's side, and testing the noodles every 2 minutes to see if they're soft and pleasant enough to bite into. Once they are, they're done. This usually ranges from 1 to 6 minutes, depending on the noodle's girth—the thicker the rice noodle, the longer the cook time. Just don't walk away and forget about them—if you do, they could become mush! Drain the noodles in a colander and rinse with cold water.

1

PARAMOUNT PASTAS

This chapter is essentially the holy grail of all the classic pasta dishes you'll find on most Italian-American restaurant menus and likely at the forefront of your mind when you think of pasta in general: marinara, Alfredo, Bolognese, vodka, and pesto.

But make no mistake—this is *my* spin on these classics and, while they may not use fancy or traditional techniques, the familiar end results are going to make you want to sing some Puccini. Not only are they outrageously good, they're so easy to make it's silly.

(DF) **Dairy-Free**

(V) **Vegetarian**

(VN) **Vegan**

+ **Compliant with Modifications**

LINGUINE MARINARA

This is the recipe I direct you to whenever another recipe calls for marinara sauce. Of course, you can absolutely be lazy and use your favorite jarred brand instead (Rao's and Victoria for the win) and then this becomes a two-ingredient meal. However, this marinara is one of the best homemade versions I've ever had and I'm very proud of it. I even think Sophia Petrillo and her catty sister, Angela, would approve since the sauce clings beautifully to pasta. The secret to the flavor is the amount of garlic. And if you want it arrabiata- or fra diavolo–style (which is spicy), check out Jeff's Tips on how to make it so!

THE PASTA
1 tablespoon salt

1 pound linguine or linguine fini/thin linguine

THE MARINARA SAUCE
¼ cup extra-virgin olive oil

1 very large Spanish or yellow onion, diced

14 cloves garlic, 6 minced or pressed and 8 sliced into slivers (see Jeff's Tips)

1 heaping tablespoon tomato paste

1 (28-ounce) can crushed tomatoes (San Marzano are best)

1 (14.5-ounce) can diced tomatoes, with their juices

1 (15-ounce) can tomato sauce (not the same as jarred pasta sauce)

1 tablespoon seasoned salt (add more to taste)

1 tablespoon Italian seasoning

1 tablespoon dried oregano

1 tablespoon garlic powder

1 tablespoon onion powder

2 teaspoons white sugar

2 teaspoons black pepper (add more to taste)

Leaves from 1 bunch fresh basil, stemmed

¼–½ cup grated Parmesan, plus more for topping (optional)

Prep Time: 10 min • **Pasta Cook Time (linguine or linguine fini/thin linguine): 6–10 min** • **Sauce Cook Time: 30 min** • **Total Time: 40 min** • **Serves: 4–6**

1. Boil the Water: Fill an 8-quart pot halfway with tap water and bring to a rolling boil over high heat.

2. Start the Sauce: Heat the oil in a nonstick 4.5- to 5-quart sauté pan over medium-high heat. Once shimmering, add the onion and sauté until translucent, about 5 minutes. Add all the garlic and sauté until browned, another 5 minutes.

3. Add the tomato paste, stir until the onion and garlic are coated, and sauté for 1 minute.

JEFF'S TIP

If you just want the sauce for future use, skip Steps 1, 5, and 7. Just let the sauce simmer for 15–20 minutes after adding everything to the pan in Step 4. The sauce will keep in the fridge in a jar or airtight container for a week, or it can be frozen for up to 3 months. And remember, the more a sauce cools and melds, the more the flavor comes out!

TO HALVE Simply halve all the ingredients. However, the salted pasta water amount remains the same. The pasta and the sauce cook times also remain the same.

4. Add the crushed tomatoes, diced tomatoes, tomato sauce, seasoned salt, Italian seasoning, oregano, garlic powder, onion powder, sugar, pepper, and basil leaves and stir. Reduce the heat to medium or medium-low and cook at a light simmer for about 10 minutes, stirring occasionally.

5. Cook the Pasta: After simmering the sauce for 10 minutes, add the salt to the pot of boiling water and reduce the heat to medium. Add the pasta and stir. Set a timer to cook until al dente (per the package instructions), or to the shortest amount of time given. When done, drain the pasta in a colander in the sink without rinsing it.

6. While the pasta is cooking, allow the sauce to continue to gently simmer in the pan, about 5–10 minutes more (all in all, the sauce should have simmered for about 15–20 minutes total). As soon as the pasta is drained, add the optional Parmesan to the sauce (start with ¼ cup and work your way up, to taste). Stir until combined into the sauce. If you want it spicy, **see Jeff's Tips**.

7. Marry It All: Turn the heat off. Add the cooked and drained pasta to the sauté pan and toss to coat with the sauce. Serve topped with additional grated Parmesan, if desired.

JEFF'S TIPS

The sauce on its own makes about 8 cups, which I think is perfect for 1 pound of pasta since I like my pasta marinara very saucy.

If you feel this is too much garlic for you (even though I believe there is no such thing as too much garlic in a marinara sauce), reduce it by half or even three quarters.

To make the sauce arrabiata/fra diavolo–style (in other words, spicy): Add a combo of any or all of the following, to taste (start with 1 teaspoon each) in Step 6:
• Cayenne pepper
• Crushed red pepper flakes
• Hot sauce of your choice

FETTUCCINE ALFREDO

RESERVE PASTA WATER!

THE PASTA
1 tablespoon salt

1 pound fettuccine

THE ALFREDO SAUCE
8 tablespoons (1 stick) salted butter

2 cups heavy cream or half-and-half

1 teaspoon garlic powder

½ teaspoon salt

½ teaspoon pepper, plus more for topping (optional)

½–1 cup grated Parmesan cheese, plus more for topping

1 (5.2-ounce) package Boursin (any flavor) or ¾ cup Herb Cheese (page 28), cut into chunks (optional)

Once upon a time around the turn of the 20th century, a man named Alfredo Di Lelio created a simple, creamy Parmesan sauce in Rome, Italy (thanks, Wikipedia). In a short span of time, it has arguably become the most iconic and well-loved white sauce in the world. Simply known today as "Alfredo," it's a very basic recipe—the original Italian version required only butter, Parmesan, and pasta water. But in America it has countless variations that build upon the flavor foundation, almost always replacing the pasta water with heavy cream (which is what I do). I like to zhuzh mine up with the optional herb cheese while tossing the pasta with the sauce. Alfredo is classically paired with fettuccine, but any pasta you have on hand will work beautifully.

Prep Time: 5 min • Pasta Cook Time (fettuccine): 10–12 min • Sauce Cook Time: 10 min • Total Time: 20 min • Serves: 4–6

1. Boil the Water and Cook the Pasta: Fill an 8-quart pot halfway with tap water and bring to a rolling boil over high heat. Add the salt and reduce the heat to medium. Add the pasta and stir. Set a timer to cook until al dente (per the package instructions), or to the shortest amount of time given. When done, **reserve 1 cup of the pasta water** and then drain the pasta in a colander in the sink without rinsing it.

2. Make the Sauce: As soon as you add the pasta to the pot, combine the butter and cream in a nonstick 4.5- to 5-quart sauté pan and set over medium heat.

3. Once the butter has melted into the cream, stir in the garlic powder, salt, and pepper (if using). Increase the heat to medium-high. Once bubbling, reduce the heat to medium or medium-low so it's at a gentle simmer. Cook, whisking occasionally, for about 5 minutes.

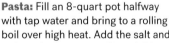

4. Add ½ cup Parmesan and whisk until fully combined into the sauce. Reduce the heat to medium-low and simmer until the sauce thickens, about 1 minute. (**NOTE:** If the sauce is done before the pasta, reduce the heat to low and cover the pan with a lid.)

5. Marry It All: Turn the heat off. Add the cooked and drained pasta to the sauté pan and toss to coat with the sauce.

JEFF'S TIPS

If you just want the sauce for future use, skip the pasta steps. The sauce will keep in the fridge in a jar or airtight container for a week. However, given that it's essentially liquified dairy, an Alfredo sauce is not the best for freezing.

Want a chicken in your Alfredo? I gotcha! In Step 5, when adding the pasta to the skillet, add 1–2 pounds rotisserie chicken meat and toss into the pasta and sauce.

If you have leftover pasta with sauce, add a few splashes of cream and stir to reconstitute the sauce while reheating in a skillet or microwave.

6. If you want a richer sauce, add up to another ½ cup Parmesan and/or the herb cheese (my signature touch!) and toss with two mixing spoons or tongs until combined into the sauce. (**NOTE:** If at this stage you decide you want a thinner sauce after adding the additional dairy, you can always add either ½–1 cup more cream, or ½–1 cup of the reserved pasta water just before draining and add it now.) Serve immediately topped with additional Parmesan and black pepper, if desired.

TO HALVE Simply halve all the ingredients. However, the salted pasta water amount remains the same. The pasta and the sauce cook times also remain the same.

RIGATONI BOLOGNESE

The ultimate red sauce, a Bolognese has it all: meat, veggies, tomatoes, wine, and in some cases—certainly mine, although optional—creamy dairy! It's a pasta lover's dream come true and easily one of the most popular recipes in my orange Instant Pot cookbook. The secret is that both dry red and white wines are infused into the meat while simmering. I find that rigatoni (or any tube-shaped pasta) is the perfect pasta pairing as the wide tubes really scoop up that loaded sauce!

  if using plant-based meat

THE PASTA

1 tablespoon salt

1 pound rigatoni

THE BOLOGNESE SAUCE

½ cup extra-virgin olive oil

1 very large Spanish or yellow onion, diced

1 large carrot (or 2 medium carrots), peeled and diced

2 ribs celery, diced

3 cloves garlic, minced or pressed

1½ pounds ground meat of your choice (see Jeff's Tips)

¾ cup dry red wine (like pinot noir, see Jeff's Tips)

¼ cup dry white wine (like chardonnay, see Jeff's Tips)

1 (28-ounce) can crushed tomatoes (San Marzano are best)

2 teaspoons seasoned salt

2 teaspoons Italian seasoning

¼ teaspoon nutmeg

OPTIONAL TOUCHES

½ cup heavy cream or half-and-half

1 (5.2-ounce) package Boursin (any flavor) or ¾ cup Herb Cheese (page 28), cut into chunks

Grated Parmesan cheese, for topping

Prep Time: 15 min • **Pasta Cook Time (rigatoni): 12–14 min** • **Sauce Cook Time: 25 min** • **Total Time: 40 min** • **Serves: 4–6**

1. Boil the Water: Fill an 8-quart pot halfway with tap water and bring to a rolling boil over high heat.

2. Start the Sauce:. Heat the oil in a nonstick 4.5- to 5-quart sauté pan over medium-high heat. Once shimmering, add the onion, carrot, and celery (this trio of chopped veggies is what the French call a "mirepoix") and sauté until slightly softened, about 5 minutes.

3. Add the garlic and ground meat and sauté until lightly browned and crumbled, another 3–5 minutes. (**NOTE:** Do *not* drain the pot of the meat's juices! We want that rich flavor in the sauce.)

Recipe Continues

4. Add both wines and reduce the heat to medium or medium-low. Allow the meat and veggies to gently simmer in the wine for 10 minutes.

5. Cook the Pasta: As soon as the wine begins to simmer in the sauté pan, add the salt to the pot of boiling water and reduce the heat to medium. Add the pasta and stir. Set a timer to cook until al dente (per the package instructions), or to the shortest amount of time given. When done, drain the pasta in a colander in the sink without rinsing it.

6. While the pasta's cooking, return to the sauté pan and add the crushed tomatoes, seasoned salt, Italian seasoning, and nutmeg. Stir to combine and let simmer for 3 minutes, stirring occasionally.

7. If using the cream and/or herb cheese, add now and stir until completely melded into the sauce. (**NOTE:** If the sauce is done before the pasta, reduce the heat to low and cover the pan with a lid.)

8. Marry It All: Turn the heat off. Add the cooked and drained pasta to the sauté pan and toss to coat with the sauce. Serve topped with grated Parmesan, if desired.

 JEFF'S TIPS

For the meat, I prefer a meatloaf mixture (usually a trio of ground beef, veal, and pork), but you can use any type of ground meat available, be it just beef, pork, veal, chicken, turkey, or plant-based.

You don't need fancy wine for this, but the general rule is don't cook with a wine you wouldn't drink (in other words, don't use cooking wine). A bottle each of cheap red and white work fine. And if you don't have two bottles of wine lying around and don't feel like buying two, you can get away with just using 1 cup red wine to make up for leaving out the white. Oh, and if wine isn't your thing, just sub a cup of a broth of your choice in its place—same 10-minute simmer time.

If you want the sauce for future use, skip the pasta steps. The sauce will keep in the fridge in a jar or airtight container for a week, or it can be frozen for up to 2–3 months. And remember, the more a sauce cools and melds, the more the flavor comes out!

TO HALVE Simply halve all the ingredients. However, the salted pasta water amount remains the same. The pasta and the sauce cook times also remain the same.

PENNE ALLA VODKA

THE PASTA

1 tablespoon salt

1 pound penne

THE VODKA SAUCE

2 tablespoons (¼ stick) salted butter

8 ounces pancetta or thick-cut bacon, diced (optional, see Jeff's Tips)

2 large shallots, diced

3 cloves garlic, minced or pressed

½ cup vodka

4 cups Marinara Sauce (page 40 or your favorite jarred brand)

1 (14.5-ounce) can diced tomatoes, with their juices

⅓ cup fresh oregano leaves, plus more for topping

½ cup heavy cream or half-and-half

1 cup grated Parmesan cheese, plus more for topping

1 (5.2-ounce) package Boursin (any flavor) or ¾ cup Herb Cheese (page 28), cut into chunks (optional)

I think if I polled a room of folks asking them what their favorite pasta sauce is, a creamy vodka sauce would win the vote. From American pubs to diners, this sauce is featured on many menus that have zero to do with Italian food. And I get why. It's a simple mix of a familiar marinara sauce, plus some cream and Parmesan. Mine is amplified with (optional) smoky pancetta and an (also optional) herb cheese thrown into the mix. As for the vodka? Once simmered and integrated into the sauce, it's flavorless. Its main purpose is to marry the creamy dairy with the acidity of the tomatoes, making for an extra smooth texture, but you can leave it out if alcohol isn't your style.

Prep Time: 10 min ● Pasta Cook Time (penne): 10–11 min ● Sauce Cook Time: 20 min ●
Total Time: 30 min ● Serves: 4–6

1. Boil the Water: Fill an 8-quart pot halfway with tap water and bring to a rolling boil over high heat.

2. Start the Sauce: Melt the butter in a nonstick 4.5- to 5-quart sauté pan over medium-high heat. Add the pancetta (if using) and sauté until it's just cooked but not quite crispy, about 5 minutes. Leave it in the pot.

3. Reduce the heat to medium. Add the shallots and garlic and sauté until just softened, another 2 minutes.

Recipe Continues

4. Add the vodka and simmer for 3 minutes, until the pungent alcohol smell clears. (**NOTE:** Don't cut this step short as it's what cooks off the alcohol and helps the sauce develop that rich flavor.)

5. Add the marinara, diced tomatoes, and oregano. Stir to combine and simmer for 3 minutes, stirring occasionally.

6. Cook the Pasta: As soon as the sauce begins to simmer in the sauté pan, add the salt to the pot of boiling water and reduce the heat to medium. Add the pasta and stir. Set a timer to cook until al dente (per the package instructions), or to the shortest amount of time given. When done, drain the pasta in a colander in the sink without rinsing it.

7. While the pasta's cooking, return to the sauté pan and add the cream or half-and-half, Parmesan, and herb cheese (if using) and stir until melded into the sauce and it turns a pretty pink color. Let simmer for 3 minutes more, stirring occasionally. (**NOTE:** If the sauce is done before the pasta, reduce the heat to low and cover the pan with a lid.)

8. Marry It All: Turn the heat off. Add the cooked and drained pasta to the sauté pan and toss to coat with the sauce. Serve topped with additional fresh oregano and Parmesan, if desired.

 JEFF'S TIPS

If not using the pancetta (or bacon), after the butter has melted in Step 2, jump right to Step 3.

Don't want the vodka? Simply leave it out and skip Step 4.

If you want the sauce for future use, skip the pasta steps. The sauce will keep in the fridge in a jar or airtight container for a week, or it can be frozen for up to 2–3 months. And remember, the more a sauce cools and melds, the more the flavor comes out!

 JEFF'S TIP

To Make Chicken Riggies: There's a popular Italian pasta in Upstate New York (Utica, specifically) called chicken riggies. It's essentially a spicy vodka sauce without the vodka and with cherry peppers and chicken tossed in. To adapt this recipe to make chicken riggies, skip Step 4 (omitting the vodka*) and add a 12- to 16-ounce jar of sliced cherry peppers (hot or mild) in Step 5 when adding the marinara. (You can also add ¼ cup of the pepper juice from the jar for extra kick.) Then, add 1½–2 pounds rotisserie chicken meat in Step 8 when marrying the pasta with the sauce. Feel free to top with some red pepper flakes. As for the pasta, riggies (as the name suggests) feature rigatoni, and you can sub that in place of the penne if you wish.
*You can keep Step 4 with the vodka as well!

TO HALVE Simply halve all the ingredients. However, the salted pasta water amount remains the same. The pasta and the sauce cook times also remain the same.

PASTA PESTO

THE PASTA

1 tablespoon salt

1 pound pipette pasta

THE PESTO SAUCE

2 cups (1–2 bunches depending on their size) packed fresh basil leaves, stemmed, plus more for garnish

1 cup extra-virgin olive oil

1 cup grated Parmesan cheese

4 cloves garlic, roughly chopped

½ cup of one of the following: pine nuts, raw sunflower seeds, raw almonds, or raw cashews

Salt, to taste (optional)

This is truly one of the simplest, yet flavor-packed and vibrant sauces that has ever been created. Originated in Genoa, Italy, during the 16th century (thanks, Google), a pesto has five key players: olive oil, Parmesan, garlic, pine nuts, and fresh basil. Now, since pine nuts can be on the pricier side and harder to find, I give you options for substitutes. And if you don't feel like making your own pesto, feel free to get some from your market or Costco (they have the best jarred) and you have a two-ingredient pasta recipe.

Prep Time: 5 min ● **Pasta Cook Time (pipette pasta): 8 min** ● **Sauce Prep Time: 5 min** ●
Total Time: 20 min ● **Serves: 4–6**

1. Boil the Water and Cook the Pasta: Fill an 8-quart pot halfway with tap water and bring to a boil over high heat. Add the salt and reduce the heat to medium. Add the pasta and stir. Set a timer to cook until al dente (per the package instructions), or to the shortest amount of time given. When done, drain the pasta in a colander in the sink without rinsing it.

2. Make the Sauce: As soon as you add the pasta to the pot, add all the sauce ingredients except the salt to a food processor or blender and pulse until pureed. Taste, and if you find you want it saltier, add salt to taste and pulse again (**see Jeff's Tips**).

3. Marry It All: Return the drained pasta to the same (now empty) pot it cooked in and add the pesto sauce.

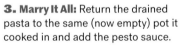

4. Toss until the pasta is coated in the sauce. Serve immediately topped with additional basil, if desired.

 JEFF'S TIPS

Want your pesto spicy? Add 1–2 teaspoons crushed red pepper flakes in Step 2 when pureeing the sauce.

After much of my own trial and error, I find this pesto's consistency to be right on the money. But when you make it, feel free to alter it to your personal tastes. After blending it, do you want it thinner? Add more olive oil. Thicker? Add more basil and/or cheese. Saltier? Add more Parmesan. Nuttier? More nuts. You get the picture. The point is that pesto is a sauce that is easily tailored to those who enjoy it so feel free to use my recipe as a blueprint and adjust it until it's the perfect pesto for you!

You can also make pesto sauce ahead of time and pop it in the fridge for a month or so.

TO HALVE Simply halve all the pesto ingredients. However, the salted pasta water amount remains the same. The pasta cook time also remains the same.

2

MEATY

If it's a meaty pasta you seek, this is the chapter where you should peek. Here I present some beloved carnivorous classics as well as some deliciously inventive new ones.

Pork, beef, veal, sausage, and pancetta (or bacon) have never been easier to prepare or more ready to toss with pasta in sauces from tomato-based to super creamy to a blend of the two. And if you're more the plant-based type, I've got you covered! Many of the recipes here can use plant-based "meats" in place of sausage or ground meat.

If you want more meaty pastas done a bit differently, check out the Stir-Fry (page 188), Al Forno (page 206), and One Pot (page 234) chapters.

ⒹⒻ **Dairy-Free**

Ⓥ **Vegetarian**

ⓋⓁ **Vegan**

✦ **Compliant with Modifications**

SPAGHETTI & MEATBALLS

Behold the most Americanized rendition of an Italian pasta dish ever! I say that because the classic spaghetti and meatball combination wasn't actually born in Italy—it was created in New York City by Italian immigrants in the late 1800s. Now beloved by virtually everyone and with countless different takes, my version of this staple gives you options for a creamier and/or spicier sauce with the melt-in-your-mouth meatballs, which not only pair perfectly with spaghetti, but can also be used for other things, such as meatball parm heroes.

 (if using plant-based meat, see Jeff's Tips)

THE PASTA
1 tablespoon salt

1 pound spaghetti

THE MEATBALLS
1 pound ground beef (the less lean, the better)

½ pound ground pork (see Jeff's Tips)

½ cup grated Parmesan cheese, plus more for serving

⅓ cup breadcrumbs

⅓ cup whole milk

6 cloves garlic, minced or pressed

2 tablespoons dried parsley

2 teaspoons seasoned salt

1 teaspoon black pepper

1 teaspoon dried oregano

1 large egg, slightly beaten

THE SAUCE
4–6 cups Marinara Sauce (page 40 or your favorite jarred brand)

1 (5.2-ounce) package Boursin (any flavor) or ¾ cup Herb Cheese (page 28), cut into chunks (optional)

¼–½ cup hot sauce (I use Frank's RedHot), optional and to taste (start with ¼ cup and add more if you like)

1–2 teaspoons crushed red pepper flakes (optional and to taste, start with 1 teaspoon and add more if you like)

Prep Time: 15 min • Pasta Cook Time (spaghetti): 9–10 min • Meatball Cook Time: 25 min • Sauce Cook Time: 10 min • Total Time: 50 min • Serves: 4–6

1. Boil the Water: Fill an 8-quart pot halfway with tap water and bring to a rolling boil over high heat.

2. Make the Meatballs: Preheat the oven to 350°F. In a large mixing bowl, combine all the meatball ingredients. Mix together with clean hands until everything is incorporated, then shape into one giant meatball.

3. Take some meat from the giant meatball and roll into a ball about 2 inches in diameter (a bit larger than a golf ball). Repeat to make 12–15 meatballs. Arrange on a nonstick foil- or parchment paper–lined baking sheet. Bake on the center rack for 25 minutes, or until cooked through to your liking—just cut one open to check. (**NOTE:** The meatballs should be fully cooked by now, but if they look slightly underdone it's fine as they'll simmer in the sauce soon. If you're making them on their own for now or later, just make sure they're fully cooked, adding 5 more minutes if needed.)

 JEFF'S TIPS If you want to save time and skip cooking the meatballs in the oven, put the raw meatballs directly in the sauce in Step 6. Just make sure you simmer on medium-high with the lid on, stirring occasionally, for 25 minutes, or until the meatballs are cooked through.

If you want to save even more the time, you can use 1–2 pounds frozen meatballs from the market. Just skip Steps 2 and 3 and add them to the marinara sauce in Step 6.

4. Cook the Pasta: Add the salt to the pot of boiling water and reduce the heat to medium. Add the pasta and stir. Set a timer to cook until al dente (per the package instructions), or to the shortest amount of time given. When done, drain the pasta in a colander in the sink without rinsing it.

5. Make the Sauce: While the pasta's cooking, combine 4 cups of the marinara sauce and any of the optional sauce ingredients in a nonstick 4.5- to 5-quart sauté pan. Cook over medium-high heat until bubbling, then reduce the heat to medium-low.

6. Add the cooked meatballs, cover the pot, and simmer for 3 minutes so the fat from the meatballs really infuses into the sauce!

7. Marry It All: Turn the heat off. Add the cooked and drained pasta to the sauté pan and toss to coat with the sauce, moving the meatballs around so they become hugged by the pasta. If at this point you find you want it saucier, stir in up to 2 cups more marinara. Serve topped with additional Parmesan, if desired.

 JEFF'S TIPS If you want just the sauce and meatballs for future use, skip the pasta steps. The sauced meatballs will keep in the fridge in an airtight container for a week, or they can be frozen for up to 2–3 months. And remember, the more a sauce cools and melds, the more the flavor comes out!

For the meat, you can use ground Italian sausage (sweet or hot), beef, veal, turkey, chicken, or a plant-based meat. Whether you combine these variations or use all of the same type of meat, 1½ pounds is the amount you want to use.

TO HALVE Simply halve all the ingredients. However, the salted pasta water amount remains the same. The pasta and the sauce cook times also remain the same.

SUNDAY SAUCE

THE PASTA
1 tablespoon salt

1 pound paccheri or schiaffoni

THE SAUCE
¼ cup extra-virgin olive oil

8 ounces pancetta or thick-cut bacon, diced

1 yellow onion, diced

1 pound ground beef (the less lean, the better)

3 pounds Italian sausage (hot, sweet, or a mix of the two), divided; 2 pounds removed from casings and 1 pound left in casings and sliced into ½-inch pieces

6 cloves garlic, minced or pressed

4 cups Marinara Sauce (page 40 or your favorite jarred brand)

Leaves from 1 bunch fresh basil, stemmed

½–1 cup grated Parmesan cheese, plus more for serving (optional)

A Sunday sauce is essentially a meat-lover's paradise, where the sauce itself takes a backseat to the meat. Traditionally made to simmer all day on Sundays, this carnivorous delight is no stranger to taking center stage at droolworthy Italian family gatherings, where family gossip and gab simmer alongside it. Because I'm impatient, my version will be done in under an hour, but is still loaded with deep, rich flavor. The meat combo I've listed in the ingredients is my personal favorite, but you can absolutely feel free to change it up if you see fit (see Jeff's Tips). Now, since there's a ton of meat in this sauce, your pan will be quite full and the sauce can serve as a meal in itself. Therefore, rather than tossing the pasta with the sauce, I prefer Sunday sauce served *over* the pasta, for which I prefer a wide, tubular shape such as paccheri, rigatoni, or macarrones.

Prep Time: 10 min • Pasta Cook Time (paccheri or schiaffoni): 14–15 min •
Sauce Cook Time: 45 min • Total Time: 55 min • Serves: 4–6

1. Boil the Water: Fill an 8-quart pot halfway with tap water and bring to a rolling boil over high heat.

2. Start the Sauce: Heat the oil in a nonstick 4.5- to 5-quart sauté pan over medium-high heat. Once shimmering, add the pancetta or bacon and sauté until just between cooked and crispy, about 5 minutes. Add the onion and cook in the pancetta oil until translucent, about 2 minutes more.

3. Add the ground beef, uncased sausage meat, and garlic. Sauté for 3–5 minutes, until crumbled and lightly browned.

TO HALVE Simply halve all the ingredients. However, the salted pasta water amount remains the same. The pasta and the sauce cook times also remain the same.

4. Add the sliced sausage, followed by the marinara, then stir in the basil. Once bubbling, reduce the heat to medium-low and cover the pot.

5. Let the sauce simmer for 15–20 minutes, removing the lid and stirring occasionally, and reducing the heat if need be (we don't want the sauce to boil, but to simmer). If using the Parmesan, stir it into the sauce after the 15–20 minutes of simmering and reduce the heat to low. Keep the lid on the pot as you cook your pasta.

6. Cook the Pasta: After 15–20 minutes of the sauce simmering, add the salt to the pot of boiling water and reduce the heat to medium. Add the pasta and stir. Set a timer to cook until al dente (per the package instructions), or to the shortest amount of time given. When done, drain the pasta in a colander in the sink without rinsing it.

7. Marry It All: Plate the cooked, naked pasta either individually or in a serving dish/pan family-style and ladle as much sauce as you want over it. You can save any leftover sauce for later (**see Jeff's Tips**). Top with additional Parmesan, if desired.

JEFF'S TIPS

For the meat, you can really use any kind you wish! Just make sure you allow the sauce to simmer long enough so the meat you've chosen is fully cooked (especially if it's a more substantial cut such as short ribs or bracciole, which will take a solid 2–3 hours).

If you just want the sauce for future use, skip the pasta steps. The sauce will keep in the fridge in an airtight container for a week, or can be frozen for up to 2–3 months. And remember, the more a sauce cools and melds, the more the flavor comes out!

PAPRIKASH RAGÙ

RESERVE PASTA WATER!

 if using plant-based meat and vegetable broth; see Jeff's Tips

THE PASTA

1 tablespoon salt

1 pound pappardelle, dried usually found in the pasta section, or fresh in the refrigerated section of your market (see Jeff's Tips)

THE SAUCE

4 tablespoons (½ stick) salted butter

1 Vidalia (sweet) onion, diced

3 cloves garlic, minced or pressed

1½ pounds ground meat of your choice (see Jeff's Tips)

2 tablespoons smoked paprika (Hungarian and regular paprika are also great), plus more for garnish

1–2 teaspoons seasoned salt

¼ cup all-purpose flour (see Jeff's Tips for GF option)

2 cups chicken or vegetable broth

1 (8-ounce) can tomato sauce (not the same as jarred pasta sauce)

½ cup heavy cream or half-and-half

½ cup sour cream

1 (5.2-ounce) package Boursin (any flavor) or ¾ cup Herb Cheese (page 28), cut into chunks

A paprikash is a super popular Hungarian sauce that dresses a protein. It's creamy and has a key ingredient that's right in the title: paprika! It inspired me to marry this wonderful sauce with some ground meat, cream, tomato sauce, and herb cheese, which amplifies it beyond the usual sour cream and gives it some ragù flair (which is similar to a Bolognese in that it's a tomato-based meat sauce). The end result makes a magnificent creamy, meaty pasta dish featuring pappardelle, a broad, long pasta noodle. As for the meat, the choice is yours as outlined in Jeff's Tips.

Prep Time: 10 min • Pasta Cook Time (pappardelle): 2–8 min • Sauce Cook Time: 20 min • Total Time: 30 min • Serves: 4–6

1. Boil the Water: Fill an 8-quart pot halfway with tap water and bring to a rolling boil over high heat.

2. Start the Sauce: Melt the butter in a nonstick 4.5- to 5-quart sauté pan over medium-high heat. Add the onion and sauté until slightly softened, about 3 minutes.

3. Add the garlic and ground meat and sauté until lightly browned and crumbled, another 3–5 minutes. Add the paprika and 1 teaspoon of the seasoned salt and sauté for 1 minute longer. (**NOTE:** Do *not* drain the pan of the meat's juices! We want that rich flavor in the sauce.)

Recipe Continues

4. Add the flour and stir until everything's fully coated. Reduce the heat to medium.

5. Add the broth and let simmer for 2 minutes, stirring occasionally.

6. Add the tomato sauce and cream or half-and-half and simmer, stirring occasionally, until thickened, another 3–5 minutes. Reduce the heat to medium-low.

7. Cook the Pasta: Add the salt to the pot of boiling water and reduce the heat to medium. Add the pasta and stir. Set a timer to cook until al dente (per the package instructions), or to the shortest amount of time given. When done, **reserve 1 cup of the pasta water** and drain the pasta in a colander in the sink without rinsing it.

8. While the pasta's cooking, return to the sauté pan and add the sour cream and herb cheese and stir until well combined with the sauce. Taste the sauce—if you find it can use some additional seasoned salt, add up to another teaspoon now.

9. Marry It All: Turn the heat off. Add the cooked and drained pasta to the sauté pan and toss to coat with the sauce. Let rest for 3–5 minutes in the pan so the sauce thickens. If you find you want a slightly thinner sauce, add ¼ cup of the reserved pasta water at a time and toss until the desired consistency is reached. Serve topped with a few more sprinkles of paprika, if desired.

 JEFF'S TIPS

For the pasta, I actually use two 9-ounce bags of refrigerated Rana brand pappardelle, which is a bit more than a pound, but it's fresh pasta and won't expand when cooked so it works here. It also only takes 2 minutes to cook. But you can also use dried pappardelle: You'll need 1 pound, and it will take a few minutes longer to cook depending on the brand.

For the meat, I prefer a meatloaf mixture (usually a trio of ground beef, veal, and pork), but you can use any type of ground meat available, be it just beef, pork, veal, chicken, turkey, or plant-based. You can also use uncased sweet or hot Italian sausage.

While sour cream is common to a paprikash and it's a nice finishing touch, you don't need to add that, nor the herb cheese, in Step 8. Give it a taste before adding either and if you're happy with how it is, feel free to leave them out.

To make the sauce gluten-free, omit the flour and mix 2 tablespoons cornstarch and 2 tablespoons cold water in a small bowl to form a slurry. Once you add the tomato sauce and heavy cream or half-and-half to the sauce in Step 6 and it begins to bubble, stir in the slurry and it will thicken perfectly! Continue the recipe as written.

TO HALVE Simply halve all the ingredients. However, the salted pasta water amount remains the same. The pasta and the sauce cook times also remain the same.

CROQUE MONSIEUR (OR MADAME) MACARONI

RESERVE PASTA WATER!

THE PASTA
1 tablespoon salt

1 pound elbow or large elbow macaroni

THE SAUCE
4 tablespoons (½ stick) salted butter

2 tablespoons all-purpose flour (see Jeff's Tips for GF option)

3 cups half-and-half or whole milk

1 teaspoon seasoned salt

1 teaspoon garlic powder

¼ teaspoon nutmeg, plus more for garnish

1 tablespoon Dijon mustard (optional)

½–1 cup (2–4 ounces) shredded Swiss or Gruyère cheese (see Jeff's Tips)

½–1 cup (2–4 ounces) shredded mozzarella cheese (see Jeff's Tips)

1 (5.2-ounce) package Boursin (any flavor) or ¾ cup Herb Cheese (page 28), cut into chunks (optional)

1 pound ham (any kind you like), sliced into slabs about ½ inch thick (ask the deli to slice it for you) and diced into bite-size cubes

FOR A CROQUE MADAME (SEE STEP 8)
Large eggs

Salted butter

Perhaps the most classic sandwich in France is one known as croque monsieur. Ham is sandwiched between two slices of white bread that are slathered with a béchamel sauce (half-and-half or milk, butter, flour, salt, and nutmeg heated and whisked together until thickened), then topped with some Swiss (or mozzarella) cheese before baking for a few minutes. It's essentially the ultimate ham and cheese sandwich (or grilled cheese with ham). Here, I transform it into the ultimate mac and cheese! Adding an egg at the end will make it Croque Madame Macaroni.

Prep Time: 10 min • Pasta Cook Time (elbow macaroni): 6–8 min • Sauce Cook Time: 10 min • Total Time: 20 min • Serves: 4–6

1. Boil the Water: Fill an 8-quart pot halfway with tap water and bring to a rolling boil over high heat.

2. Start the Sauce: Melt the butter in a nonstick 4.5- to 5-quart sauté pan over medium heat. Add the flour and whisk until a lightly browned (almost peanut butter–colored) and fragrantly nutty roux has formed, 1–2 minutes.

3. Slowly pour the half-and-half or milk into the pan while whisking. Once bubbling, reduce the heat to medium-low.

Recipe Continues

4. Cook the Pasta: Once the half-and-half in the pan begins to simmer, add the salt to the pot of boiling water and reduce the heat to medium. Add the pasta and stir. Set a timer to cook until al dente (per the package instructions), or to the shortest amount of time given. When done, **reserve 1 cup of the pasta water** and then drain the pasta in a colander in the sink without rinsing it.

5. While the pasta's cooking, return to the sauté pan and add the seasoned salt, garlic powder, nutmeg, and Dijon (if using) and whisk into the béchamel that's forming. Let simmer for 3–5 minutes, until it's nicely thickened and coats the back of a spoon.

6. Whisk a third of the cheeses into the béchamel. Once melded in, repeat the process twice more until all the cheese is blended and the béchamel begins to stretch like a very thin taffy. If using, add the herb cheese and whisk until combined into the stretchy cheesy sauce.

7. Marry It All: Turn the heat off. Add the cooked and drained pasta and the ham to the sauté pan and stir into the rich, cheesy sauce until all is coated. If at this point you find you want your sauce thinner, add ¼ cup pasta water at a time to thin it out. Serve immediately with a very light sprinkle of additional nutmeg, if desired.

8. For a Croque Madame Finish: Use as many eggs as those who want one to top their bowl of pasta. In a skillet, melt 1 tablespoon butter over medium heat (this is good for 1–4 eggs at a time). Crack the eggs into the pan and cook until the egg whites are solid and even a bit crispy on the bottom, 3–5 minutes. Top individual bowls of pasta with one egg, madame-style.

 JEFF'S TIPS When whisking the Swiss and mozzarella cheeses into the béchamel in Step 6, start with ½ cup (4 ounces) each. If you're happy with your transformed Mornay sauce at that point, you're good. But if you want it cheesier, you can always add ½ cup (4 ounces) more of each.

Feel free to sub smoked or honey turkey if ham isn't your thing.

To make the sauce gluten-free, omit the flour and mix 1 tablespoon cornstarch and 1 tablespoon cold water in a small bowl to form a slurry. Set aside. Then, begin the sauce by placing both the butter and the half-and-half or milk in the pan and heating it up. Once the butter's melted into the half-and-half or milk and comes to a bubble in Step 3, stir in the slurry and it will thicken perfectly! Continue the recipe from there as written.

TO HALVE Simply halve all the ingredients. However, the salted pasta water amount remains the same. The pasta and the sauce cook times also remain the same.

REUBEN ROTINI

RESERVE PASTA WATER!

THE PASTA
1 tablespoon salt

1 pound rotini

THE SAUCE
2 tablespoons (¼ stick) salted butter

2 tablespoons all-purpose flour (see Jeff's Tips for GF option)

½ cup chicken broth

1½ cups heavy cream

½ cup Thousand Island or Russian salad dressing

1–2 cups (4–8 ounces) shredded Swiss cheese, plus more for optional al forno finish (see Jeff's Tips)

2 teaspoons caraway seeds, plus more for garnish (optional)

1 pound deli-thin slices pastrami or corned beef, diced

1 cup sauerkraut, drained and squeezed until dry (optional)

I initially developed this recipe for my yellow Instant Pot cookbook, and it was very well-received. As such (and because it's so dang delicious), I knew I had to adapt it for this pasta book—especially since it features out-of-the-box recipes. It is exactly what it sounds like: your favorite Reuben sandwich transformed into a pasta. And, while the classic Reuben is made with corned beef, it tastes just as delish with pastrami (which I prefer) so feel free to use either, or a mix of the two.

Prep Time: 10 min • Pasta Cook Time (rotini): 7–10 min • Sauce Cook Time: 10 min • Total Time: 25 min • Serves: 4–6

1. Boil the Water and Cook the Pasta: Fill an 8-quart pot halfway with tap water and bring to a rolling boil over high heat. Add the salt and reduce the heat to medium. Add the pasta and stir. Set a timer to cook until al dente (per the package instructions), or to the shortest amount of time given. When done, **reserve 1 cup of the pasta water** and then drain the pasta in a colander in the sink without rinsing it.

2. Make the Sauce: As soon as you add the pasta to the pot, melt the butter in a nonstick 4.5- to 5-quart sauté pan over medium heat. Add the flour and whisk until a lightly browned (almost peanut butter–colored) and fragrantly nutty roux has formed, 1–2 minutes.

3. Add the broth and stir or whisk for 1 minute, until thickened.

4. Stir in the cream. Once bubbling, reduce the heat to medium-low and cook, whisking, until thickened into a Reuben-esque béchamel or until the sauce coats the back of a spoon, 3–5 minutes.

5. Turn the heat off. Add the dressing, shredded cheese (start with 1 cup/4 ounces), and caraway seeds (if using) and stir until combined. If you want it cheesier, add up to 1 cup more of the cheese.

6. Marry It All: Add the cooked and drained pasta to the sauté pan, followed by the pastrami or corned beef and the sauerkraut (if using). Toss to coat with the sauce. If you find you want a slightly thinner, creamier sauce, add ½ cup of the reserved pasta water at a time and stir until the desired consistency is reached. Serve immediately topped with caraway seeds, if desired.

JEFF'S TIPS

If you want to give this an al forno (aka baked) finish, put the completed pasta in a casserole dish, top with 1–2 cups (4–8 ounces) more shredded cheese, and broil in the oven until the top is bubbly and crusty (this shouldn't take more than 3–5 minutes—just keep an eye on it as all broilers vary).

To make the sauce gluten-free, omit the flour and mix 1 tablespoon cornstarch and 1 tablespoon cold water in a small bowl to form a slurry. After melting the butter, add the broth and cream at the same time. Once it begins to bubble, stir in the slurry and it will thicken perfectly! Continue the recipe as written. Also, be sure to use a gluten-free salad dressing.

TO HALVE Simply halve all the ingredients. However, the salted pasta water amount remains the same. The pasta and the sauce cook times also remain the same.

CAVATELLI STROGANOFF

 (if using plant-based meat; see Jeff's Tips)

THE PASTA
1 tablespoon salt

1 pound cavatelli

THE SAUCE
4 tablespoons (½ stick) salted butter

1 yellow onion, diced

1 pound baby bella or white mushrooms, sliced

1½ pounds ground meat of your choice (see Jeff's Tips)

¼ cup all-purpose flour (see Jeff's Tips for GF option)

2 cups beef broth

1 (1-ounce) packet onion dip mix

½ cup sour cream

1 (5.2-ounce) package Boursin (any flavor) or ¾ cup Herb Cheese (page 28), cut into chunks

1 tablespoon Dijon mustard (optional, but suggested)

Stroganoff is a Russian dish in which tender chunks of beef are served over egg noodles and then tossed in a sour cream–based sauce. My Instant Pot take upped the flavor profile by adding an herb cheese, which we'll also do here. But I wanted the version for this book to have more of a ground beef consistency mixed with Italian-style pasta. So in lieu of using chunks of beef, we'll use ground beef, and in place of the egg noodles, we'll use a scoopy-shaped pasta called cavatelli that will better trap that creamy, dreamy sauce. But shells or spaghetti are also nice pasta pairings for this glorious dish!

Prep Time: 10 min • Pasta Cook Time (cavatelli): 3–10 min • Sauce Cook Time: 15 min • Total Time: 25 min • Serves: 4–6

1. Boil the Water: Fill an 8-quart pot halfway with tap water and bring to a rolling boil over high heat.

2. Start the Sauce: Melt the butter in a nonstick 4.5- to 5-quart sauté pan over medium-high heat. Add the onion and mushrooms and sauté until the mushrooms have browned and softened a bit, about 5 minutes.

3. Add the ground meat and sauté until lightly browned and crumbled, another 3–5 minutes. (**NOTE:** Do *not* drain the pan of the meat's juices! We want that rich flavor in the sauce).

4. Add the flour and stir until everything's fully coated. Then, add the broth and onion dip mix. Once bubbling, reduce the heat to medium-low, and simmer for 3–5 minutes, stirring occasionally, until thickened.

5. Cook the Pasta: Add the salt to the pot of boiling water and reduce the heat to medium. Add the pasta and stir. Set a timer to cook until al dente (per the package instructions), or to the shortest amount of time given. When done, drain the pasta in a colander in the sink without rinsing it.

6. While the pasta's cooking, return to the sauté pan and reduce the heat to low. Add the sour cream, herb cheese, and Dijon (if using—and you really should). Stir until well combined. (**NOTE:** If the sauce is done before the pasta, reduce the heat to low and cover the pan with a lid.)

7. Marry It All: Turn the heat off. Add the cooked and drained pasta to the sauté pan and toss to coat with the sauce. Let rest a few minutes in the pan before serving.

JEFF'S TIPS

For the meat, you can use any type of ground meat available, be it beef, pork, veal, chicken, turkey, or plant-based. Your choice!

To make the sauce gluten-free, omit the flour and mix 2 tablespoons cornstarch and 2 tablespoons cold water in a small bowl to form a slurry. Once the broth begins to bubble in Step 4, stir in the slurry and it will thicken perfectly! Continue the recipe as written.

TO HALVE Simply halve all the ingredients. However, the salted pasta water amount remains the same. The pasta and the sauce cook times also remain the same.

PASTA ITALIA

 (if using plant-based meat; see Jeff's Tips)

THE PASTA

1 tablespoon salt

1 pound mezze penne or ziti rigati

THE SAUCE

2 tablespoons extra-virgin olive oil

1 pound Italian sausage (hot, sweet, or a mix of the two), sliced into ½-inch pieces

2 cups Marinara Sauce (page 40 or your favorite jarred brand), plus more for topping

1½ cups Alfredo Sauce (page 42 or your favorite jarred brand), plus more for topping

½ cup Pesto Sauce (page 50 or your favorite jarred brand), plus more for topping

1–1½ pounds meatballs (see Jeff's Tips)

Grated Parmesan cheese, for topping (optional)

If you can't decide between a pesto, Alfredo, or marinara sauce (which happen to sport the three colors of the Italian flag), go a bit crazy and use all three in the same pasta! To make it even more exciting, we're going to add some Italian sausage and meatballs to the mix. For an optional and fun finishing touch, I like to plate the finished pasta in a large serving dish and top with an extra layer of the sauce trio to pay homage to the Italian flag.

Prep Time: 10 min • Pasta Cook Time (mezze penne or ziti rigati): 7–9 min • Sauce Cook Time: 10–30 min • Total Time: 20–40 min • Serves: 4–6

1. Boil the Water: Fill an 8-quart pot halfway with tap water and bring to a rolling boil over high heat.

2. Start the Sauce: Heat the oil in a nonstick 4.5- to 5-quart sauté pan over medium-high heat. Once shimmering, add the sausage and sauté until lightly browned, 3–5 minutes. (**NOTE:** Do *not* drain the pan of the meat's juices! We want that rich flavor in the sauce.)

3. Cook the Pasta: Add the salt to the pot of boiling water and reduce the heat to medium. Add the pasta and stir. Set a timer to cook until al dente (per the package instructions), or to the shortest amount of time given. When done, drain the pasta in a colander in the sink without rinsing it.

4. While the pasta's cooking, return to the sauté pan and add the three sauces to the pot and stir to combine.

5. Nestle in the meatballs. Once bubbling, cover the pot halfway and reduce the heat to medium-low. Let simmer, stirring occasionally, for 5–10 minutes if using frozen pre-cooked meatballs, or 25–30 minutes for uncooked meatballs. (**NOTE:** If using uncooked meatballs, begin cooking the pasta 15 minutes after the balls have simmered in the sauce.)

6. Marry It All: Turn the heat off. Add the cooked and drained pasta to the sauté pan and toss to coat with the sauce. Serve as is or transfer to a large serving dish and spoon on additional stripes of pesto, Alfredo, and marinara (they should be at room temp or heated in the microwave separately), forming the Italian flag right on top! Feel free to add some grated Parmesan as well.

JEFF'S TIPS

For the meatballs, you have options:
- For a quick cook, use 1–2 pounds of bagged frozen meatballs.
- For sausage-based meatballs, make the Italian mini meatballs from my Italian & Jewish Wedding Soup (page 262) before beginning the recipe.
- For traditional meatballs, make the meatballs from my Spaghetti & Meatballs (page 54) before beginning the recipe.

To make it vegetarian, use a plant-based meat and sausage.

TO HALVE Simply halve all the ingredients. However, the salted pasta water amount remains the same. The pasta and the sauce cook times also remain the same.

HALUSKI
(NOODLES WITH FRIED CABBAGE & BACON)

 (see Jeff's Tip)

THE PASTA

1 tablespoon salt

12 ounces egg noodles (I use wide)

THE SAUCE

8 tablespoons (1 stick) salted butter, divided

1 pound thick-cut bacon, diced

1 large yellow onion, diced

½ head green cabbage, cored and chopped

6 cloves garlic, minced or pressed

1 teaspoon seasoned salt

1 teaspoon garlic powder

1 teaspoon black or ½ teaspoon white pepper

As I was cleaning out my fridge one day, I found a head of perfectly fine cabbage sitting in the vegetable hospice drawer—you know, the place veggies we buy are forgotten about and then go bad. But this head of cabbage was still vibrant and begging to be used. I also found some egg noodles in the pantry and bacon in the fridge and decided to make a rendition of haluski—a fantastically simple and light yet satisfying Polish noodle dish—for dinner!

Prep Time: 10 min • **Pasta Cook Time (wide egg noodles): 6–11 min** • **Sauce Cook Time: 35–40 min** • **Total Time: 45–50 min** • **Serves: 4–6**

1. Boil the Water: Fill an 8-quart pot halfway with tap water and bring to a rolling boil over high heat.

2. Start the Sauce: Melt 2 tablespoons of the butter in a nonstick 4.5- to 5-quart sauté pan over medium-high heat. Add the bacon and sauté until just between cooked and crispy, 8–10 minutes. Remove with a slotted spoon and drain in a paper towel–lined bowl. Set aside. (**NOTE:** Leave the oil in your pan—it's a huge key to the sauce's flavor!)

3. Add the remaining 6 tablespoons butter to the pan. Once melted, add the onion and sauté until lightly browned, 3–5 minutes.

 JEFF'S TIP If you want this dish vegetarian, simply skip the bacon and melt all the butter in Step 3 just before adding the onion.

4. Add the cabbage, garlic, seasoned salt, garlic powder, and pepper and sauté until lightly wilted and lightly browned, 15–20 minutes. Once the cabbage is done to your liking, turn the heat off the sauté pan.

5. Cook the Pasta: After 10 minutes of sautéing the cabbage, add the salt to the pot of boiling water and reduce the heat to medium. Add the pasta and stir. Set a timer to cook until al dente (per the package instructions), or to the shortest amount of time given. When done, drain the pasta in a colander in the sink without rinsing it.

6. Marry It All: Add the cooked noodles to the sauté pan followed by the cooked bacon. Toss until combined and serve.

TO HALVE Simply halve all the ingredients. However, the salted pasta water amount remains the same. The pasta and the sauce cook times also remain the same.

BUCATINI CARBONARA

RESERVE PASTA WATER!

THE PASTA

1 tablespoon salt

1 pound bucatini or perciatelli

THE SAUCE

2 large eggs plus 2 large egg yolks

½ cup freshly grated Pecorino Romano cheese, plus more for serving

½ cup freshly grated Parmesan cheese, plus more for serving

1 teaspoon freshly ground pepper, plus more for serving

1 teaspoon garlic powder (optional)

2 tablespoons extra-virgin olive oil

8 ounces pancetta, guanciale, or thick-cut bacon, diced

All you need to do is add bacon, eggs, and cheese to some pasta to make what is essentially the breakfast of the pasta world. Although known for taking classics and putting my own spin on them (like the carbonara recipe in my orange Instant Pot book), I'm going to make this one more traditional in terms of the ingredients, but I do supply some options in Jeff's Tips. Carbonara is most commonly made with spaghetti, but any long noodle works great. That said, I personally prefer bucatini or perciatelli for carbonara, as I like to slurp the sauce simultaneously with the noodles.

Prep Time: 10 min • **Pasta Cook Time (bucatini or perciatelli): 7–11 min** • **Sauce Cook Time: 10 min** • **Total Time: 20 min** • **Serves: 4–6**

1. Boil the Water and Cook the Pasta: Fill an 8-quart pot halfway with tap water and bring to a rolling boil over high heat. Add the salt and reduce the heat to medium. Add the pasta and stir. Set a timer to cook until al dente (per the package instructions), or to the shortest amount of time given. When done, **reserve 2 cups of the pasta water** and then drain the pasta in a colander in the sink without rinsing it.

2. Make the Sauce: As soon as you add the pasta to the pot, add the eggs and yolks, both cheeses, the pepper, and garlic powder (if using) to a mixing bowl and whisk until combined into a thick paste. Set aside.

Recipe Continues

3. Heat the olive oil in a nonstick 4.5- to 5-quart sauté pan over medium-high heat. Once shimmering, add the pancetta, guanciale, or bacon and sauté until just between cooked and crispy, 5–8 minutes. (**NOTE:** Leave the oil from the pancetta, guanciale, or bacon in your pan—it's a huge key to the sauce's flavor!) Remove the pan from the heat and place on a cool part of the stove or a trivet on the counter as the pasta finishes cooking.

4. Marry It All: Add the cooked and drained pasta to the sauté pan and toss with the pancetta, guanciale, or bacon and the oil.

5. Then pour the cheesy egg mixture over it, followed by ½ cup of the reserved starchy pasta water.

6. Using tongs, toss for 1–2 minutes, until the egg mixture is lightly cooked into the pasta and a creamy consistency forms. And don't worry, the heat of the pan and the pasta combined is enough to gently cook the eggs. If, when done tossing, you want the dish creamier, add more pasta water in ½-cup increments until the desired consistency is reached. Serve immediately topped with additional grated cheese and pepper, if desired.

 JEFF'S TIPS

Only have Parmesan or Pecorino Romano on hand? Just use 1 cup of either (so you have 1 cup of grated cheese, total). Just know that using only Pecorino Romano will make for a slightly saltier carbonara.

Some like their carbonara with onion and peas. If that's you, sauté a diced small yellow onion or shallot with the pancetta, guanciale, or bacon in Step 3 and/or add up to ½ cup peas (thawed from a frozen bag) in Step 4 when tossing the pasta with the sauce.

If you have leftovers, the best way to reheat and reconstitute the sauce is to add a few splashes of heavy cream to the pasta and zap in the microwave in 30-second intervals until heated, then mix until a rich and creamy sauce is formed. Allow it to rest for 1–2 minutes before serving and the sauce will be perfect.

TO HALVE Simply halve all the ingredients. However, the salted pasta water amount remains the same. The pasta and the sauce cook times also remain the same.

SAUSAGE & SHELLS

This is the most popular pasta dish I've ever created. In fact, it has become so popular worldwide, I saw many other iterations of it pop up after I released mine. But just like Alfredo Di Lelio invented the iconic fettuccine Alfredo, Jeffrey Eisner invented this unmistakably decadent Sausage & Shells. There used to be only one way to make it: In the Instant Pot and using the recipe in my orange book...until now! Welcome to one of the most addicting pastas you'll ever make.

 (if using plant-based meat; see Jeff's Tips)

THE PASTA
1 tablespoon salt

1 pound medium shells

THE SAUCE
2 tablespoons (¼ stick) salted butter

2 large shallots, diced

3 cloves garlic, minced or pressed

2 pounds Italian sausage (hot, sweet, or a mix of the two), sliced into ½-inch pieces (see Jeff's Tips)

2 tablespoons all-purpose flour (see Jeff's Tips for GF option)

½ cup dry white wine (like chardonnay, or see Jeff's Tips)

½ cup chicken or garlic broth (e.g., made from Better Than Bouillon Roasted Garlic Base)

1½ teaspoons Italian seasoning

2 cups heavy cream

5 ounces spinach

½ cup grated Parmesan or Pecorino Romano cheese, plus more for serving

1 (5.2-ounce) package Boursin (any flavor) or ¾ cup Herb Cheese (page 28), cut into chunks

Garlic salt or seasoned salt, to taste (optional)

1 (14-ounce) can artichoke hearts, drained and ripped up by hand

1 (16-ounce or so) jar sun-dried tomatoes, drained and roughly chopped

---

Prep Time: 15 min • Pasta Cook Time (medium shells): 8–9 min • Sauce Cook Time: 15 min • Total Time: 30 min • Serves: 4–6

1. Boil the Water: Fill an 8-quart pot halfway with tap water and bring to a rolling boil over high heat.

2. Start the Sauce: Melt the butter in a nonstick 4.5- to 5-quart sauté pan over medium-high heat. Add the shallots and sauté for 2 minutes.

3. Add the garlic and sausage and sauté until the meat is browned, about 5 minutes.

Recipe Continues

4. Cook the Pasta: Add the salt to the pot of boiling water and reduce the heat to medium. Add the pasta and stir. Set a timer to cook until al dente (per the package instructions), or to the shortest amount of time given. When done, drain the pasta in a colander in the sink without rinsing it.

5. While the pasta's cooking, return to the sauté pan. Add the flour and stir to coat the sausage and shallots. Reduce the heat to medium.

6. Add the wine, broth, and Italian seasoning and stir. Simmer for 1–2 minutes, until thickened.

7. Stir in the cream and top with the spinach. Once bubbling, reduce the heat to medium-low and let simmer for 3–5 minutes, stirring occasionally, until the sauce begins to thicken and the spinach is wilted.

8. Stir in the Parmesan or Pecorino Romano and herb cheese until combined into the sauce. Taste the sauce. If you want it saltier, feel free to stir in garlic salt or seasoned salt in 1-teaspoon increments until you're content.

9. Marry It All: Turn the heat off. Add the cooked and drained pasta, artichokes, and sun-dried tomatoes to the sauté pan and toss to coat with the sauce. Serve immediately, topped with additional grated Parmesan, if desired.

JEFF'S TIPS

While I feel Italian sausage works best with this dish, you can use literally any sausage variety, be it raw or pre-cooked. And to make it vegetarian, use a plant-based sausage, although it can greatly change the flavor profile depending on which you use.

If you don't want wine, just use 1 cup broth instead of ½ cup.

To make the sauce gluten-free, omit the flour and mix 1 tablespoon cornstarch and 1 tablespoon cold water in a small bowl to form a slurry. Once the wine and broth begin to simmer in Step 6, stir in the slurry and it will thicken perfectly! Continue the recipe as written.

TO HALVE Simply halve all the ingredients. However, the salted pasta water amount remains the same. The pasta and the sauce cook times also remain the same.

FUSILLI ALL'AMATRICIANA

 (see Jeff's Tips)

THE PASTA

1 tablespoon salt

1 pound fusilli col buco

THE SAUCE

2 tablespoons (¼ stick) salted butter

8 ounces pancetta or thick-cut bacon, diced

1 large yellow onion, diced

3 cloves garlic, minced or pressed

3 cups Marinara Sauce (page 40 or your favorite jarred brand)

¼ cup hot sauce of your choice

½–2 teaspoons cayenne pepper

1–3 teaspoons crushed red pepper flakes (optional)

¼ cup grated Parmesan or Pecorino Romano cheese, plus more for serving

This well-known pasta dish is essentially an arrabbiata (or spicy) red sauce embedded with onion and pancetta. It's definitely for those who enjoy some zing in their pasta. I like to add some hot sauce to the mix, which gives the sauce a richer undertone. The common pasta for amatriciana is bucatini, but my choice is a long fusilli col buco, which is like a squiggly, more fun bucatini or perciatelli.

Prep Time: 10 min • **Pasta Cook Time (fusilli col buco): 13 min** • **Sauce Cook Time: 20 min** •
Total Time: 30 min • **Serves: 4–6**

1. Boil the Water: Fill an 8-quart pot halfway with tap water and bring to a rolling boil over high heat.

2. Start the Sauce: Melt the butter in a nonstick 4.5- to 5-quart sauté pan over medium-high heat. Add the pancetta or bacon and sauté until it's just between being cooked and crisped, 5–8 minutes. Reduce the heat to medium. (**NOTE:** Leave the oil from the pancetta or bacon in your pan—it's a huge key to the sauce's flavor!)

3. Cook the Pasta: Add the salt to the pot of boiling water and reduce the heat to medium. Add the pasta and stir. Set a timer to cook until al dente (per the package instructions), or to the shortest amount of time given. When done, drain the pasta in a colander in the sink without rinsing it.

JEFF'S TIPS

To keep this vegetarian, omit the pancetta or bacon. You'll have more of a fra diavolo (spicy) sauce.

If you don't want this amatriciana spicy, leave out the hot sauce and cayenne and don't add the optional red pepper flakes.

TO HALVE Simply halve all the ingredients. However, the salted pasta water amount remains the same. The pasta and the sauce cook times also remain the same.

4. While the pasta's cooking, return to the sauté pan. Add the onion and garlic and sauté until translucent, another 2–3 minutes.

5. Add the marinara, hot sauce, cayenne (start with ½ teaspoon), and red pepper flakes, if using (again, start with less and add more). Stir to combine and let simmer for 5 minutes, stirring occasionally. Taste it and feel free to add more of the spicy ingredients now, if you dare (do it to taste so you don't go overboard).

6. Marry It All: Turn the heat off. Stir in the grated cheese and then add the cooked and drained pasta and use tongs to toss and coat with the sauce. Serve topped with additional cheese, if desired.

PUMPKIN & SAUSAGE PASTA

 (see Jeff's Tips)

THE PASTA

1 tablespoon salt

1 pound zucca/zucchette pasta

THE SAUCE

2 tablespoons (¼ stick) salted butter

2 large shallots, diced

3 cloves garlic, minced or pressed

2 pounds Italian sausage (hot, sweet, or a mix of the two), casings removed

2 cups heavy cream

¼ teaspoon nutmeg, plus more for topping (see Jeff's Tips)

1 (15-ounce) can pumpkin puree (I use Libby's 100% Pure Pumpkin)

½ cup grated Pecorino Romano cheese, plus more for topping

1 (5.2-ounce) package Boursin (any flavor) or ¾ cup Herb Cheese (page 28), cut into chunks (optional)

Toasted pumpkin seeds, for topping (optional)

It's The Great Pumpkin & Sausage Pasta, Charlie Brown! One fall, I was in the market and a box of a pumpkin-shaped pasta, known as "zucca," immediately grabbed my attention. This was the first I'd heard of it, but I just knew I had to do something creative with this pasta shape—so I infused a creamy Parmesan sauce with some canned pumpkin. Perfect for Halloween and Thanksgiving alike, Pumpkin & Sausage Pasta has no tricks but is all treat—making you mouth a lusty "thank you" to it after each bite. If you can't find zucca, don't fret! Any scoopy pasta (see page 33) will work great!

Prep Time: 10 min • Pasta Cook Time (zucca/zucchette): 10 min • Sauce Cook Time: 15 min • Total Time: 25 min • Serves: 4–6

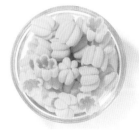

1. Boil the Water: Fill an 8-quart pot halfway with tap water and bring to a rolling boil over high heat.

2. Start the Sauce: Melt the butter in a nonstick 4.5- to 5-quart sauté pan over medium-high heat. Add the shallots, garlic, and sausage and sauté until the meat is crumbled and browned and the oils have been released, about 5 minutes. Reduce the heat to medium.

3. Cook the Pasta: Add the salt to the pot of boiling water and reduce the heat to medium. Add the pasta and stir. Set a timer to cook until al dente (per the package instructions), or to the shortest amount of time given. When done, drain the pasta in a colander in the sink without rinsing it.

4. While the pasta's cooking, return to the sauté pan and stir in the cream and nutmeg.

5. Once bubbling, reduce the heat to medium-low and simmer for 5–7 minutes, stirring occasionally, until the sauce is moderately thickened and coats the back of a spoon.

6. Stir in the pumpkin puree, Pecorino Romano, and herb cheese (if using) until combined into the sauce.

7. Marry It All: Turn the heat off. Add the cooked and drained pasta to the sauté pan and toss to coat with the sauce. Serve topped with additional grated cheese, nutmeg, and toasted pumpkin seeds, if desired.

 JEFF'S TIPS To make it vegetarian, use a plant-based sausage, although depending on which you use, it can greatly change the flavor profile.

To change things up a bit, if you have some apple pie spice lying around, feel free to use that in place of the nutmeg!

TO HALVE Simply halve all the ingredients. However, the salted pasta water amount remains the same. The pasta and the sauce cook times also remain the same.

SPICY SAUSAGE LEMON NOODLES

 (see Jeff's Tips)

THE PASTA

1 tablespoon salt

1 pound mafaldine

THE SAUCE

2 tablespoons (¼ stick) salted butter

2 pounds hot Italian sausage, casings removed

2 large shallots, diced

1 pound baby bella or white mushrooms, sliced

6 cloves garlic, minced or pressed

Juice of 3 lemons (plus grated zest for garnish, if desired)

½ cup chicken or garlic broth (e.g., made from Better Than Bouillon Roasted Garlic Base)

1 teaspoon dried oregano

1 teaspoon dried parsley flakes

½ cup heavy cream

5 ounces spinach

1 cup grated Parmesan, plus more for serving

1 (5.2-ounce) package Boursin (any flavor) or ¾ cup Herb Cheese (page 28), cut into chunks

½–1 teaspoon cayenne pepper

½–1 teaspoon crushed red pepper flakes, plus more for serving

1 tablespoon cornstarch + 1 tablespoon cold water

In case you couldn't tell with this chapter, I absolutely love pasta with sausage. Mostly because it creates such a vibrant taste when the oils seep into the sauce, setting the stage for a truly deep flavor experience. Once you add a lemon-infused Parmesan sauce and then pepper it with zesty seasonings, you have one seriously sassy pasta dish that awaits the twirl of your fork. Mafaldine is my noodle of choice since it makes this pasta as fun to look at as it is to devour.

Prep Time: 10 min • **Pasta Cook Time (mafaldine): 8–9 min** • **Sauce Cook Time: 20 min** • **Total Time: 30 min** • **Serves: 4–6**

1. Boil the Water: Fill an 8-quart pot halfway with tap water and bring to a rolling boil over high heat.

2. Start the Sauce: Melt the butter in a nonstick 4.5- to 5-quart sauté pan over medium-high heat. Add the sausage and sauté until the meat is crumbled and browned and the oils have been released, 3–5 minutes.

3. Add the shallots, mushrooms, and garlic and sauté another 5 minutes, until softened.

Recipe Continues

4. Reduce the heat to medium. Add the lemon juice, broth, oregano, and parsley flakes, stir, and simmer for 2 minutes.

5. Cook the Pasta: Add the salt to the pot of boiling water and reduce the heat to medium. Add the pasta and stir. Set a timer to cook until al dente (per the package instructions), or to the shortest amount of time given. When done, drain the pasta in a colander in the sink without rinsing it.

6. While the pasta's cooking, return to the sauté pan, add the cream, and top with the spinach. Once bubbling, reduce the heat to medium-low and simmer, stirring occasionally, for another 3–5 minutes, until the spinach is wilted.

7. Stir in the Parmesan, herb cheese, and the lesser amounts of cayenne and red pepper flakes until combined. Taste the sauce. If you want more spice, add it now.

8. In a small bowl, whisk the cornstarch and water to form a slurry. Increase the heat to medium, add the cornstarch slurry to the sauté pan, and stir until the sauce thickens.

9. Marry It All: Turn the heat off. Add the cooked and drained pasta and use tongs to toss and coat with the sauce. Serve topped with the lemon zest and additional grated Parmesan and red pepper flakes, if desired.

 JEFF'S TIPS Even though this dish is designed to be on the spicy side, you can keep it totally mild by using sweet sausage instead of hot and omitting the cayenne and red pepper flakes.

To make it vegetarian, use a plant-based sausage, although depending on which you use, it can greatly change the flavor profile.

TO HALVE Simply halve all the ingredients. However, the salted pasta water amount remains the same. The pasta and the sauce cook times also remain the same.

GNOCCHI IN SAUSAGE GRAVY

THE PASTA

1 tablespoon salt

2 pounds gnocchi (a room-temperature sealed package is preferred)

THE SAUCE

1 pound ground breakfast sausage (get the kind found in a wrapped tube, not solid pre-cooked links—either regular or spicy) (see Jeff's Tips)

2 tablespoons (¼ stick) salted butter

¼ cup all-purpose flour

3 cups whole milk or half-and-half

½ teaspoon seasoned salt

½ teaspoon garlic powder

½–1 teaspoon black pepper, plus more for serving

One morning while I was making a basic breakfast of biscuits and gravy for some friends, I was just too lazy to make the biscuits (nor did I have a can of Pillsbury Grands in the fridge). But I did have gnocchi on hand and realized they would probably go really well with the gravy. And let me tell you, that fluffy potato gnocchi in sausage (or "sauce-age") gravy was the perfect brunch pasta, and it's since been requested over and over again. A star is born with this fast and easy breakfast or brunch pasta!

Prep Time: 10 min • Pasta Cook Time (gnocchi): 2–3 min • Sauce Cook Time: 10 min • Total Time: 20 min • Serves: 4–6

1. Boil the Water: Fill an 8-quart pot halfway with tap water and bring to a rolling boil over high heat.

2. Start the Sauce: Sauté the sausage meat in a nonstick 4.5- to 5-quart sauté pan over medium-high heat until crumbled and browned, 3–5 minutes. (**NOTE:** Do *not* drain the pot of the meat's juices! We want that rich flavor in the sauce.)

3. Stir in the butter until melted. Add the flour and stir until the sausage is fully coated.

Recipe Continues

4. Cook the Gnocchi: Add the salt to the pot of boiling water and reduce the heat to medium. Add the gnocchi and stir. Set a timer to cook until al dente (per the package instructions), or to the shortest amount of time given. When done, **reserve 1 cup of the pasta water** and drain the gnocchi in a colander in the sink without rinsing them.

5. While the gnocchi are cooking, return to the sauté pan and add the milk or half-and-half, seasoned salt, garlic powder, and pepper and whisk. Once bubbling, reduce the heat to medium-low so it becomes a gentle simmer.

6. Cook, whisking occasionally, for 1–2 minutes, until thickened; turn off the heat.

7. Marry It All: Add the cooked and drained gnocchi to the sauté pan and toss to coat with the sauce. If you find you want a slightly thinner, creamier sauce, add ¼ cup of the reserved pasta water at a time and stir until the desired consistency is reached. Serve topped with more pepper, if desired.

JEFF'S TIPS

Want this cheesy? Toward the end of Step 5, as you're whisking and the gravy thickens, add a few sprinkles of shredded Cheddar.

If you just want to use this recipe for a great biscuit gravy over actual biscuits, just skip the pasta steps!

If you want a thinner gravy that's also a bit richer, sub more milk or cream for the pasta water in Step 7.

You can use any kind of breakfast sausage you like, be it mild, spicy, or sagey. Tubes of breakfast sausage (also known as a "chub") can be found in the meat or frozen section of some markets.

TO HALVE Simply halve all the ingredients. However, the salted pasta water amount remains the same. The pasta and the sauce cook times also remain the same.

VEAL PARMINARA

THE PASTA
1 tablespoon salt

1 pound cascatelli

THE SAUCE
2 tablespoons extra-virgin olive oil

2 pounds ground veal (see Jeff's Tips)

3 cups Marinara Sauce (page 40 or your favorite jarred brand)

2 large eggs, slightly beaten

⅔ cup heavy cream or half-and-half

1 cup grated Parmesan cheese

1 cup (4 ounces) shredded mozzarella cheese, optional, plus more for optional al forno finish (see Jeff's Tips)

This pasta is a special creation I whipped up one winter's day when I was craving some veal Parmesan and carbonara (page 72). After rummaging through the deep freezer, I couldn't find veal cutlets, but I *did* find some ground veal I'd forgotten about. It was then that a light bulb went off in my head. I knew this would make for a very interesting pasta in which I could combine my love of a Parmesan (hence the "parm") and carbonara (hence the "ara") using a sensational and meaty parm-egg-marinara sauce!

Prep Time: 10 min • **Pasta Cook Time (cascatelli): 13–15 min** • **Sauce Cook Time: 15 min** • **Total Time: 25 min** • **Serves: 4–6**

1. Boil the Water and Cook the Pasta: Fill an 8-quart pot halfway with tap water and bring to a rolling boil over high heat. Add the salt and reduce the heat to medium. Add the pasta and stir. Set a timer to cook until al dente (per the package instructions), or to the shortest amount of time given. When done, drain the pasta in a colander in the sink without rinsing it.

2. Make the Sauce: As soon as you add the pasta to the pot, heat the oil in a nonstick 4.5- to 5-quart sauté pan over medium-high heat. Once shimmering, add the ground veal and sauté until crumbled and browned, 3–5 minutes. (**NOTE:** Do *not* drain the pot of the meat's juices! We want that rich flavor in the sauce.)

3. Reduce the heat to medium. Add the marinara and let simmer for 3–5 minutes, stirring occasionally. Reduce the heat to medium-low.

TO HALVE Simply halve all the ingredients. However, the salted pasta water amount remains the same. The pasta and the sauce cook times also remain the same.

4. In a bowl, whisk together the eggs, cream, and Parmesan cheese.

5. Add the cheesy egg mixture to the sauce in the pan and stir for 1-2 minutes as the egg cooks and the sauce thickens.

6. Marry It All: Turn the heat off. Add the cooked and drained pasta and the mozzarella (if using) to the sauté pan and toss to coat with the sauce. <u>See Jeff's Tips</u> for an al forno finish.

JEFF'S TIPS

If veal isn't your style, use any ground meat you desire!

If you want to give this an al forno (aka baked) finished, put the completed pasta in a casserole dish and top with an additional 1-2 cups (4-8 ounces) shredded mozzarella. Broil in the oven until the top is bubbly and crusty (this shouldn't take more than 3-5 minutes—just keep an eye on it as all broilers vary).

3

CLUCKY

Why did the chicken cross the road?

   To not end up in this chapter!

   I just love a pasta that's loaded with poultry and tossed in basically any variety of sauce. This chapter will feature both tender and juicy white and dark variations of chicken. Some will have the chicken pan-seared prior to making the sauce and others will have it cooked directly in the sauce, which can range from tomato-based to creamy to light and oil-based.

   If you want even more clucky pastas done a bit differently, check out the Stir-Fry (page 188), Al Forno (page 206), and One Pot (page 234) chapters.

🅳🅵 **Dairy-Free**

🆅 **Vegetarian**

🆅🅽 **Vegan**

✦ **Compliant with Modifications**

CHICKEN PARMESAN PASTA

If you're a lover of crispy, golden chicken Parmesan served over a bed of pasta, this is probably going to become your new all-time favorite recipe. It's very easy to make, and what time you spend breading and cooking the cutlets is made up by the simplicity of the sauce. Just use a homemade marinara or one of your favorite jarred brands (Victoria or Rao's for me), or see Jeff's Tips for other sauce options. What's more, the completely addicting cutlets are perfection on their own over any pasta, rice, or veggie dish! See Jeff's Tips for how to make this a classic chicken Parm.

THE PASTA
1 tablespoon salt

1 pound angel hair or capellini

THE CHICKEN
½ cup all-purpose flour

2 large eggs

1 cup panko breadcrumbs (don't use regular breadcrumbs here, panko makes a difference)

¾ cup grated Parmesan cheese

1 teaspoon dried parsley flakes

1 teaspoon garlic powder

½ teaspoon onion powder

½ teaspoon seasoned salt

½ teaspoon black pepper

1 cup extra-virgin olive oil

2 pounds boneless, skinless chicken breasts, sliced into ¼-inch-thick cutlets (but no thicker; this is so the chicken cooks all the way through)

THE SAUCE
4 cups Marinara Sauce (page 40 or your favorite jarred brand, or see Jeff's Tips)

Leaves from 1 bunch fresh basil, stemmed, some reserved for serving (optional)

1 cup grated Parmesan cheese, plus more for serving

Mozzarella cheese, sliced, for serving

Prep Time: 15 min • **Pasta Cook Time (angel hair/capellini):** 2–4 min • **Chicken Cook Time:** 10 min • **Sauce Cook Time:** 5 min • **Total Time:** 30–35 min • **Serves:** 4–6

1. Boil the Water: Fill an 8-quart pot halfway with tap water and bring to a rolling boil over high heat.

2. Cook the Chicken: Set up a dredging line (stations A, B, and C, in that order):

a. Spread the flour on a large plate.

b. Beat the eggs in a shallow bowl.

c. Whisk the breadcrumbs, Parmesan, parsley flakes, garlic powder, onion powder, seasoned salt, and pepper together on a large plate until combined.

3. Heat the oil in a nonstick 4.5- to 5-quart sauté pan over medium-high heat. Once heated and shimmering, reduce the heat to medium to medium-low.

Recipe Continues

4. It's time to bread the chicken! Just make sure to do so only *just* before pan-frying each batch of them (two or three at a time). In assembly-line fashion, place each chicken cutlet in the flour (Station A) and dredge both sides until fully coated, then coat both sides in the eggs (Station B), and finally dredge in the breadcrumb mixture (Station C), fully coating both sides.

5. Add the chicken directly from the assembly line to the hot oil and cook for 3–5 minutes, flipping the cutlets every 30 seconds or so to make sure the breadcrumb crust doesn't burn. When done, the crust of the cutlets should be mostly golden brown in color with a few darker specks or shades here and there. Transfer the chicken to a cutting board and slice into a piece to ensure it's fully cooked (165°F with fully white meat and no traces of pink). Keep the cutlets whole (or **see Jeff's Tips**) and set aside on a paper towel–lined plate. Repeat the process until all the chicken is cooked. (**NOTE:** When done pan-frying, there will still be oil in the pan. Keeping some is fine, but if there appears to be more than ¼ cup, you can transfer the excess hot oil to a Pyrex dish until cool and either save for later or dispose.)

6. Start the Sauce: With the heat on medium, add the marinara, basil (if using), and Parmesan to the sauté pan, stir, and bring to a simmer. Heat until the basil is wilted into the sauce, 3–5 minutes.

 JEFF'S TIPS

Feel free to change the sauce up to a Vodka Sauce (page 47) or Alfredo Sauce (page 42)!

You can also cut your chicken up and toss it with the pasta, if you like.

For a classic chicken Parm finish: Put the cooked chicken cutlets on a parchment- or foil-lined baking sheet. Top each cutlet with an additional drizzle of marinara (not too much so the breading doesn't get soggy) and a slice or two of mozzarella cheese (⅛–¼ inch thick) and broil in the oven until the cheese is bubbly brown (this shouldn't take more than 3 minutes—just keep an eye on it as all broilers vary). When done, top those cheesy, crispy cutlets with additional sauce and a sprinkle of Parmesan before serving over the pasta, or simply on their own.

You can also forego the pasta steps and just make the chicken parm on its own!

TO HALVE Simply halve all the ingredients. However, the salted pasta water amount remains the same. The pasta and the sauce cook times also remain the same.

7. Cook the Pasta: While the sauce is simmering, add the salt to the pot of boiling water and reduce the heat to medium. Add the pasta and stir. Set a timer to cook until al dente (per the package instructions), or to the shortest amount of time given. When done, drain the pasta in a colander in the sink without rinsing it.

8. Marry It All: Turn the heat off under the sauté pan. Add the cooked and drained pasta to the sauté pan and toss to coat. Serve the pasta topped with a chicken cutlet and mozzarella, Parmesan, and basil, if desired. Or **see Jeff's Tips** on how to give it a really impressive finish.

MARDI GRAS CHICKEN PASTA

RESERVE PASTA WATER!

There's a certain pasta dish on the menu at one of my happiest places on earth, also known as the Cheesecake Factory, that I love (okay, actually there are many pasta dishes there that are amazing). This recipe is inspired by their Louisiana Chicken Pasta, except instead of breaded chicken cutlets, I prefer chicken sausage to give it that extra Southern flair. However, if you wish to use breaded or blackened chicken, check out Jeff's Tips in the recipes on pages 92 and 114, respectively. Or see Jeff's Tips in this recipe for other chicken options.

THE PASTA
1 tablespoon salt

1 pound farfalle (bow ties)

THE SAUCE
2 tablespoons (¼ stick) salted butter

2 pounds chicken sausage of your choice (pre-cooked or raw), sliced into ½-inch-thick disks (or **see Jeff's Tips**)

1 red onion, diced

2 bell peppers of your choice (I use red and yellow), seeded and diced

3 cloves garlic, minced or pressed

2 teaspoons Cajun/Creole/Louisiana seasoning (I use Tony Chachere's)

1½ teaspoons smoked or regular paprika

3 tablespoons all-purpose flour (**see Jeff's Tips** for GF option)

2 cups heavy cream

1 (14.5-ounce) can diced tomatoes, with their juices

½ cup grated Parmesan cheese, plus more for serving

1–2 teaspoons crushed red pepper flakes (optional and to taste), plus more for serving

1–2 teaspoons cayenne pepper (optional and to taste), plus more for serving

**Prep Time: 10 min • Pasta Cook Time (farfalle): 10–11 min • Sauce Cook Time: 15 min •
Total Time: 25 min • Serves: 4–6**

1. Boil the Water: Fill an 8-quart pot halfway with tap water and bring to a rolling boil over high heat.

2. Start the Sauce: Melt the butter in a nonstick 4.5- to 5-quart sauté pan over medium-high heat. Add the chicken sausage and sauté for 3–5 minutes. (**NOTE:** Do *not* drain the pot of any sausage juices! We want that rich flavor in the sauce.)

3. Cook the Pasta: Add the salt to the pot of boiling water and reduce the heat to medium. Add the pasta and stir. Set a timer to cook until al dente (per the package instructions), or to the shortest amount of time given. When done, **reserve 1 cup of the pasta water** and then drain the pasta in a colander in the sink without rinsing it.

x

4. While the pasta's cooking, return to the sauté pan and add the onion, peppers, garlic, Cajun/Creole/Louisiana seasoning, and paprika. Sauté until slightly softened, about 5 minutes. Reduce the heat to medium.

5. Add the flour and stir to coat the chicken and veggies.

6. Add the cream and diced tomatoes and stir. Once bubbling, reduce the heat to medium-low and simmer for 2–3 minutes, until the sauce thickens.

7. Add the Parmesan and stir until melded into the sauce. If you want it spicy, now's the time to do a taste test and add the red pepper flakes and/or cayenne to taste.

8. Marry It All: Turn the heat off. Add the cooked and drained pasta to the sauté pan and toss to coat with the sauce. If you find you want a slightly thinner, creamier sauce, add ¼ cup of the reserved pasta water at a time and stir until the desired consistency is reached. Serve topped with additional Parmesan and cayenne and/or red pepper flakes, if desired.

JEFF'S TIPS

You can also use chicken tenders or chicken nuggets instead of chicken sausage and cook according to the package instructions while the pasta is cooking. However, instead of adding them in Step 2, add any of these options in Step 8, just after adding the pasta and tossing together with the sauce.

To make the sauce gluten-free, omit the flour and mix 1½ tablespoons cornstarch and 1½ tablespoons cold water in a small bowl to form a slurry. Once the cream and tomatoes begin to bubble in Step 6, stir in the slurry and it will thicken perfectly! Continue the recipe as written.

TO HALVE Simply halve all the ingredients. However, the salted pasta water amount remains the same. The pasta and the sauce cook times also remain the same.

CHAMPAGNE CHICKEN CAVATAPPI

RESERVE **PASTA** WATER!

I made my famous Champagne Chicken on the *Rachael Ray Show* a few years ago and she and I had the best time. And I guess fun combined with flavor pays off: It quickly became one of my readers' go-to chicken dishes. This is another one of those recipes that I originally designed to be a chicken dish served over pasta but then I figured, why not just cut to the chase and marry them together right from the get-go? Ta-da! The cutlets are perfection on their own as well; try them over any pasta, rice, or veggie dish!

THE PASTA
1 tablespoon salt

1 pound cavatappi or cellentani

THE CHICKEN
½ cup all-purpose flour

1½ tablespoons seasoned salt

2 teaspoons garlic powder

2 teaspoons Italian seasoning

1 teaspoon black pepper

2 pounds boneless, skinless chicken breasts, sliced into cutlets about ¼ inch thick

¼ cup extra-virgin olive oil

THE SAUCE
2 tablespoons (¼ stick) salted butter

2 large shallots, diced

1 pound baby bella or white mushrooms, sliced

3 cloves garlic, minced or pressed

2 teaspoons seasoned salt

1 teaspoon black pepper

1 teaspoon Italian seasoning

½ cup dry champagne or prosecco (see Jeff's Tip)

3 tablespoons all-purpose flour

2 cups heavy cream

5 ounces spinach

¼ cup grated Pecorino Romano cheese

1 (16-ounce or so) jar sun-dried tomatoes, drained and roughly chopped, plus some of the oil for drizzling

---

Prep Time: 15 min • Pasta Cook Time (cavatappi or cellentani): 6–11 min • Chicken Cook Time: 10 min • Sauce Cook Time: 15 min • Total Time: 40 min • Serves: 4–6

1. Boil the Water: Fill an 8-quart pot halfway with tap water and bring to a rolling boil over high heat.

2. Cook the Chicken: On a plate, whisk the flour, seasoned salt, garlic powder, Italian seasoning, and pepper with a fork until combined. Dredge (coat) each chicken cutlet in the flour mixture on both sides.

3. Heat the oil in a nonstick 4.5- to 5-quart sauté pan over medium-high heat. Once shimmering, reduce the heat to medium. Add the chicken in batches (two or three cutlets at a time should fit) and cook on each side for about 2 minutes. Transfer the chicken to a cutting board and slice into a piece to ensure it's fully cooked (no pink). Slice the cutlets into either bite-size pieces or strips and set aside on a plate. (**NOTE:** Do *not* drain the pot of the meat's juices! We want that rich flavor in the sauce.)

Recipe Continues

4. Start the Sauce: With the heat on medium-high, melt the butter in the sauté pan. Add the shallots, mushrooms, and garlic and sauté until slightly softened, about 5 minutes. Add the seasoned salt, pepper, and Italian seasoning and stir into the sautéed veggies.

5. Cook the Pasta: Add the salt to the pot of boiling water and reduce the heat to medium. Add the pasta and stir. Set a timer to cook until al dente (per the package instructions), or to the shortest amount of time given. When done, **reserve 1 cup of the pasta water** and then drain the pasta in a colander in the sink without rinsing it.

6. While the pasta's cooking, return to the sauté pan, add the champagne, and simmer for 1–2 minutes, until the intense alcohol scent has burned off.

7. Add the flour and stir to coat all the veggies. Reduce the heat to medium.

8. Stir in the cream and top with the spinach. Once bubbling, reduce the heat to medium-low and simmer for 3–5 minutes, stirring occasionally, until the spinach is wilted and the sauce is moderately thickened and coats the back of a spoon.

9. Add the Pecorino Romano and stir until melded into the thickened sauce.

10. Marry It All: Turn the heat off. Add the cooked and drained pasta and sun-dried tomatoes to the sauté pan and toss to coat with the sauce. If you find you want a slightly thinner sauce, add ¼ cup of the reserved pasta water at a time and stir until the desired consistency is reached.

11. If you sliced the chicken into bite-size pieces, toss them with the pasta and sauce. **If you sliced the cutlets into strips,** top each pasta portion with a sliced chicken cutlet and with a drizzle of oil from the jar of sun-dried tomatoes, if desired.

JEFF'S TIP If you don't feel like opening a whole bottle of champagne for only ½ cup's worth, drink the rest with the meal! But seriously, you can get a small bottle of champagne called a "split," which is perfect for this. And if you aren't feeling like popping open a bottle of cheap bubbly for whatever reason, use ½ cup broth.

TO HALVE Simply halve all the ingredients. However, the salted pasta water amount remains the same. The pasta and the sauce cook times also remain the same.

CHICKEN CACCIATORE CAMPANELLE

THE PASTA

1 tablespoon salt

1 pound campanelle

THE SAUCE

3 tablespoons extra-virgin olive oil

2 pounds boneless, skinless chicken: 1 pound breasts, sliced into cutlets about ¼ inch thick and then into bite-size pieces, and 1 pound thighs, cut into bite-size pieces

1 Vidalia (sweet) onion, diced

6 cloves garlic, minced or pressed

2 green bell peppers, seeded and diced

8 ounces baby bella or white mushrooms, sliced

1 heaping tablespoon tomato paste

¼ cup dry red wine (like pinot noir) or ¼ cup beef broth

2 teaspoons red wine vinegar

3½ cups Marinara Sauce (page 40 or your favorite jarred brand)

1 cup pitted olives of your choice (I use a combo of Spanish and kalamata, either whole and/or sliced, or **see Jeff's Tip**), plus more for serving

A cacciatore ("hunter" in Italian) is a dish featuring chicken in a bell pepper, mushroom, and olive-filled tomato sauce. A borderline hearty tomato-based stew, it cried out to me for the pasta treatment to make it even more of a complete meal. This is easily one of my favorite go-to dinners when I'm craving a lighter yet protein-filled pasta dish!

Prep Time: 15 min • **Pasta Cook Time (campanelle): 10 min** • **Sauce Cook Time: 20 min** • **Total Time: 35 min** • **Serves: 4–6**

1. Boil the Water: Fill an 8-quart pot halfway with tap water and bring to a rolling boil over high heat.

2. Start the Sauce: Heat the oil in a nonstick 4.5- to 5-quart sauté pan over medium-high heat. Once shimmering, add the chicken and sauté until mostly cooked but a little pinkish-white in color, 3–5 minutes. (**NOTE:** Do *not* drain the pan of the meat's juices! We want that rich flavor in the sauce.)

3. Add the onion, garlic, peppers, and mushrooms and sauté until slightly softened, about 5 minutes. Reduce the heat to medium.

Recipe Continues

4. Cook the Pasta: Add the salt to the pot of boiling water and reduce the heat to medium. Add the pasta and stir. Set a timer to cook until al dente (per the package instructions), or to the shortest amount of time given. When done, drain the pasta in a colander in the sink without rinsing it.

5. While the pasta's cooking, return to the sauté pan. Add the tomato paste and stir until all is coated in the pan. Sauté for 1 minute.

6. Add the wine (or broth) and vinegar and simmer for 3–5 minutes, until slightly reduced.

7. Add the marinara and, once bubbling, reduce the heat to medium-low and simmer for 2 minutes longer.

8. Marry It All: Turn the heat off. Add the cooked and drained pasta to the sauté pan along with the olives and toss to coat with the sauce. Serve topped with more olives, if desired.

JEFF'S TIP Feel free to sub some capers for the olives. They'll work perfectly, as the role of the olives is to provide a nice burst of savory flavor. And if olives or capers aren't your thing, just leave them out or sub in some diced roasted red peppers from a jar!

TO HALVE Simply halve all the ingredients. However, the salted pasta water amount remains the same. The pasta and the sauce cook times also remain the same.

SOUR CREAM & CHEDDAR CHICKEN TWISTS

RESERVE PASTA WATER!

THE PASTA
1 tablespoon salt

1 pound gemelli

THE SAUCE
2 tablespoons (¼ stick) salted butter

2 pounds boneless, skinless chicken thighs, cut into bite-size pieces

2 teaspoons garlic salt

2 cups heavy cream

½ cup sour cream

1–2 cups (4–8 ounces) shredded sharp Cheddar cheese

1 (5.2-ounce) package Boursin (any flavor) or ¾ cup Herb Cheese (page 28), cut into chunks

⅓ cup sliced fresh chives, plus more for garnish

Cheddar & sour cream potato chips, crumbled, for serving (optional)

Can a pasta dish really be inspired by a potato chip? It sure can if you're snowed in with nothing but a big bag of them (along with a cheap bottle of wine) and the creative juices start flowing. Featuring a fun and twisty pasta called gemelli, this mega-creamy, cheesy, chicken-filled pasta party I conjured up is right on the money. For good measure, top it off with some crumbled potato chips (Cheddar & sour cream, of course). And if you want it sour cream & onion style, check out Jeff's Tip!

Prep Time: 10 min • Pasta Cook Time (gemelli): 12 min • Sauce Cook Time: 20 min • Total Time: 30 min • Serves: 4–6

1. Boil the Water: Fill an 8-quart pot halfway with tap water and bring to a rolling boil over high heat.

JEFF'S TIP

Want to make it a cheesy sour cream & onion pasta? Use ½ cup of a refrigerated onion dip (you can get this in the market by the dairy section) in place of the sour cream, use shredded Swiss or white Cheddar for the cheese, and top with sour cream & onion potato chips instead!

2. Start the Sauce: Melt the butter in a nonstick 4.5- to 5-quart sauté pan over medium-high heat. Add the chicken and garlic salt and sauté until fully cooked, 7–10 minutes. (**NOTE:** Do *not* drain the pan of the meat's juices! We want that rich flavor in the sauce.) Reduce the heat to medium.

3. Cook the Pasta: Add the salt to the pot of boiling water and reduce the heat to medium. Add the pasta and stir. Set a timer to cook until al dente (per the package instructions), or to the shortest amount of time given. When done, **reserve 1 cup of the pasta water** and drain the pasta in a colander in the sink without rinsing it.

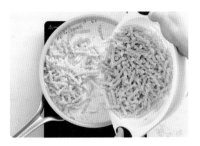

4. While the pasta's cooking, return to the sauté pan and stir in the cream. Once bubbling, reduce the heat to medium-low and simmer for 7–10 minutes, stirring occasionally, until the sauce is just slightly thickened and coats the back of a spoon.

5. Reduce the heat to low. Add the sour cream, Cheddar (start with 1 cup), herb cheese, and chives and whisk or stir until well combined and the sauce thickens. If you find you want it cheesier, add up to an additional cup of cheese.

6. Marry It All: Turn the heat off. Add the cooked and drained pasta to the sauté pan and toss to coat with the sauce. If you find you want a slightly thinner, creamier sauce, add ¼ cup of the reserved pasta water at a time and stir until the desired consistency is reached. Serve topped with additional chives and the potato chips, if desired.

TO HALVE Simply halve all the ingredients. However, the salted pasta water amount remains the same. The pasta and the sauce cook times also remain the same.

CREAMY CURRY CHICKEN CRESTS

THE PASTA

1 tablespoon salt

1 pound creste di gallo

THE SAUCE

2 tablespoons (¼ stick) salted butter

2 pounds boneless, skinless chicken thighs, cut into bite-size pieces

1 tablespoon minced or crushed fresh ginger

1 large yellow onion, diced

6 cloves garlic, minced or pressed

1 heaping tablespoon tomato paste

3 tablespoons all-purpose flour (see Jeff's Tips for GF option)

½ cup unsweetened coconut milk (it should be thin like water and not thick and lumpy)

1 (14.5-ounce) can diced tomatoes, with their juices

1 tablespoon garam masala (I like the Rani or Swad brands)

1 tablespoon seasoned salt

2 teaspoons curry powder (see Jeff's Tips)

1 teaspoon cumin

1 cup heavy cream or half-and-half

Fresh cilantro, for garnish (optional)

Inspired by the deep flavors of Indian cuisine, this pasta dish combines the creamy, tomato-based elements of a tikka masala and butter chicken. A key spice to giving this pasta its flavor is garam masala, which can easily be found in many markets in the spice section. If you can't find it there, you certainly will at an Indian market or online. My pasta shape of choice is creste di gallo or cascatelli, as they both scoop up the thick and rich sauce nicely, with ruffles to add to the fun!

Prep Time: 10 min • Pasta Cook Time (creste di gallo): 8–10 min • Sauce Cook Time: 15 min • Total Time: 25 min • Serves: 4–6

1. Boil the Water: Fill an 8-quart pot halfway with tap water and bring to a rolling boil over high heat.

2. Start the Sauce: Melt the butter in a nonstick 4.5- to 5-quart sauté pan over medium-high heat. Add the chicken and ginger and sauté until mostly cooked but a little pinkish-white in color, 3–5 minutes. (**NOTE:** Do *not* drain the pot of the meat's juices! We want that rich flavor in the sauce.)

3. Reduce the heat to medium. Add the onion, garlic, and tomato paste and sauté for 3–5 minutes.

Recipe Continues

4. Add the flour and stir until everything's fully coated.

5. Cook the Pasta: Add the salt to the pot of boiling water and reduce the heat to medium. Add the pasta and stir. Set a timer to cook until al dente (per the package instructions), or to the shortest amount of time given. When done, drain the pasta in a colander in the sink without rinsing it.

6. While the pasta's cooking, return to the sauté pan and add the coconut milk, diced tomatoes, garam masala, seasoned salt, curry powder, and cumin. Simmer for 1 minute, stirring occasionally, until slightly thickened.

7. Stir in the cream and increase the heat to medium-high. Once bubbling, reduce the heat to medium-low and simmer for 3 minutes, stirring occasionally, until the sauce is thickened and coats the back of a spoon.

8. Marry It All: Turn the heat off. Add the cooked and drained pasta to the sauté pan and toss to coat with the sauce. Serve topped with fresh cilantro, if desired.

JEFF'S TIPS

Although this is a curry chicken pasta dish, you can leave out the curry powder for a less intense curry flavor.

To make the sauce gluten-free, omit the flour and mix 1½ tablespoons cornstarch and 1½ tablespoons cold water in a small bowl to form a slurry. Once the cream begins to bubble in Step 7, stir in the slurry and it will thicken perfectly! Continue the recipe as written.

TO HALVE Simply halve all the ingredients. However, the salted pasta water amount remains the same. The pasta and the sauce cook times also remain the same.

BASIL CHICKEN RAGÙ

 (see Jeff's Tips)

THE PASTA

1 tablespoon salt

1 pound spaghetti rigati

THE SAUCE

3 tablespoons extra-virgin olive oil

2 pounds ground chicken, or raw chicken sausage, casings removed

10 cloves garlic, thinly sliced (see Jeff's Tips)

Leaves from 1 bunch fresh basil, stemmed, some reserved for garnish

3 cups Marinara Sauce (page 40 or your favorite jarred brand)

5 ounces spinach

THE CHEESE DOLLOPS

1 cup ricotta cheese

½ cup (2 ounces) shredded mozzarella cheese

½ cup grated Pecorino Romano cheese, plus more for garnish

2 teaspoons dried parsley flakes

This easy, delightful, light spaghetti dish features ground chicken, basil, and spinach in a marinara sauce. I prefer ground chicken here to give the red-meets-green marinara sauce that sort of ragù vibe. I also like to serve it up topped with dollops of a simple ricotta-Pecorino mixture at the end—or just stir it all into the married pasta and sauce just before serving.

Prep Time: 10 min • **Pasta Cook Time (spaghetti rigati): 6 min** • **Sauce Cook Time: 15 min** •
Total Time: 25 min • **Serves: 4–6**

1. Boil the Water: Fill an 8-quart pot halfway with tap water and bring to a rolling boil over high heat.

2. Start the Sauce: Heat the oil in a nonstick 4.5- to 5-quart sauté pan over medium-high heat. Once shimmering, add the chicken and garlic. Sauté until the chicken meat is crumbled and lightly browned, about 5 minutes. (**NOTE:** Do *not* drain the pot of the meat's juices! We want that rich flavor in the sauce.)

3. Reduce the heat to medium. Add the basil and sauté until slightly wilted into the chicken and olive oil, about 3 minutes.

Recipe Continues

4. Cook the Pasta: Add the salt to the pot of boiling water and reduce the heat to medium. Add the pasta and stir. Set a timer to cook until al dente (per the package instructions), or to the shortest amount of time given. When done, drain the pasta in a colander in the sink without rinsing it.

5. While the pasta's cooking, return to the sauté pan and add the marinara and, once bubbling, reduce the heat to medium-low. Stir and let simmer for 5 minutes.

6. Stir in the spinach until wilted into the sauce.

7. Meanwhile, in a medium bowl, combine the cheese dollops ingredients and set aside.

8. Marry It All: Turn the heat off. Add the cooked and drained pasta to the sauté pan and toss to coat with the sauce. Serve topped with some cheese dollops and more basil and Pecorino Romano, if desired. **Alternatively, for a really cheesy finish,** you can add all the cheese dollops mixture directly into the pan and mix until combined with the pasta and sauce.

JEFF'S TIPS To cut down on prep time (and avoid some sticky fingers), you can use 3 tablespoons of jarred thinly sliced garlic instead of slicing the cloves yourself. Speaking of the garlic slices, I chose to cook them directly with the ground chicken because I like them substantial and not browned in this dish. But if you'd rather get them browned, add them just before the chicken. Once browned to your liking, add the chicken and continue as written.

Keep this dairy-free by omitting the cheese dollops altogether.

TO HALVE Simply halve all the ingredients. However, the salted pasta water amount remains the same. The pasta and the sauce cook times also remain the same.

CHICKEN MARSALA TORTELLINI

THE PASTA
1 tablespoon salt

20–24 ounces chicken tortellini of your choice

THE SAUCE
4 tablespoons (½ stick) salted butter

2 large shallots, diced

1 pound baby bella or white mushrooms, sliced

3 cloves garlic, minced or pressed

2 tablespoons all-purpose flour, divided (see Jeff's Tip for GF option)

½ cup Marsala wine (see Jeff's Tips)

1 cup chicken or garlic broth (e.g., made from Better Than Bouillon Roasted Garlic Base)

½ cup heavy cream or half-and-half

½ cup grated Parmesan cheese, plus more for serving

Being a mushroom lover, one of my all-time favorite chicken dishes is chicken Marsala. Featuring tender chicken cutlets dressed in a lush sauce of mushrooms and a dry or sweet Marsala wine (see Jeff's Tips), it's a special treat for those who love a savory, yet slightly sweet poultry experience. Here, I marry the classic mushroom-wine sauce with a light Parmesan-cream sauce and toss it with chicken-filled tortellini, amplifying it to the next level while keeping it simple.

Prep Time: 10 min • Pasta Cook Time (tortellini): 2–4 min • Sauce Cook Time: 15 min • Total Time: 25 min • Serves: 4–6

1. Boil the Water: Fill an 8-quart pot halfway with tap water and bring to a rolling boil over high heat.

2. Start the Sauce: Melt the butter in a nonstick 4.5- to 5-quart sauté pan over medium-high heat. Add the shallots, mushrooms, and garlic and sauté until the mushrooms are browned and begin to release their juices, about 5 minutes.

3. Reduce the heat to medium. Add 1 tablespoon of the flour and stir until everything is coated. Add the wine and broth and let simmer for 3 minutes.

TO HALVE Simply halve all the ingredients. However, the salted pasta water amount remains the same. The pasta and the sauce cook times also remain the same.

JEFF'S TIP To make the sauce gluten-free, omit the flour and mix 1 tablespoon cornstarch and 1 tablespoon cold water in a small bowl to form a slurry. Once the cream begins to bubble in Step 5, stir in the slurry and it will thicken perfectly! Continue the recipe as written.

4. Cook the Pasta: Add the salt to the pot of boiling water and reduce the heat to medium. Add the pasta and stir. Set a timer to cook until al dente (per the package instructions), or to the shortest amount of time given. When done, drain the pasta in a colander in the sink without rinsing it.

5. While the pasta's cooking, return to the sauté pan and stir in the cream and the remaining 1 tablespoon flour. Simmer for 2–3 minutes over medium heat, stirring occasionally, until the sauce is thickened and coats the back of a spoon.

6. Reduce the heat to low. Add the Parmesan and stir until combined into the sauce.

7. Marry It All: Turn the heat off. Add the cooked and drained pasta to the sauté pan and toss to coat with the sauce. Serve topped with additional Parmesan, if desired.

 JEFF'S TIPS For the Marsala wine, you can use either the cooking variety found in the oil and vinegar section of most markets or get fancy with a sweet or dry Marsala wine from a liquor store. The sweeter wine will, of course, give you a slightly sweeter pasta sauce over the dry.

And if you don't want wine, you can leave it out and use 1½ cups chicken or garlic broth instead. Of course, the Marsala flavor won't be present—it will be more of a delicious Parmesan-cream sauce instead.

CHICKEN FAJITA PASTA

Oh my *lawd*, fajitas! There is nothing I love more than sitting in a Mexican restaurant (with a margarita-filled pitcher) and hearing the sizzle of a cast-iron pan loaded with juicy chicken, peppers, and onion coming my way! The aroma of this sizzlin' sensation is all it takes for me to be instantly overcome with hunger vibes. After one occasion of eating them (and after the margarita pitcher was nearly empty), I thought of turning fajitas into a pasta using mouthwatering blackened chicken cutlets. Best thing that ever could have happened. And if you want this fajita pasta done shrimp- or steak-style, check out Jeff's Tips.

THE PASTA
- 1 tablespoon salt
- 1 pound rigatoni

THE CHICKEN
- 4 teaspoons garlic powder
- 4 teaspoons onion powder
- 4 teaspoons cumin
- 4 teaspoons Cajun/Creole/Louisiana seasoning (I use Tony Chachere's) or seasoned salt
- 4 teaspoons chili powder
- 2 pounds boneless, skinless chicken breasts, sliced into cutlets about ¼ inch thick
- ¼ cup extra-virgin olive oil

THE SAUCE
- 1 large yellow onion, sliced into ¼-inch-thick strands
- 2 bell peppers (I use one green and one red), seeded and sliced into ¼-inch-thick strands
- ½ cup taco or fajita sauce (I use Ortega brand), plus more for serving
- 2 cups heavy cream
- 1–2 cups (4–8 ounces) shredded Mexican or taco cheese blend
- Crumbled cotija cheese, for serving (optional)

Prep Time: 15 min ● **Pasta Cook Time (rigatoni): 12–14 min** ● **Chicken Cook Time: 10 min**
Sauce Cook Time: 25 min ● **Total Time: 50 min** ● **Serves: 4–6**

1. Boil the Water: Fill an 8-quart pot halfway with tap water and bring to a rolling boil over high heat.

2. Make the Chicken: Mix all the chicken seasonings on a plate with a fork until combined. Lightly rub the seasonings on both sides of each chicken cutlet. Set aside on the plate.

3. Heat the oil in a nonstick 4.5- to 5-quart sauté pan over medium-high heat. Once shimmering, add the chicken in batches (two or three cutlets at a time should fit) and cook on each side for about 2 minutes. Transfer the chicken to a cutting board and cut into it to ensure it's fully cooked. Slice into bite-size pieces and set aside on a plate. (**NOTE:** Do *not* drain the pan of the chicken's juices and seasonings! We want that rich flavor in the sauce.)

Recipe Continues

4. Start the Sauce: Add the onion and peppers to the pan and sauté until slightly softened, about 10–15 minutes total.

5. Cook the Pasta: Ten minutes after sautéing the veggies in the pan, add the salt to the pot of boiling water and reduce the heat to medium. Add the pasta and stir. Set a timer to cook until al dente (per the package instructions), or to the shortest amount of time given. When done, drain the pasta in a colander in the sink without rinsing it.

6. While the pasta's cooking and when the veggies are sautéed to your liking, return to the sauté pan and add the taco sauce and cream. Once bubbling, reduce the heat to medium-low and simmer for 5–7 minutes, until the sauce slightly thickens.

7. Reduce the heat to low. Add the shredded cheese by starting with 1 cup (4 ounces) and stir until melded into the sauce. If you find you want a thicker, richer sauce, stir in up to 1 more cup (4 ounces) cheese until the desired consistency is reached.

8. Marry It All: Turn the heat off. Add the cooked and drained pasta to the sauté pan along with the cooked chicken and toss to coat with the sauce. Serve topped with crumbled cotija cheese and additional taco sauce, if desired.

JEFF'S TIPS

For Shrimp Fajita Pasta: Sub 1½–2 pounds peeled and deveined raw shrimp for the chicken in Steps 2–3. Sauté for 2–3 minutes. Once curled and opaque, they're cooked! Remove to a plate and set aside until adding to the pasta in Step 8.

For Steak Fajita Pasta: Sub 1½–2 pounds thinly sliced (¼ to ½ inch thick) skirt or flank steak for the chicken in Steps 2–3. Sauté for 5–8 minutes (or cook it how you like your steak's temperature, between 130°F and 160°F). Transfer to a plate, slice into bite-size pieces, and set aside until adding it along with its juices to the pasta in Step 8.

To make the blackened chicken only, follow Steps 2 and 3 and skip the pasta steps. It's great over salads, veggies, sandwiches (with lettuce, tomato, mayo, and bacon) or simply on its own!

TO HALVE Simply halve all the ingredients. However, the salted pasta water amount remains the same. The pasta and the sauce cook times also remain the same.

CREAMY PESTO CHICKEN PENNE

THE PASTA

1 tablespoon salt

1 pound penne

THE SAUCE

4 tablespoons (½ stick) salted butter

2 pounds boneless, skinless chicken breasts or thighs (or a mix of the two), sliced into bite-size chunks and sprinkled with 2 teaspoons garlic salt

2 tablespoons all-purpose flour (see Jeff's Tips for GF option)

2 cups heavy cream

1½ cups Pesto Sauce (page 50 or your favorite jarred brand, I like Costco's)

This dish speaks to me because it combines two of my favorite things: a green pesto sauce and a white béchamel sauce, making for a super creamy pesto experience. Here, the béchamel is slightly thinner than usual because I don't want it to be too thick and overwhelming, but rather complement the pesto nicely—especially when chicken and pasta are added to the mix and everything comes together into one unforgettable dish.

Prep Time: 10 min • Pasta Cook Time (penne): 9–11 min • Sauce Cook Time: 15 min • Total Time: 25 min • Serves: 4–6

1. Boil the Water: Fill an 8-quart pot halfway with tap water and bring to a rolling boil over high heat.

2. Start the Sauce: Melt the butter in a nonstick 4.5- to 5-quart sauté pan over medium-high heat. Add the garlic salt–coated chicken and sauté for 7–10 minutes, until the chicken is fully cooked. Using a slotted spoon, transfer the chicken to a bowl and set aside. (**NOTE:** Do *not* drain the pan of the meat's juices! Not only do we want that rich flavor in the sauce, but it will also be needed for our roux.)

3. Cook the Pasta: Add the salt to the pot of boiling water and reduce the heat to medium. Add the pasta and stir. Set a timer to cook until al dente (per the package instructions), or to the shortest amount of time given. When done, drain the pasta in a colander in the sink without rinsing it.

Recipe Continues

4. While the pasta's cooking, return to the sauté pan and reduce the heat to medium. Whisk the flour into the juices in the pot for 30 seconds. It will become like a very thick and chunky roux.

5. Slowly pour in the cream and increase the heat to high. As soon as it bubbles, reduce the heat to medium and whisk until a béchamel is formed and the sauce is thickened, 3–5 minutes. It's okay if it's still slightly lumpy, but it should be mostly smooth.

6. Reduce the heat to low. Add the pesto and whisk until combined into the béchamel, heating for about 2 minutes. Turn the heat off and, if the pasta isn't done cooking by now, cover the pan with a lid until it is.

7. Marry It All: Add the cooked and drained pasta and cooked chicken to the sauté pan and toss to coat with the sauce. Dig in!

JEFF'S TIPS

If you want to skip the béchamel steps and create a thinner creamy pesto sauce, skip Steps 4 and 5, but add ½–1 cup heavy cream or half-and-half with the pesto in Step 6.

To make the sauce gluten-free, omit the flour and mix 1 tablespoon cornstarch and 1 tablespoon cold water in a small bowl to form a slurry. Skip Step 4 and stir the slurry into the cream in Step 5 once it begins to bubble. Continue the recipe as written.

TO HALVE Simply halve all the ingredients. However, the salted pasta water amount remains the same. The pasta and the sauce cook times also remain the same.

4

FARM & GARDEN

This large chapter is all things vegetarian, which in itself is a whole gold mine of pasta dishes. When I designed the book's structure, I figured it best to divide this portion into three separate sections.

Five Ingredient Sauces

Simple, yet vibrant flavors—many of which are olive oil–based and take no time at all to whip up.

Creamy & Cheesy

Rich, creamy, and cheesy sauces for the ultimate cheese lover.

Veggie Variations

Pastas that are made with delicious vegetables and grains: tomatoes, asparagus, Brussels sprouts, peppers, onion, and even buckwheat.

Welcome to the **MEAT-FREE** chapter!

DF **Dairy-Free**

V **Vegetarian**

VN **Vegan**

✦ **Compliant with Modifications**

CACIO E PEPE AMERICANO

THE PASTA

1 tablespoon salt

1 pound spaghetti

THE SAUCE

2 cups (8 ounces) Monterey Jack or white Cheddar cheese, grated or shredded (see Jeff's Tips)

6 slices (deli-size) white American cheese, grated, shredded, or ripped into small pieces

1–2 tablespoons freshly ground pepper, plus more for serving

RESERVE **PASTA** WATER!

Perhaps one of the trendiest pasta dishes made today, the Roman classic known as cacio e pepe (which translates as "cheese and pepper") uses only four ingredients: cheese, pepper, pasta, and pasta water. The creamy sauce is created by nothing more than the marriage of cheese melting into a cup or two of the pasta water and pepper, all then tossed over pasta. Finely grated salty Pecorino Romano is the traditional "cacio" for the dish, but I've found it's not as easy to make as it sounds. It requires eyeballing the pasta-water-to-cheese ratio for proper heat tempering to form a cheesy paste which, if done wrong, can often result in a botched and clumpy cheese sauce. Because I want you to have the creamiest, easiest version possible (and because there are countless recipes for the classic version already out there), I'm taking liberties with the cheese used. Remaining true to the key ingredients, I choose a "cacio" blend of Monterey Jack (or white Cheddar) and white American cheeses. While this is definitely an Americanized version, I promise you it's one of the tastiest, most foolproof iterations of this dish you'll experience. If you want an homage to the classic, feel free to top it off with some grated Pecorino Romano just before serving. Spaghetti is the typical noodle used, and so I do the same, but check out Jeff's Tips to go the way of the stars (literally) with pastina.

Prep Time: 5 min • Pasta Cook Time (spaghetti): 9–10 min • Total Time: 15 min • Serves: 4–6

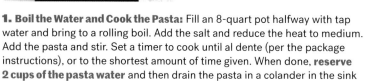

1. Boil the Water and Cook the Pasta: Fill an 8-quart pot halfway with tap water and bring to a rolling boil. Add the salt and reduce the heat to medium. Add the pasta and stir. Set a timer to cook until al dente (per the package instructions), or to the shortest amount of time given. When done, reserve **2 cups of the pasta water** and then drain the pasta in a colander in the sink without rinsing it.

2. Heat a nonstick 4.5- to 5-quart sauté pan over medium-low heat and add the cooked and drained pasta.

FIVE INGREDIENT SAUCES

TO HALVE Simply halve all the ingredients. However, the salted pasta water amount remains the same. The pasta and the sauce cook times also remain the same.

3. Marry It All: Add the cheeses and pepper followed by 1 cup of the reserved pasta water.

4. Use tongs to toss continuously until a creamy consistency forms, 2–3 minutes. If you want it creamier, add up to 1 cup more of the pasta water and toss until combined. Turn the heat off. Serve immediately topped with additional pepper and some additional cheese, if desired.

JEFF'S TIPS My main choice for the Jack/white Cheddar here is any variety of Natural Viking cheese from the Washington State University Creamery (you can order it online—get it directly through WSU Creamery by Googling), but that's definitely not required and any white Cheddar or Jack cheese will work great.

Of course, there's also the classic and iconic way to make this dish using Pecorino Romano. But if you want that, I suggest you do an old-fashioned Google search for a reputable recipe; you'll find countless choices. Some use olive oil to toast the pepper and others throw butter into the mix, proving that no two recipes are alike or always follow the rules.

If you want to give this dish the star treatment (I'm talking the tiny star-shaped pastina, which some may say is the equivalent of Italian penicillin), boil a 12-ounce package of pastina (one of the few pastas sold in that size versus 1 pound) according to the package instructions and follow the recipe as written.

LINGUINE AGLIO E OLIO

 DF V

THE PASTA

1 tablespoon salt

1 pound linguine (or any pasta you prefer)

THE SAUCE

½ cup extra-virgin olive oil, plus more for drizzling

12 cloves garlic, thinly sliced, minced, or pressed

1–3 teaspoons crushed red pepper flakes (optional)

1–2 teaspoons Better Than Bouillon base of your choice (I like Roasted Garlic and Italian Herb from the Culinary Collection)

½–1 cup grated Parmesan cheese, plus more for serving

¼ cup fresh Italian (flat-leaf) parsley, chopped, plus more for serving

I'm going to keep this headnote as short and simple as this beautiful and light recipe. This Neapolitan dish focuses on two main ingredients: garlic (aglio), and olive oil (olio). I also add Parmesan and parsley when tossing with the pasta, as well as some optional red pepper flakes. It's done in minutes, and I'm willing to bet many of you already have these ingredients in your kitchen to make this simple, yet flavorful-filled classic!

Prep Time: 10 min • Pasta Cook Time (linguine): 10 min • Sauce Cook Time: 10 min • Total Time: 25 min • Serves: 4–6

1. Boil the Water and Cook the Pasta: Fill an 8-quart pot halfway with tap water and bring to a boil over high heat. Add the salt and reduce the heat to medium. Add the pasta and stir. Set a timer to cook until al dente (per the package instructions), or to the shortest amount of time given. When done, **reserve 1 cup of the pasta water** and then drain the pasta in a colander in the sink without rinsing it.

2. Make the Sauce: As soon as you add the pasta to the pot, heat the oil in a nonstick 4.5- to 5-quart sauté pan over medium-high heat. Once shimmering, add the garlic, red pepper flakes (if using—start with 1 teaspoon and work your way up), and Better Than Bouillon (if using—start with 1 teaspoon and work your way up). Sauté for 3–5 minutes, until the garlic is lightly browned. Remove the pan from the heat as the pasta finishes cooking. (**NOTE:** This prevents the garlic from continuing to cook and burn.)

3. Marry It All: Add the cooked and drained pasta to the sauté pan along with the Parmesan (start with ½ cup), the parsley, and ½ cup of the reserved pasta water.

TO HALVE Simply halve all the ingredients. However, the salted pasta water amount remains the same. The pasta and the sauce cook times also remain the same.

FIVE INGREDIENT SAUCES

4. Use tongs to toss to coat in the oil. Feel free to add up to ½ cup more Parmesan and more pasta water, if desired. Let rest for 5 minutes for everything to come together.

5. Serve immediately, topped with more grated Parmesan, red pepper flakes, parsley, and a drizzle of olive oil, if desired.

I provide a range in quantity for the red pepper flakes because how spicy you want this dish is up to you. Even 1 teaspoon will be a bit spicy. Feel free to taste the oil before adding more until you've reached your spicy heart's content. And in place of red pepper flakes from the market, this is the perfect dish to use those hot spices you may have gotten and forgotten about after a trip to Italy! If you don't want it spicy at all, leave them out altogether.

LEMON, ARTICHOKE & OLIVE WHEELS

THE PASTA

1 tablespoon salt

1 pound wagon wheel or mini wagon wheel pasta

THE SAUCE

½ cup extra-virgin olive oil, plus more for drizzling

6 cloves garlic, minced or pressed

Grated zest and juice of 1 lemon

1 cup kalamata olives, pitted, sliced, and halved lengthwise (or kept whole)

1 (14-ounce) can artichoke hearts, ripped up by hand (see Jeff's Tips)

OPTIONAL TOPPINGS

Grated Parmesan cheese

Chopped fresh parsley

Due to its versatility in the kitchen, lemon is one of my favorite ingredients. While it can make your lips pucker on its own, once lemon juice squeezed over pasta and then tossed with olive oil and olives, it gives the pasta a sprightly and tangy essence. This simple dish is lightning-quick, packs a flavor punch, and is just "wheely" wonderful.

Prep Time: 10 min • **Pasta Cook Time (wagon wheels or mini wheels): 6–7 min** • **Sauce Cook Time: 5 min** • **Total Time: 20 min** • **Serves: 4–6**

1. Boil the Water and Cook the Pasta: Fill an 8-quart pot halfway with tap water and bring to a rolling boil over high heat. Add the salt and reduce the heat to medium. Add the pasta and stir. Set a timer to cook until al dente (per the package instructions), or to the shortest amount of time given. When done, drain the pasta in a colander in the sink without rinsing it.

2. Make the Sauce: As soon as you add the pasta to the pot, heat the oil in a nonstick 4.5- to 5-quart sauté pan over medium heat. Once shimmering, add the garlic and sauté for 2 minutes, until browned. Remove the pan from the heat as the pasta finishes cooking. (**NOTE:** This will prevent the garlic from continuing to cook and burn.)

3. Marry It All: Add the cooked and drained pasta, lemon juice, olives, and artichokes to the sauté pan.

FIVE INGREDIENT SAUCES

JEFF'S TIPS

If you want to cheese this pasta up a bit, add up to ½ cup of grated Parmesan when tossing the pasta in the oil with the olives and lemon juice in Step 3.

Want more artichokes and olives? Add up to an additional 14-ounce can of artichokes and an additional 1 cup olives. (By the way, you can use any type of olive; just make sure they're pitted so you don't crack a tooth!)

If you want to give your artichokes a bit of a toasty crisp, after draining them from the can and ripping them up by hand, spread them on a baking sheet, lightly brush with some olive oil, and bake for about 10 minutes at 450°F, until slightly crispy. Add them in Step 3 as instructed.

4. Toss to coat the pasta in the oil. Feel free to toss in a few extra drizzles of olive oil. Serve immediately, topped with lemon zest, grated Parmesan, and parsley, if desired.

TO HALVE Simply halve all the ingredients. However, the salted pasta water amount remains the same. The pasta and the sauce cook times also remain the same.

SHAKSHUKA SPAGHETTI

THE PASTA

1 tablespoon salt

1 pound thick spaghetti

THE SAUCE

3 tablespoons extra-virgin olive oil

2 large green bell peppers, seeded and diced

4 cups Marinara Sauce (page 40 or your favorite brand—get a chunky one if possible)

1 tablespoon paprika (regular or smoked)

¼ cup hot sauce (I use Frank's RedHot), plus more for serving (optional)

6 large eggs

OPTIONAL TOPPINGS

Crumbled feta cheese

Chopped fresh cilantro

Crushed red pepper flakes

Shakshuka is a Middle Eastern tomato and egg dish where eggs are cooked, poach-style, in little wells created in the sauce! It usually has a spicy flair, but it doesn't have to (so omit the hot sauce if you want it mild). I thought shakshuka would work really well turned into a pasta. Here, I use marinara for the sauce and skip making wells in the sauce for the eggs, because they just aren't necessary. When tossed together with the spaghetti, the runny egg yolks cloak the pasta beautifully, making for a delicious and simple pasta dish.

Prep Time: 10 min • Pasta Cook Time (thick spaghetti): 11 min • Sauce Cook Time: 15 min • Total Time: 25 min • Serves: 4–6

1. Boil the Water: Fill an 8-quart pot halfway with tap water and bring to a rolling boil over high heat.

2. Start the Sauce: Heat the oil in a nonstick 4.5- to 5-quart sauté pan over medium-high heat. Once shimmering, add the bell peppers and sauté for 5–7 minutes, until slightly softened.

3. Cook the Pasta: Add the salt to the pot of boiling water and reduce the heat to medium. Add the pasta and stir. Set a timer to cook until al dente (per the package instructions), or to the shortest amount of time given. When done, drain the pasta in a colander in the sink without rinsing it.

JEFF'S TIP If you want to keep your (mostly) cooked eggs intact instead of stirring them into the sauce and pasta in Step 7, gently remove them (be it all or some) with a serving spoon before adding the pasta to the pan and put them on a plate. Then, once the sauce and pasta are tossed together, place any reserved eggs on top of the sauced pasta in individual bowls upon serving.

TO HALVE Simply halve all the ingredients. However, the salted pasta water amount remains the same. The pasta and the sauce cook times also remain the same.

FIVE INGREDIENT SAUCES

4. While the pasta's cooking, return to the sauté pan and add the marinara, paprika, and hot sauce (if using). Stir until combined and bubbling, about 1 minute.

5. Reduce the heat to medium-low. Add each egg, one at a time, to the sauce (**see Jeff's Tips**), so they're evenly spaced apart from each other.

6. Cover the pan and cook the eggs until the whites become opaque, 4–5 minutes at most as we don't want our yolks overcooked—they should be runny. Feel free to pierce an egg to test it out. Once it looks good, remove the pan from the burner.

7. Marry It All: Add the cooked and drained pasta to the sauté pan and use tongs to toss everything together. The egg yolks should break and run through the pasta (**see Jeff's Tip** on page 128). Serve immediately with a drizzle of additional hot sauce and/or any of the optional toppings, if desired.

JEFF'S TIPS

To avoid any eggshells in your sauce, I suggest cracking each egg into a separate small bowl or ramekin first and then sliding each into the sauce in Step 5.

Want this pasta extra eggy? Add up to six additional eggs in Step 5, making it a full dozen. Due to the extra eggs, you may need to increase the simmer time from 4–5 minutes to 5–7 minutes, until cooked but still a bit runny in the yolks.

PASTA POMODORO

THE PASTA

1 tablespoon salt

1 pound medium shells

THE SAUCE

½ cup extra-virgin olive oil

2 pounds cherry or grape tomatoes, halved

1 teaspoon seasoned salt

½ teaspoon black pepper

9 cloves garlic, crushed or pressed

OPTIONAL TOPPINGS

Chopped fresh basil

Grated Parmesan or Pecorino Romano cheese

Even though I'm admittedly not a fan of raw tomatoes, I love them when cooked. One of the sweetest and brightest types are cherry tomatoes. Whether you have a garden and grow your own, or go to the market to get them (Costco for me), here we are going to make use of fresh cherry or grape tomatoes (see Jeff's Tip). It's a super simple sauce where the tomatoes are combined with garlic and olive oil to create a wonderful and memorable pomodoro sauce. Light and bright never tasted so delicious. I use pasta shells here, but a long pasta is also nice, be it thin (angel hair), medium (spaghetti), or fat (bucatini).

Prep Time: 10 min • **Pasta Cook Time (medium shells): 8-9 min** • **Sauce Cook Time: 10-15 min** • **Total Time: 20-25 min** • **Serves: 4-6**

1. Boil the Water: Fill an 8-quart pot halfway with tap water and bring to a rolling boil over high heat.

2. Start the Sauce: Heat the oil in a nonstick 4.5- to 5-quart sauté pan over medium-high heat. Once shimmering, add the tomatoes, seasoned salt, pepper, and garlic and sauté in the oil for 2 minutes.

3. Cook the Pasta: Add the salt to the pot of boiling water and reduce the heat to medium. Add the pasta and stir. Set a timer to cook until al dente (per the package instructions), or to the shortest amount of time given. When done, drain the pasta in a colander in the sink without rinsing it.

JEFF'S TIP

While pomodoro is a red sauce because it uses red tomatoes, you can also feel free to use a colorful medley of grape and cherry tomatoes that vary from red to orange to yellow! The sauce will take on a slightly different color with a slightly different flavor profile but will be just as delightful.

FIVE INGREDIENT SAUCES

4. While the pasta's cooking, return to the sauté pan and reduce the heat to medium. Cover the pan with a lid and let simmer for 6-8 minutes.

5. As the tomatoes simmer in the covered pan, they'll begin to soften and release their juices. Check on them occasionally (every 2 minutes or so) by removing the lid and giving them a stir. While stirring, lightly press on them with a wooden spatula.

6. Once a chunky, light sauce is formed, loaded with the delicious skins of the tomatoes, it's done. Turn the heat off. If the sauce is done before the pasta's finished cooking, cover the pan until it's ready.

7. Marry It All: Add the cooked and drained pasta to the sauté pan and toss to coat with the sauce. Serve immediately topped with basil and grated Parmesan or Pecorino Romano, if desired.

JEFF'S TIPS

The sauce is the right amount for 1 pound of pasta as written because it is meant to be light, yet loaded with a fresh sweet and savory flavor. To that point, if you want it extra saucy, double up on the sauce ingredients and cook as written.

For a really indulgent and rich touch: While tossing the sauce in Step 7, add the soft inside of a ball of burrata or 4 ounces thinly sliced mozzarella (smoked or regular) and toss until melty and stretchy.

TO HALVE Simply halve all the ingredients. However, the salted pasta water amount remains the same. The pasta and the sauce cook times also remain the same.

GINGER-SCALLION NOODLES

THE PASTA

1 tablespoon salt	
1 pound vermicelli (the Italian kind)	

THE SAUCE

6-inch knob fresh ginger, peeled and roughly chopped
1 bunch scallions, sliced
1 cup vegetable oil
1 teaspoon salt
1 teaspoon soy sauce, tamari, or coconut aminos

This recipe is in my green *Super Shortcut Instant Pot* cookbook and it's *so* easy and *so* delicious—and without requiring a pan—that I simply had to include it here. It uses a Cantonese ginger-scallion oil that's typically served with steamed chicken and rice—but when I first had a taste of the oil, I knew it needed the pasta treatment. Since it's an oil-based sauce, it's far better suited to starchy Italian pasta rather than slicker rice noodles, as it will cling beautifully to the pasta.

Prep Time: 5 min • **Pasta Cook Time (vermicelli): 5–6 min** • **Sauce Prep Time: 5 min** • **Total Time: 20 min** • **Serves: 4–6**

1. Boil the Water and Cook the Pasta: Fill an 8-quart pot halfway with tap water and bring to a rolling boil over high heat. Add the salt and reduce the heat to medium. Add the pasta and stir. Set a timer to cook until al dente (per the package instructions), or to the shortest amount of time given. When done, drain the pasta in a colander in the sink without rinsing it.

TO HALVE Simply halve all the ingredients. However, the salted pasta water amount remains the same. The pasta cook time also remains the same.

2. Make the Sauce: As soon as you add the pasta to the pot, add all the sauce ingredients to a food processor or blender and pulse until pureed.

3. Marry It All: In a large bowl, add the cooked pasta followed by the ginger-scallion oil and use tongs to toss until the pasta is coated in the oil. Serve.

FIVE INGREDIENT SAUCES

You can use any long-form noodle, such as angel hair/ capellini, spaghetti, linguine, fettuccine, tagliatelle, mafaldine, or pappardelle, and simply cook according to the package instructions. Since the pasta is cooked in the first step and the ginger-scallion oil requires no pan to cook it in, the type of pasta you choose won't have any bearing on the timing.

Want it with some chicken? Add up to 1 pound shredded rotisserie meat in Step 3 and toss with the pasta and oil.

THE ULTIMATE BUTTER NOODLES

RESERVE PASTA WATER!

(if using garlic broth)

THE PASTA
1 tablespoon salt

1 pound mafaldine

THE SAUCE
8 tablespoons (1 stick) salted butter

¼ cup all-purpose flour (see Jeff's Tips for GF option)

2½ cups broth of your choice (I like chicken or garlic broth, e.g., made from Better Than Bouillon Roasted Garlic Base)

1–2 tablespoons dried parsley flakes (optional)

¼–½ cup grated Parmesan cheese, plus more for serving (optional)

I think the most common pasta dish for kids is "butter noodles." That's definitely the case for my niece and nephews! Well, my friends, those noodles just got amplified to the next level. I take the basics of a béchamel but reduce the flour-to-fat ratio so it's not quite as thick, and sub broth for the milk. What we have now is a rich broth-based, buttery sauce that really clings to the noodles. Kids and adults alike will love it. This recipe can be made with just three ingredients for the sauce, but I like to add some dried parsley flakes and Parmesan for added oomph.

Prep Time: 5 min • Pasta Cook Time (mafaldine): 8-9 min • Sauce Cook Time: 8 min • Total Time: 20 min • Serves: 4-6

1. Boil the Water and Cook the Pasta: Fill an 8-quart pot halfway with tap water and bring to a rolling boil over high heat. Add the salt and reduce the heat to medium. Add the pasta and stir. Set a timer to cook until al dente (per the package instructions), or to the shortest amount of time given. When done, **reserve 1 cup of the pasta water** and then drain the pasta in a colander in the sink without rinsing it.

2. Make the Sauce: As soon as you add the pasta to the pot, melt the butter in a nonstick 4.5- to 5-quart sauté pan over medium heat. Add the flour and whisk until fragrantly nutty and a roux has formed, 1–2 minutes.

3. Add the broth to the pan. Once bubbling, reduce the heat to medium-low and simmer while whisking for 3–5 minutes, until the sauce is slightly thickened and coats the back of a spoon. Turn the heat off. If the sauce is done before the pasta's finished cooking, cover the pan until it's ready.

FIVE INGREDIENT SAUCES

4. Marry It All: Add the cooked and drained pasta to the sauté pan and use tongs to toss everything together. If using parsley flakes (start with 1 tablespoon) and Parmesan (start with ¼ cup), add them now while tossing. If you want more parsley flakes, add up to 1 tablespoon more, and for Parmesan, add up to ¼ cup more. And if you want a thinner sauce, add the reserved pasta water in ¼-cup increments until the desired consistency is reached. Serve immediately, with more Parmesan if desired.

 JEFF'S TIPS

Some prefer a tubular pasta for this. My niece and nephews love ziti rigati (ziti with ridges).

For a thinner sauce from the start, you can use 2 tablespoons all-purpose flour in Step 2. If you want it thicker, you can always whisk in more flour in Step 3 when adding the broth.

To make the sauce gluten-free, omit the flour and mix 2 tablespoons cornstarch and 2 tablespoons cold water in a small bowl to form a slurry. Set aside. Then, begin the sauce by placing both the butter and the broth in the pan and heating it up. Once the butter's melted into the simmering broth in Step 3, stir in the slurry and it will thicken perfectly! Continue the recipe from there as written.

TO HALVE

Simply halve all the ingredients. However, the salted pasta water amount remains the same. The pasta and the sauce cook times also remain the same.

CREAM & CRIMSON PASTA

THE PASTA

1 tablespoon salt

1 pound macarrones or short rigatoni

THE SAUCE

4 tablespoons (½ stick) salted butter

1 cup heavy cream or half-and-half

½ teaspoon garlic powder

2 cups Marinara Sauce (page 40 or your favorite jarred brand)

½–1 cup grated Parmesan cheese, plus more for serving

Burrata balls, for serving (optional)

As an alumnus of Indiana University (go, Hoosiers!), I often think about a pizza joint I used to order from at 2 a.m., while cramming for a class that served me absolutely no purpose in life. They had a pizza, known as the Cream & Crimson (which are the colors of IU), that was everything. I knew I had to make it into a pasta, where short tubes of pasta bathe in an Alfredo-marinara blend. Even better? It's a regal meal on a college student budget.

Prep Time: 5 min ● Pasta Cook Time (macarrones or short rigatoni): 10–15 min ● Sauce Cook Time: 8 min ● Total Time: 25 min ● Serves: 4–6

1. Boil the Water and Cook the Pasta: Fill an 8-quart pot halfway with tap water and bring to a rolling boil over high heat. Add the salt and reduce the heat to medium. Add the pasta and stir. Set a timer to cook until al dente (per the package instructions), or to the shortest amount of time given. When done, drain the pasta in a colander in the sink without rinsing it.

2. Make the Sauce: As soon as you add the pasta to the pot, heat the butter and cream in a nonstick 4.5- to 5-quart sauté pan over medium-low heat. Once the butter has melted into the cream, stir in the garlic powder. Bring the cream and butter to a gentle simmer, whisking occasionally, and simmer until the sauce is slightly thickened and coats the back of a spoon, 4–6 minutes.

3. Stir in the marinara and increase the heat to medium. Add the Parmesan and whisk until fully combined into the sauce (start with ½ cup and go up to 1 cup, if desired). Once bubbling, reduce the heat to medium-low and simmer for 2 minutes, until well-blended. Turn the heat off, cover with a lid, and wait for the pasta to finish cooking if it hasn't.

FIVE INGREDIENT SAUCES

4. Marry It All: Add the cooked and drained pasta to the sauté pan and toss to coat with the sauce. Serve immediately, topped with additional Parmesan or a sliced-open ball of burrata, if desired.

JEFF'S TIP You can really play this one easy and just heat up 1 cup jarred Alfredo sauce (or make mine ahead of time, page 42), along with 2 cups marinara in the pan. Toss in the pasta and done-zo! Parmesan is optional here as the Alfredo sauce already includes it.

TO HALVE Simply halve all the ingredients. However, the salted pasta water amount remains the same. The pasta and the sauce cook times also remain the same.

MACARONI & CHEESE

THE PASTA

1 tablespoon salt

1 pound cavatappi or cellentani

THE SAUCE

8 tablespoons (1 stick) salted butter

¼ cup all-purpose flour (see Jeff's Tips for GF option)

4–6 cups half-and-half or whole milk, divided

1 teaspoon seasoned salt

1 teaspoon garlic powder

1 teaspoon pepper

⅛ teaspoon nutmeg

4–6 cups (1–1½ pounds) shredded melty cheese of your choice (I use a mix of shredded sharp yellow Cheddar and white or yellow American cut into small pieces—see Jeff's Tips)

1 tablespoon Dijon mustard (optional)

1–2 tablespoons hot sauce (optional)

FOR OPTIONAL CRUST

1 sleeve Ritz crackers, crumbled

4 tablespoons (½ stick) salted butter, melted in the microwave (30–45 seconds will do it)

Here it is—the holy grail of American pasta dishes: mac & cheese! There are countless ways to vary this classic, be it the cheese used (see Jeff's Tips on that) or the way it comes together. But at the end of the day, the two components that are required are in the title of the recipe itself. In my pull-out-all-the-stops version, I am going with a French béchamel-based cheese sauce called Mornay. It maximizes the creamy factor where, once the initial thick and rich Mornay is formed, *you* get to control how cheesy and how thick or thin it will be. I'm also providing an optional, yet supreme, buttery Ritz cracker–crusted baked finish. I assure you it will be one of the cheesiest, smoothest, and most memorable mac & cheeses you've ever experienced.

Prep Time: 10 min • Pasta Cook Time (cavatappi or cellentani): 6–11 min • Sauce Cook Time: 10–15 min •
Optional Bake Time: 15 min • Total Time: 20–40 min • Serves: 4–6

1. Boil the Water: Fill an 8-quart pot halfway with tap water and bring to a rolling boil over high heat. (**NOTE:** If adding the optional Ritz crust, preheat your oven to 350°F now.)

2. Start the Sauce: Melt the butter in a nonstick 4.5- to 5-quart sauté pan over medium heat. Add the flour and whisk until fragrantly nutty and a light brown roux has formed, 1–2 minutes.

3. Cook the Pasta: Add the salt to the pot of boiling water and reduce the heat to medium. Add the pasta and stir. Set a timer to cook until al dente (per the package instructions), or to the shortest amount of time given. When done, drain the pasta in a colander in the sink without rinsing it.

Recipe Continues

CREAMY & CHEESY

4. While the pasta's cooking, return to the sauté pan and slowly pour 4 cups of the half-and-half or milk into the pan, while whisking constantly. Once it's bubbling, add the seasoned salt, garlic powder, pepper, and nutmeg and whisk into the béchamel that's forming. Continue to whisk for 3–5 minutes, until the sauce is nicely thickened and coats the back of a spoon. You now have a lovely béchamel sauce! Reduce the heat to medium-low.

5. Choose Your Cheesiness: Start with 4 cups of cheese and add in batches. First, whisk a third of the cheese into the béchamel. Once it's melded in, repeat the process twice until all the cheese is smoothly blended into the béchamel, which has now turned it into a thick, rich, and cheesy Mornay sauce! If you want to go even further with the cheese level, whisk up to 2 cups more into the sauce. (**NOTE:** Rule #1—There's no such thing as too much cheese in a mac & cheese. If you worry it will get or has gotten too thick, worry not because...)

6. Choose Your Thickness: At this point, *you* get to control how thick your sauce is! Whisk ¼ cup of the 2 remaining cups of half-and-half or milk at a time into the Mornay sauce until you've achieved the consistency that's right for you.

JEFF'S TIPS

For the cheese, you can use any melty variety your heart desires. My main choice of Cheddar is Cougar Gold or Smoky Cheddar cheese from the Washington State University Creamery (you can order it online—get it directly through WSU Creamery by Googling), but that's definitely not required and any will work great. Some other suggestions are: Gruyère/Swiss, Monterey Jack, Cheddar Jack, Cheddar blend, or Mexican cheese blend.

Let's talk leftovers. If you have any, you'll notice that once the mac & cheese cools, and especially once refrigerated, the sauce will firm up and become super thick—like a glue. To reheat the pasta, simply put in a bowl and add a few splashes of half-and-half, milk, or cream. Microwave in 30-second increments, stirring in between, until the sauce becomes creamy once again! The more cream you add while reheating, the thinner the sauce will become.

To make the sauce gluten-free, omit the flour and mix 2 tablespoons cornstarch and 2 tablespoons cold water in a small bowl to form a slurry. Set aside. Then, begin the sauce by placing both the butter and the half-and-half or milk in the pan and heating it up. Once the butter's melted into the half-and-half or milk and comes to a bubble in Step 4, stir in the slurry and it will thicken perfectly!

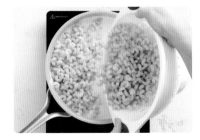 

7. Marry It All: Turn the heat off. Add the cooked and drained pasta and stir into the velvety, cheesy sauce. If using the Dijon and/or hot sauce, add them now (you can also add it to taste). Serve as is or...

TO HALVE Simply halve all the ingredients. However, the salted pasta water amount remains the same. The pasta and the sauce cook times also remain the same.

8. For the Optional Crust: Put the mac & cheese in a large, deep casserole dish (about 9x13 inches and 3 inches deep). Mix the crumbled Ritz crackers with the butter in a bowl and sprinkle evenly on top. Bake on the center rack of the 350°F preheated oven, uncovered, for 10–15 minutes, until the crust is golden brown (keep an eye on it as all ovens vary). Remove from the oven and dig in!

STRAW & HAY

RESERVE PASTA WATER!

THE PASTA

1 tablespoon salt

1 pound fresh tagliatelle or dried fettuccine/linguine (I use about ½ pound yellow pasta for the straw and ½ pound spinach pasta for the hay; see Jeff's Tips)

THE SAUCE

2 tablespoons (¼ stick) salted butter

6 cloves garlic, minced or pressed

2 tablespoons all-purpose flour (see Jeff's Tips for gluten-free option)

3 cups half-and-half or milk

2 teaspoons seasoned salt

2 teaspoons garlic powder

½ teaspoon black pepper

½ cup grated Parmesan cheese, plus more for serving

1 (5.2-ounce) package Boursin (any flavor) or ¾ cup Herb Cheese (page 28), cut into chunks (optional)

10–12 ounces frozen peas, thawed by rinsing

When I was introduced to this pasta, I fell deeply in love. It combines two types of tagliatelle—egg and spinach—to symbolize the colors of straw and hay respectively (but you can also just use one or the other). The very creamy, mouthwatering garlic-Parmesan sauce, once combined with the two-toned pasta and sweet peas, creates a pasta that is as delicious as it is Instagrammable. Check out Jeff's Tips to give it a smoky, porky touch.

Prep Time: 10 min ● **Pasta Cook Time (fresh tagliatelle or dried fettuccine/linguine): 2-12 min** ●
Sauce Cook Time: 15 min ● **Total Time: 25 min** ● **Serves: 4-6**

1. Boil the Water: Fill an 8-quart pot halfway with tap water and bring to a rolling boil over high heat.

2. Start the Sauce: Melt the butter in a nonstick 4.5- to 5-quart sauté pan over medium heat. Add the garlic and sauté until lightly browned, about 2 minutes.

3. Add the flour and whisk until golden brown and a chunky roux has formed, about 30 seconds.

Recipe Continues

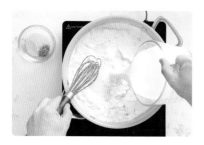

4. Slowly pour in the half-and-half or milk, then add the seasoned salt, garlic powder, and black pepper. Once bubbling, reduce the heat to medium-low and simmer for 5–7 minutes, whisking occasionally, until the sauce is moderately thickened and coats the back of a spoon.

5. Cook the Pasta: Just before the sauce is thickened, add the salt to the pot of boiling water and reduce the heat to medium. Add the pasta and stir. Set a timer to cook until al dente (per the package instructions), or to the shortest amount of time given. When done, **reserve 1 cup of the pasta water** and drain the pasta in a colander in the sink without rinsing it.

6. While the pasta's cooking, return to the sauté pan and add the Parmesan and herb cheese (if using). Stir until melded into the sauce. Turn the heat off, cover the pan, and wait for the pasta to finish cooking if it hasn't.

7. Marry It All: Add the cooked and drained pasta along with the peas to the sauté pan and use tongs to toss and coat with the sauce. If you find you want a slightly thinner, creamier sauce, add ¼ cup of the pasta water at a time and stir until the desired consistency is reached. Serve topped with additional Parmesan, if desired.

JEFF'S TIPS

For the pasta, I use two 9-ounce bags of the Rana fresh tagliatelle that already mixes green and yellow noodles together. It can be found in the deli section of many markets and only takes 2 minutes to cook since it's fresh pasta. That's why I start the pasta to cook between Steps 4 and 6. If using dried fettuccine or linguine, begin cooking the pasta in Step 1 and start the sauce as soon as you add the pasta to the water.

This is a vegetarian dish as written, but feel free to rip up some thinly sliced prosciutto and toss into the pasta with the peas in Step 7.

To make the sauce gluten-free, omit the flour and mix 1 tablespoon cornstarch and 1 tablespoon cold water in a small bowl to form a slurry. Set aside. Skip Step 3 and once the half-and-half or milk is bubbling in Step 4, stir in the slurry and it will thicken perfectly! Continue the recipe from there as written.

TO HALVE Simply halve all the ingredients. However, the salted pasta water amount remains the same. The pasta and the sauce cook times also remain the same.

LEMON-POPPY MASCARPONE PAPPARDELLE

RESERVE PASTA WATER!

THE PASTA
1 tablespoon salt

1 pound pappardelle, dried usually found in the pasta section, fresh in the refrigerated section of your market (see Jeff's Tips)

THE SAUCE
4 tablespoons (½ stick) salted butter

Grated zest and juice of 1 lemon, plus more juice and zest to taste

½ cup grated Pecorino Romano cheese, plus more to taste

½ cup mascarpone cheese, divided, plus more for serving (see Jeff's Tips)

Seasoned salt, to taste

2 teaspoons poppy seeds, plus more for topping

I initially developed this idea from a sun-speckled risotto that I just love. Lemon with cheese is a beautiful combo: The savory and slightly sour lemon complements the sweet creaminess of the mascarpone. The sauce takes practically no time to make and at the end we give a little sprinkle of poppy seeds—and dinner is served.

Prep Time: 5 min • Pasta Cook Time (pappardelle): 2–8 min • Sauce Cook Time: 5 min • Total Time: 15 min • Serves: 4–6

1. Boil the Water and Cook the Pasta: Fill an 8-quart pot halfway with tap water and bring to a rolling boil over high heat. Add the salt and reduce the heat to medium. Add the pasta and stir. Set a timer to cook until al dente (per the package instructions), or to the shortest amount of time given. When done, **reserve 1 cup of the pasta water** and drain the pasta in a colander in the sink without rinsing it.

2. Make the Sauce: As soon as you add the pasta to the pot, melt the butter in a nonstick 4.5- to 5-quart sauté pan over medium heat. Add the lemon juice, Pecorino Romano, and ¼ cup of the mascarpone.

3. Whisk for 2 minutes, until blended and heated. Taste the sauce. If you find you want it more savory, add some seasoned salt, to taste (start with ¼ teaspoon to not overdo it). Turn the heat off and, if the pasta isn't done cooking, cover the sauté pan until it is.

CREAMY & CHEESY

4. **Marry It All:** Add the cooked and drained pasta to the sauté pan followed by the poppy seeds.

5. Add the remaining ¼ cup mascarpone and ½ cup of the pasta water.

6. Use tongs to toss the pasta until combined with the sauce. If you want it thinner, add up to an additional ½ cup pasta water; if you want it cheesier, add up to ¼ cup additional Pecorino Romano; and if you want it more lemony, add additional juice in teaspoon increments, to taste. Serve immediately, topped with additional grated Pecorino Romano, some lemon zest, a small dollop of mascarpone, and more poppy seeds.

 JEFF'S TIPS For the pasta, I use two 9-ounce bags of Rana pappardelle, which is a bit more than a pound but it's fresh pasta and won't expand when cooked so it works here. It also only takes 2 minutes to cook. But you can also use dried pasta; you need 1 pound, and it will take a few minutes longer to cook depending on the brand.

Make sure you get the mascarpone that's **not** espresso flavored—that's used for tiramisu!

TO HALVE Simply halve all the ingredients. However, the salted pasta water amount remains the same. The pasta and the sauce cook times also remain the same.

GARLIC-PARMESAN ZITI

RESERVE PASTA WATER!

THE PASTA

1 tablespoon salt

1 pound ziti or ziti rigati

THE SAUCE

8 tablespoons (1 stick) salted butter

6 cloves garlic, minced or pressed

¼ cup all-purpose flour (see Jeff's Tips for GF option)

4 cups heavy cream, half-and-half, or whole milk (I always use cream for the richest sauce)

2 teaspoons seasoned salt, iodized salt, or Tony Chachere's Creole seasoning

2 teaspoons garlic powder

½ teaspoon pepper

1 teaspoon Better Than Bouillon Roasted Garlic Base (optional)

1 cup grated Parmesan cheese

O.M.Ziiiiti! This is a SUPER garlicky and creamy pasta that will destroy vampires, so if you know of any you value, keep them far away from it. I use the recipe as a base for a slew of rich Parmesan-cream pastas. It's fully customizable in terms of proteins, spices, and seasonings, so it's a great blueprint for you to play around with and ultimately make your own. See Jeff's Tips to get started.

Prep Time: 5 min • Pasta Cook Time (ziti or ziti rigati): 7–11 min • Sauce Cook Time: 15 min • Total Time: 20 min • Serves: 4–6

1. Boil the Water and Cook the Pasta: Fill an 8-quart pot halfway with tap water and bring to a rolling boil over high heat. Add the salt and reduce the heat to medium. Add the pasta and stir. Set a timer to cook until al dente (per the package instructions), or to the shortest amount of time given. When done, **reserve 1½ cups of the pasta water**, then drain the pasta in a colander in the sink without rinsing it.

2. Make the Sauce: While the pasta's cooking, melt the butter in a nonstick 4.5- to 5-quart sauté pan over medium heat. Add the garlic and sauté for about 2–3 minutes, until lightly browned.

3. Whisk the flour into the butter until a roux is formed, 1–2 minutes. Once it's fragrantly nutty and the color of peanut butter, you're good.

Recipe Continues

CREAMY & CHEESY

4. Increase the heat to medium-high. Add the cream, half-and-half, or milk, whisking as you pour it into the pan, and bring to a light boil. Once bubbling, reduce the heat to medium or medium-low and let the cream, half-and-half, or milk simmer for 3 minutes, whisking often, until the sauce is thickened and coats the back of a spoon.

5. Add the seasoned salt, garlic powder, pepper, Parmesan, and Better Than Bouillon (if using).

6. Whisk until combined, let simmer 1 minute more, then turn off the heat. If the pasta's not ready yet, cover the pan with a lid until it is, whisking every so often to keep the sauce nice and fortified.

7. Marry It All: Turn the heat off. Add the cooked and drained pasta to the sauté pan, toss to coat with the sauce, and serve. For a thinner sauce, add ¼–½ cup of the reserved pasta water at a time and toss to combine into the finished pasta until the desired consistency is reached.

JEFF'S TIPS

If you want some chicken, be my guest! Add about 1 pound of rotisserie chicken meat while marrying the pasta with the sauce in Step 7. If shrimp's more your style, rub a light dusting of garlic salt on 1 pound of raw (tail-on or -off) shrimp and sauté with the garlic in Step 2. Once curled and opaque, remove with a slotted spoon to a bowl, then return it when marrying the pasta with the sauce in Step 7.

You can feel free to use any other seasonings you wish in Step 5, including spicy ones—just start with ½ teaspoon of each so as to not overdo it. Have fun and experiment!

To reheat any leftovers, add some cream when microwaving to reconstitute the sauce. While reheating, adding a few splashes of marinara (page 40, or your favorite jarred brand) transforms the sauce into something extra special!

To make the sauce gluten-free, omit the flour, skip Step 3, and mix 2½ tablespoons cornstarch and 2½ tablespoons cold water in a small bowl to form a slurry. Once you add the heavy cream, half-and-half, or milk to the sauce in Step 4 and it begins to bubble, stir in the slurry and it will thicken perfectly! Continue the recipe as written.

TO HALVE Simply halve all the ingredients. However, the salted pasta water amount remains the same. The pasta and the sauce cook times also remain the same.

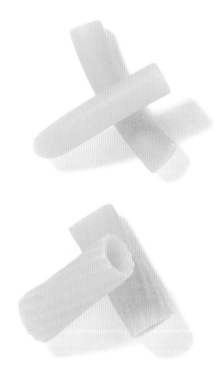

AVGOLEMONO ANGEL HAIR

RESERVE PASTA WATER!

 (if using garlic broth)

THE PASTA

1 tablespoon salt

1 pound angel hair or capellini

THE SAUCE

4 large eggs

Juice of 2 lemons

2 teaspoons salt, seasoned salt, or Cavender's Greek seasoning

8 tablespoons (1 stick) salted butter

2 tablespoons all-purpose flour (see Jeff's Tips for GF option)

2 cups broth of your choice (I like chicken or garlic broth, e.g., made from Better Than Bouillon Roasted Garlic Base)

OPTIONAL FINISHES

Up to 1 cup shredded rotisserie chicken meat

Up to 1 cup crumbled feta or blue cheese

2–3 tablespoons dried dill

Aphrodite, the Greek goddess of love, is often depicted with long-flowing hair and because this book focuses on a love for pasta, this one is for her. Here, I take a Greek avgolemono soup made up of lemon, egg, broth, and usually orzo or rice (speaking of which, check out my Avgolemon-Os on page 276), and give it the most amazing pasta sauce treatment that would make Apollo strum his lyre. Since this is the Creamy & Cheesy section of this chapter, feel free to toss in some crumbled feta (or even blue cheese) at the end. And for some additional protein, some shredded rotisserie chicken is a nice touch as well.

Prep Time: 5 min • Pasta Cook Time (angel hair/capellini): 2–4 min • Sauce Cook Time: 10 min • Total Time: 20 min • Serves: 4–6

1. Boil the Water: Fill an 8-quart pot halfway with tap water and bring to a rolling boil over high heat.

2. Make the Sauce: Whisk the eggs, lemon juice, and salt in a bowl and set aside.

3. Melt the butter in a nonstick 4.5- to 5-quart sauté pan over medium heat. Add the flour and whisk until fragrantly nutty and a roux has formed, 1–2 minutes.

Recipe Continues

4. While whisking, add the broth to the pan and increase the heat to medium-high. Once bubbling, reduce the heat to medium and simmer for 3–5 minutes, until slightly thickened. Turn the heat off, cover with a lid, and cook the pasta.

5. Cook the Pasta: Add the salt to the pot of boiling water and reduce the heat to medium. Add the pasta and stir. Set a timer to cook until al dente (per the package instructions), or to the shortest amount of time given. When done, **reserve 2 cups of the pasta water** and then drain the pasta in a colander in the sink without rinsing it.

6. Marry It All: Add 1 cup of the reserved pasta water to the egg-lemon mixture and gently whisk for 30 seconds to temper the eggs.

7. Add the cooked and drained pasta to the sauté pan and use tongs to toss everything together. (**NOTE:** It's going to feel like there's a LOT of sauce in the pan at first, but as soon as you add the tempered egg mixture in the next step, it's all going to quickly come together and thicken into the perfect sauce.)

8. Add the tempered egg-lemon mixture while continuing to toss. If you want a thinner sauce, add the reserved pasta water in ½-cup increments until you've reached the desired consistency.

9. If using, add the optional chicken, crumbled cheese, and/or dill, toss with the pasta, and serve immediately.

JEFF'S TIPS

For a thinner sauce from the start, you can use 1 tablespoon all-purpose flour in Step 3.

To make the sauce gluten-free, omit the flour and mix 1 tablespoon cornstarch and 1 tablespoon cold water in a small bowl to form a slurry. Set aside. Then, begin the sauce by heating both the butter and broth in the pan. Once the butter's melted into the broth and bubbling in Step 4, stir in the slurry and it will thicken perfectly! Continue the recipe from there as written.

TO HALVE Simply halve all the ingredients. However, the salted pasta water amount remains the same. The pasta and the sauce cook times also remain the same.

CREAM OF MUSHROOM MOSTACCIOLI

RESERVE PASTA WATER!

THE PASTA
1 tablespoon salt

1 pound mostaccioli or penne

THE SAUCE
6 tablespoons (¾ stick) salted butter

1½ pounds baby bella mushrooms (see Jeff's Tip), sliced

2 teaspoons garlic salt

½ teaspoon black pepper

2 tablespoons all-purpose flour

2 cups heavy cream or half-and-half

¼ cup grated Parmesan cheese, plus more for serving

Truffle oil, for drizzling (optional)

If buttery, browned mushrooms in a slightly cheesy sauce is your game, get ready to play. Think of mushrooms as a sponge—they like to sop up every liquid that comes their way, including melted butter. And then they release their butter-laced juices and the angels sigh. If the recipe seems to include a lot of butter, it's because there's a lotta mushrooms! I like to use mostaccioli as the pasta for this one as it's essentially penne without the ridges. (And if you find a mostaccioli rigati, it's essentially just penne.)

Prep Time: 10 min • Pasta Cook Time (mostaccioli or penne): 9–11 min • Sauce Cook Time: 15 min • Total Time: 25 min • Serves: 4–6

1. Boil the Water: Fill an 8-quart pot halfway with tap water and bring to a rolling boil over high heat.

2. Start the Sauce: Melt the butter in a nonstick 4.5- to 5-quart sauté pan over medium-high heat. Add the mushrooms and sauté until they begin to brown, soften, and release their juices, 5–8 minutes.

3. Cook the Pasta: Just when the mushrooms begin to release their juices, add the salt to the pot of boiling water and reduce the heat to medium. Add the pasta and stir. Set a timer to cook until al dente (per the package instructions), or to the shortest amount of time given. When done, **reserve 1 cup of the pasta water** and drain the pasta in a colander in the sink without rinsing it.

CREAMY & CHEESY

4. While the pasta's cooking, return to the sauté pan and add the garlic salt, pepper, and flour and stir into the mushrooms until they're coated.

5. Add the cream and stir well. Once bubbling, reduce the heat to medium-low and simmer for 5 minutes, or until the sauce is thickened and coats the back of a spoon. Add the Parmesan and stir until combined into the sauce. Turn the heat off, covering the pan with a lid if the pasta isn't done cooking yet.

6. Marry It All: Add the cooked and drained pasta to the sauté pan and toss to coat with the sauce. If you want a thinner sauce, add ¼ cup of the reserved pasta water at a time and stir until it's the desired consistency. Serve topped with additional Parmesan and a few drizzles of truffle oil, if desired.

JEFF'S TIP The recipe may call for baby bella mushrooms but you can use a blend of any kind up to 1½ pounds. Also, don't rinse your mushrooms before cooking! They will absorb the first thing they come into contact with and it should be the delicious ingredients you're cooking them with, not boring water! If you see dirt on them before cooking, use a damp paper towel to clean them.

TO HALVE Simply halve all the ingredients. However, the salted pasta water amount remains the same. The pasta and the sauce cook times also remain the same.

WHITE PIZZA PASTA

THE PASTA

1 tablespoon salt

1 pound radiatore (or any pasta you prefer)

THE SAUCE

2 cups (8 ounces) shredded mozzarella cheese

2 cups ricotta cheese (a 15-ounce container is fine)

1 cup grated Parmesan cheese

3 large eggs

1 tablespoon dried basil

1 teaspoon seasoned salt

Extra-virgin olive oil, for drizzling (optional)

This dish is one of my favorites, mostly because I love cheese (mozzarella), cheese (ricotta), and more cheese (Parmesan). It's similar to a white pizza, with no red sauce present, and works really nicely as a pasta. (But if you want some red sauce action for a tomatoey touch, I've got you taken care of in Jeff's Tip.) Don't forget to save some of that pasta water because it's going to create a silky, smooth texture once combined with the eggy ricotta mixture!

Prep Time: 10 min • **Pasta Cook Time (radiatore): 5–8 min** • **Sauce Cook Time: 5 min** •
Total Time: 20 min • **Serves: 4–6**

1. Boil the Water and Cook the Pasta: Fill an 8-quart pot halfway with tap water and bring to a rolling boil over high heat. Add the salt and reduce the heat to medium. Add the pasta and stir. Set a timer to cook until al dente (per the package instructions), or to the shortest amount of time given. When done, **reserve 1 cup of the pasta water** and drain the pasta in a colander in the sink without rinsing it.

2. Make the Sauce: As soon as you add the pasta to the pot, combine the cheeses, eggs, dried basil, and seasoned salt in a large mixing bowl and mix to combine.

3. As soon as the pasta is done cooking and drained, return its pot to the stove and set over low heat.

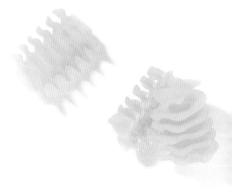

JEFF'S TIP Want this white pizza pasta with some red sauce? Add 1–2 cups marinara sauce in Step 4 after the sauce is married to the pasta. Stir to combine and enjoy!

4. Marry It All: Return the drained pasta to its pot followed by the cheese mixture and ½ cup of the pasta water. Stir to combine for 1–2 minutes (the heat of the pasta and the pot will cook the eggs through).

5. If you want a creamier sauce, add up to an additional ½ cup of the pasta water. Once the cheesy pasta is to your liking, turn the heat off and serve immediately with some drizzles of olive oil, if desired.

TO HALVE Simply halve all the ingredients. However, the salted pasta water amount remains the same. The pasta and the sauce cook times also remain the same.

PASTA PRIMAVERA

RESERVE PASTA WATER!

This chapter wouldn't be complete without the inclusion of the nonna of all vegetable pastas: primavera! From red onion to broccoli and bell pepper to zucchini—you name it, it's in here (literally, see Jeff's Tip). And while the name translates as "spring pasta," it can be made any time of year! What really makes the pasta pop are the colors of the veggies. And while it will feel like you're putting an entire garden into this pasta, trust me—the veggies will become pliable like the pasta itself and will shrink down, creating the perfect balance once tossed together.

THE PASTA
1 tablespoon salt

1 pound tri-color penne

THE VEGGIES
3 cups cherry tomatoes (I like a colorful variety), sliced in half

2 large carrots, peeled and sliced into ¼-inch-thick matchsticks about 1 inch long

1 medium red onion, sliced into thin strands

2 large bell peppers (any color, or a mix), seeded and sliced into thin strands

1 large zucchini, sliced into ½-inch-thick disks and quartered

1 large yellow squash, sliced into ½-inch-thick disks and quartered

2 cups broccoli florets, cut into bite-size pieces

6 cloves garlic, thinly sliced, minced, or pressed

½ cup extra-virgin olive oil

2 teaspoons Italian seasoning

2 teaspoons seasoned salt

1 teaspoon black pepper

THE FINISHING TOUCHES
½–1 cup grated Parmesan cheese, plus more for serving

Chopped fresh basil leaves, for garnish (optional)

Prep Time: 20 min • Pasta Cook Time (tri-color penne): 9–11 min • Roasting Time: 15–25 min • Total Time: 35–45 min • Serves: 4–6

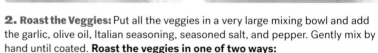
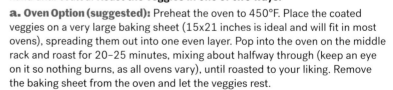

1. Boil the Water: Fill an 8-quart pot halfway with tap water and bring to a rolling boil over high heat.

2. Roast the Veggies: Put all the veggies in a very large mixing bowl and add the garlic, olive oil, Italian seasoning, seasoned salt, and pepper. Gently mix by hand until coated. **Roast the veggies in one of two ways:**

a. Oven Option (suggested): Preheat the oven to 450°F. Place the coated veggies on a very large baking sheet (15x21 inches is ideal and will fit in most ovens), spreading them out into one even layer. Pop into the oven on the middle rack and roast for 20–25 minutes, mixing about halfway through (keep an eye on it so nothing burns, as all ovens vary), until roasted to your liking. Remove the baking sheet from the oven and let the veggies rest.

b. Air Fryer Option: Preheat the air fryer to 390°F. Place the coated veggies in the air fryer basket. (The veggies will be on top of each other, and that's fine. However, you may need to do this in two batches.) Air fry for 15–20 minutes, tossing a few times to ensure even roasting and making sure nothing burns, until roasted to your liking. Remove the basket from the air fryer and let the veggies rest.

VEGGIE VARIATIONS

3. Cook the Pasta: After 10 minutes of the veggies roasting, add the salt to the pot of boiling water and reduce the heat to medium. Add the pasta and stir. Set a timer to cook until al dente (per the package instructions), or to the shortest amount of time given. When done, **reserve 1 cup of the pasta water**, then drain the pasta in a colander in the sink without rinsing it.

4. Marry It All: Return the cooked and drained pasta to the pot it cooked in and set over low heat. Add the roasted veggies.

5. Toss until the vegetables are combined with the pasta. Follow with ½ cup of the Parmesan and ½ cup of the reserved pasta water. If you want it cheesier, add up to ½ cup more Parmesan; if you want it thinner, add more pasta water until the desired consistency is reached. Serve immediately, topped with additional grated Parmesan and basil, if desired.

 JEFF'S TIP The beautiful thing about this recipe is you can really add any vegetable you love. If you see one you don't like, leave it out. And if you want one I don't mention, add it in!

TO HALVE Simply halve all the ingredients. However, the salted pasta water amount remains the same. The pasta and the vegetable cook times remain the same.

FRENCH ONION TORTELLINI

RESERVE PASTA WATER!

V+ (if using vegetable broth)

THE PASTA

1 tablespoon salt

24 ounces tortellini of your choice

THE SAUCE

4 tablespoons (½ stick) salted butter

2 large Vidalia (sweet) onions, thinly sliced into strands

1 tablespoon light or dark brown sugar

1 tablespoon garlic salt

2 teaspoons dried thyme, plus more for topping

½ teaspoon black pepper

1½ cups vegetable or beef broth

1½ cups (6 ounces) shredded Swiss or Gruyère cheese

1 (5.2-ounce) package Boursin (any flavor) or ¾ cup Herb Cheese (page 28), cut into chunks

Doing a variation of anything French onion has become a signature of mine. In my blog and other cookbooks, I've covered French onion chicken, pot roast, risotto, mac & cheese, and, of course, soup. This recipe takes the best elements of golden-brown caramelized onions and marries them to tortellini with a sauce made from the onions and their sweet syrup, plus shredded Swiss or Gruyère, a creamy herb cheese, and some of the pasta water. If you're a lover of French Onion Anything, prepare yourself for something very special.

Prep Time: 10 min • Pasta Cook Time (tortellini): 2–4 min • Caramelizing Time: 20–30 min • Sauce Cook Time: 5 min • Total Time: 35–45 min • Serves: 4–6

1. Boil the Water: Fill an 8-quart pot halfway with tap water. Place on the stove over high heat and bring to a rolling boil as you caramelize the onions.

2. Caramelize the Onions: While the water comes to a boil, melt the butter in a nonstick 4.5- to 5-quart sauté pan over medium-high heat. Add the onions, followed by the brown sugar, garlic salt, thyme, and black pepper. Sauté for 20–30 minutes, stirring occasionally, until the onions begin to caramelize (which means they become syrupy and golden brown in color).

3. Cook the Pasta: When the onions are just about done caramelizing, add the salt to the pot of boiling water and reduce the heat to medium. Add the pasta and stir. Set a timer to cook until al dente (per the package instructions), or to the shortest amount of time given. When done, **reserve 2 cups of the pasta water,** then drain the pasta in a colander in the sink without rinsing it.

VEGGIE VARIATIONS

4. Make the Sauce: While the pasta's cooking, return to the sauté pan, add the broth to the onions, and reduce the heat to medium. Simmer until slightly reduced, about 2 minutes. Turn the heat off and wait for the pasta to be done if it isn't by now.

5. Marry It All: Add the cooked and drained pasta to the sauté pan of caramelized onions, followed by the shredded cheese and herb cheese.

6. Gently toss until the sauce is combined with the pasta. If you want the sauce to be thinner, add ½ cup of the reserved pasta water at a time and toss until the desired consistency is reached. Serve immediately, topped with additional thyme, if desired.

JEFF'S TIP The beautiful thing about this dish is you can use tortellini stuffed with any filling you want—be it just cheese or something fancier, such as chicken, sausage, or even lobster!

TO HALVE Simply halve all the ingredients. However, the salted pasta water amount remains the same. The pasta, onion, and sauce cook times remain the same.

BALSAMIC BRUSSELS SPROUTS ORECCHIETTE

RESERVE PASTA WATER!

THE PASTA
1 tablespoon salt

1 pound orecchiette

THE BRUSSELS SPROUTS
1 pound Brussels sprouts, hard bottom stalks removed, shredded (see Jeff's Tips)

2 tablespoons extra-virgin olive oil

1 teaspoon salt

½ teaspoon black pepper

¼ cup balsamic vinegar

THE SAUCE
½ cup sour cream or Greek yogurt (see Jeff's Tips), at room temperature

2 tablespoons balsamic glaze, plus more for drizzling

Brussels sprouts are a prime example of a food that can be a turn-off in its raw state versus cooked. I know this first-hand because the thought of them on their own is something that makes my lips purse, but tell me they've been roasted and crisped in some olive oil, salt, and pepper (that's all it takes, folks!), and I'll eat them anytime! This recipe takes them to new heights when we add some balsamic vinegar *and* balsamic glaze (yum) and then combine with pasta and a touch of sour cream or Greek yogurt. If you never thought you'd enjoy eating Brussels sprouts, I implore you to try this recipe. They may just become your go-to veggie.

Prep Time: 10 min • Pasta Cook Time (orecchiette): 9 min • Roasting Time: 5–20 min • Total Time: 25–45 min • Serves: 4–6

1. Boil the Water: Fill an 8-quart pot halfway with tap water and bring to a boil over high heat.

2. Roast the Brussels Sprouts: Put the Brussels sprouts in a large mixing bowl, add the olive oil, salt, and pepper, and toss until combined. **Choose one of the following ways to roast:**

a. Oven Option: Preheat the oven to 425°F. Place the coated Brussels sprouts on a large baking sheet lined with parchment paper, shaking them into a single layer. Pop into the oven on the middle rack and roast for 15–20 minutes (keep an eye on them so nothing burns, as all ovens vary). About 10 minutes in, drizzle the balsamic vinegar (*not* the glaze) over the sprouts and continue to roast. When done, the Brussels sprouts should be slightly charred and crispy. Remove the baking sheet from the oven and let the sprouts rest.

b. Air Fryer Option: Preheat the air fryer to 390°F. Place the coated Brussels sprouts in the air fryer basket in a single layer as best as possible (it's fine if they rest on top of each other a bit). Air fry for 5–10 minutes. About 3 minutes in, drizzle the balsamic vinegar (*not* the glaze) over the sprouts, mix together, and continue to air fry. Check on them a few times and stir to make sure they don't burn. When done, they should be slightly charred and crispy. Remove the basket from the air fryer and let the sprouts rest.

VEGGIE VARIATIONS

3. Cook the Pasta: When the Brussels sprouts are just about done roasting, add the salt to the pot of boiling water and reduce the heat to medium. Add the pasta and stir. Set a timer to cook until al dente (per the package instructions), or to the shortest amount of time given. When done, **reserve 2 cups of the pasta water** and then drain the pasta in a colander in the sink without rinsing it.

4. Marry It All: Return the cooked and drained pasta to the pot it cooked in and set over low heat. Add the roasted Brussels sprouts, sour cream or Greek yogurt, and balsamic glaze.

5. Toss until combined with the pasta. If you want the sauce thinned out a bit, add ½ cup of the reserved pasta water at a time until the desired consistency is reached. Serve immediately topped with an additional drizzle of balsamic glaze, if desired.

 As for shredding the Brussels sprouts, you can sometimes find them already shredded in the produce section of your market. But if not, you can either grate or chop them yourself or do what I do and pulse them (in batches if necessary) in a food processor until shredded.

For a more decadent creamy ending, use ¼–¾ cup Herb Cheese (page 28) in place of the sour cream or yogurt in Step 4. And if you want a *really* decadent touch, add the herb cheese to the sour cream or yogurt. But note that if you use both, you may need to use the full 2 cups of pasta water to thin out the rich and cheesy sauce. In fact, feel free to reserve 3 cups of the pasta water just in case.

TO HALVE Simply halve all the ingredients. However, the salted pasta water amount remains the same. The pasta and the vegetable cook times remain the same.

RAVIOLI IN ROASTED CARROT SAUCE

   (see Jeff's Tips)

THE PASTA

1 tablespoon salt

24–30 ounces ravioli of your choice

THE CARROTS

2 pounds medium carrots, each sliced lengthwise down the center and cut into thirds (or see Jeff's Tips)

¼ cup extra-virgin olive oil

1 teaspoon kosher salt

1 teaspoon dried thyme

1 teaspoon light or dark brown sugar (optional)

½ teaspoon dried oregano

¼ teaspoon black pepper

THE SAUCE

2 cups heavy cream or half-and-half, divided

1 tablespoon pure maple syrup, or more to taste (optional)

¼ cup sour cream or Greek yogurt, at room temperature (optional)

In an effort to eat lighter, I developed an obsession with roasted carrots. A simple seasoned olive oil marinade and an oven or air fryer were all it took to make carrots that were fork tender and tasting like candy! In fact, they were so tender, I thought they would be the perfect suitor to blend with some cream into a sauce to dress up ravioli. So carrot lovers (and Docs), if you really wanna know what's up, it's this outrageously good chunky, sweet, and savory dish.

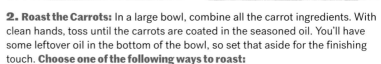

Prep Time: 15 min ● Pasta Cook Time (ravioli): 4–5 min ● Roasting Time: 20–40 min ● Sauce Cook Time: 5 min ● Total Time: 40 min–1 hour ● Serves: 4–6

1. Boil the Water: Fill an 8-quart pot halfway with tap water and bring to a boil over high heat.

2. Roast the Carrots: In a large bowl, combine all the carrot ingredients. With clean hands, toss until the carrots are coated in the seasoned oil. You'll have some leftover oil in the bottom of the bowl, so set that aside for the finishing touch. **Choose one of the following ways to roast:**

a. Oven Option: Preheat the oven to 425°F. Line a large baking sheet with parchment paper and arrange the oiled carrots on it in a single layer. Roast on the center rack for 30–40 minutes. After 30 minutes of baking, check on the carrots by sticking a fork in one. If it's soft and tender, they're done. If not, bake for 10 minutes more, or until fork tender.

b. Air Fryer Option: Preheat the air fryer to 390°F. Place the oiled carrots in a single layer in the air fryer basket. (**NOTE:** Depending on the size of your air fryer, you may need to do this in a few batches.) Air fry for 20–25 minutes. After 20 minutes, check on the carrots by sticking a fork in one. If it's soft and tender, they're done. If not, air fry for 10 minutes more, or until fork tender.

Recipe Continues

VEGGIE VARIATIONS

3. Start the Sauce: Cut one-fourth of the roasted carrots into smaller pieces and set aside.

4. Put the remaining carrots in a food processor with 1 cup of the heavy cream and the maple syrup (if using, start 1 with tablespoon). Blend until pureed. It will be slightly chunky even when blended, which is exactly what this sauce should be. Taste it. If you decide you want more maple syrup, add it now to taste and blend.

5. Heat a nonstick 4.5- to 5-quart sauté pan over medium heat. Add the roasted carrot puree, reserved cut carrots, and sour cream or yogurt, if using, and stir until combined.

6. Cook the Pasta: As the carrot puree is heating up in the sauté pan, add the salt to the pot of boiling water and reduce the heat to medium. Add the pasta and stir. Set a timer to cook until al dente (per the package instructions), or to the shortest amount of time given. When done, drain the pasta in a colander in the sink without rinsing it.

7. While the pasta's cooking, return to the sauté pan and stir the remaining 1 cup heavy cream into the carrot puree until combined into a creamy orange sauce. Once bubbling, reduce the heat to medium-low and simmer for 1–2 minutes.

 JEFF'S TIPS Want to save time? You can use baby carrots that are already peeled for you, are the right size, *and* achieve quicker cooking! Keep them whole and roast for 30 minutes in the oven or 15–20 minutes in the air fryer (at the same temps as specified in the recipe). Just make sure they're fork tender. If not, cook a little longer until they are.

If you want to make this pasta vegan and dairy-free, sub an unsweetened nondairy milk for the cream and use a vegan and dairy-free ravioli or other pasta.

8. Marry It All: Turn the heat off. Add the cooked and drained pasta to the sauté pan and toss to coat with the sauce. Serve immediately, topped with an additional drizzle of the reserved seasoned oil (from Step 2), if desired.

TO HALVE Simply halve all the ingredients. However, the salted pasta water amount remains the same. The pasta, vegetable, and sauce cook times remain the same.

KASHA VARNISHKES

As a Jewish person, I am telling you that a part of my wanting to do a pasta book was so I could include this recipe. In fact, there are three main pasta dishes in the Jewish cooking arsenal, and they're all here: Noodle Pudding (aka Kugel, page 231), Chicken Noodle Soup (page 272), and Kasha Varnishkes. But what exactly is this dish that you may not know how to pronounce? Kasha varnishkes ("VAR-nish-kuhz") is an Ashkenazi dish that typically features either regular or mini bow ties combined with buckwheat groats (kasha) in a caramelized onion, mushroom, and garlic medley. It is light, yet super delicious, and unlike anything you've ever had. While butter or vegetable oil will do, schmaltz, which is rendered chicken fat, is the preferred fat for this dish; it can be found at many a kosher butcher and some markets, but I show you how to make your own in Jeff's Tip.

 (if using schmaltz, vegetable oil, or margarine)

 (if using vegetable or garlic broth and not using schmaltz)

THE PASTA

1 tablespoon salt

1 pound farfalle (bow ties) or mini farfalle

THE VEGGIES

6 tablespoons schmaltz (rendered chicken or duck fat, see Jeff's Tip), vegetable oil, margarine, or salted butter, plus more to taste

4 yellow onions, roughly chopped

8 ounces baby bella or white mushrooms, sliced (optional)

THE KASHA

1 cup medium-size granulated kasha (buckwheat groats; I use Wolff's brand)

1 large egg, lightly beaten

6 cloves garlic, minced or pressed

2½ cups chicken, vegetable, or garlic broth (e.g., made from Better Than Bouillon Roasted Garlic Base)

2 teaspoons seasoned salt, plus more to taste

½ teaspoon white pepper, plus more to taste

Prep Time: 10 min • **Pasta Cook Time (farfalle/bow ties or mini farfalle): 7–11 min** • **Caramelizing Time: 20–30 min** • **Kasha Cook Time: 15 min** • **Total Time: 45 min–1 hour** • **Serves: 4–6**

1. Boil the Water: Fill an 8-quart pot halfway with tap water and bring to a rolling boil over high heat.

TO HALVE Simply halve all the ingredients. However, the salted pasta water amount remains the same. The pasta and the vegetable cook times remain the same.

2. Caramelize the Onions: Heat the schmaltz (or other fat) in a nonstick 4.5- to 5-quart sauté pan over medium-high heat. Once melted or shimmering, add the onions and sauté for 20–30 minutes, stirring occasionally, until they caramelize (which means they become syrupy and golden in color).

3. If using, add the mushrooms and sauté for another 5 minutes, until they are browned and their juices have released.

Recipe Continues

4. Transfer the cooked veggies to a bowl to rest and place the pan back on the stove.

5. Start the Kasha: In a mixing bowl, mix the kasha, egg, and garlic until combined.

6. Transfer the coated kasha to the now-empty sauté pan and cook, stirring, over medium-high heat until it begins to break up, toast, and separate, 3–5 minutes.

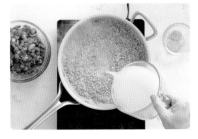

7. Add the broth, seasoned salt, and white pepper to the kasha and bring to a boil. Return the onion mixture to the pan and stir well.

8. Cook the Pasta: Add the salt to the pot of boiling water and reduce the heat to medium. Add the pasta and stir. Set a timer to cook until al dente (per the package instructions), or to the shortest amount of time given. When done, drain the pasta in a colander in the sink without rinsing it.

9. As the pasta cooks, cover the sauté pan, reduce the heat to medium-low, and let simmer for 10–12 minutes. After 10 minutes, remove the cover and see if the broth has been absorbed by the kasha. If not, cover again for a few minutes until it has. If the kasha is done before the pasta, just remove from the heat and keep the pan covered.

10. Marry It All: Add the cooked and drained pasta to the sauté pan of cooked kasha, onions, and (maybe) mushrooms and toss until combined. Feel free to add more schmaltz (or vegetable oil or butter), seasoned salt, or white pepper to taste before serving.

JEFF'S TIP

To Make Schmaltz

- 2–4 cups chicken or duck fat and skin (this can be collected from a chicken you've peeled the skin off; you can also collect it over time and freeze in a ziplock freezer bag for the future)
- 1 large Vidalia (sweet) or yellow onion, peeled and quartered

Add the chicken or duck fat and skin in an enamel-coated Dutch oven or large nonstick pan (with no oil or butter added) and cook over low heat until the skin begins to render the fat into liquid and starts to lightly brown, about 20 minutes. Add the onion, raise the heat to medium-high, and cook, allowing the onion to break up and soften as the fat from the chicken skin continues to render. You want to cook this until the onion begins to really soften and the chicken skin is crispy and begins to get quite browned, but not burned, another 10–15 minutes. From there, use tongs to remove the crisped skin and syrupy onions and discard (or transfer to a bowl and lightly salt for a crunchy, comforting snack). Let the fat cool for 10–15 minutes. If the fat has browned bits in it, place cheesecloth over a mason jar and pour the fat through it, discarding the cheesecloth when done. Cover the jar and place in the fridge where it will congeal and become schmaltz! It'll keep for up to 1 week in the fridge or 6 months in the freezer.

PASTA ALLA NORMA

THE PASTA
1 tablespoon salt

1 pound ziti rigati

THE EGGPLANT
1 large or 2 small eggplants, skin-on and sliced into ½-inch-thick disks, then cut into bite-size chunks

⅓ cup extra-virgin olive oil

1½ teaspoons salt

1 teaspoon black pepper

THE SAUCE
5 cups Marinara Sauce (page 40 or use your favorite jarred brand)

Leaves from 1 bunch fresh basil, stemmed, some reserved for serving

½–1 cup grated or shredded ricotta salata (see Jeff's Tip), Pecorino Romano, or Parmesan, plus more for serving

½–1 cup black olives, pitted and sliced, with some for serving (optional)

This classic Sicilian pasta dish is one of my all-time favorites. It features roasted eggplant in a marinara sauce that's combined with fresh basil and cheese. The first time I ever tried pasta alla Norma was in a now long-gone Italian joint in Queens, but they did it a bit differently from most others I've tried since. They tossed pitted black olives into the pasta, which really elevated the savory elements, so I'm doing that as well—but keeping them optional as I know olives are not for everyone. The common cheese used here is ricotta salata (check out Jeff's Tip for more info on that).

Prep Time: 10 min • **Pasta Cook Time (ziti rigati): 7–8 min** • **Roasting Time: 10–25 min** • **Sauce Cook Time: 10 min** • **Total Time: 30–55 min** • **Serves: 4–6**

1. Boil the Water: Fill an 8-quart pot halfway with tap water and bring to a boil over high heat.

TO HALVE Simply halve all the ingredients. However, the salted pasta water amount remains the same. The pasta, vegetable, and sauce cook times remain the same.

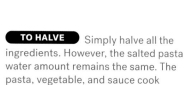

2. Roast the Eggplant in one of the following ways:

a. Oven Option: Preheat the oven to 425°F. Lay the eggplant chunks on a large, parchment paper–lined baking sheet. Brush with the oil and then sprinkle on the salt and pepper. Pop into the oven on the middle rack and roast for 15–25 minutes (keep an eye on things so nothing burns, as all ovens vary). When done, they should look nice and roasted and feel tender to the touch. Remove the baking sheet from the oven and let the eggplant rest.

b. Air Fryer Option: Preheat the air fryer to 390°F. Place the eggplant in a very large mixing bowl and add the oil, salt, and pepper. Mix by hand until well-coated. Transfer the coated eggplant to the basket in a single layer as best as possible and air fry for 10–15 minutes. Check on it a few times to make sure the eggplant doesn't burn. When done, they should look nicely roasted and feel tender to the touch. Remove the basket from the air fryer and let the eggplant rest.

VEGGIE VARIATIONS

3. Cook the Pasta: When the eggplant is done roasting and resting, add the salt to the pot of boiling water and reduce the heat to medium. Add the pasta and stir. Set a timer to cook until al dente (per the package instructions), or to the shortest amount of time given. When done, drain the pasta in a colander in the sink without rinsing it.

4. Make the Sauce: While the pasta's cooking, heat the marinara in a nonstick 4.5- to 5-quart sauté pan over medium-high heat. Once bubbling, reduce the heat to medium-low and stir in the fresh basil (reserving some for garnish) and grated cheese and stir until the basil wilts. Let simmer for 3–5 minutes. Reduce the heat to low.

5. Add the roasted eggplant to the sauce. If using the olives, add them now as well. Stir gently to combine. If the pasta isn't ready yet, turn the heat off and cover the pan, letting the sauce rest until it is.

6. Marry It All: If you haven't already, turn the heat off under the sauté pan and add the cooked and drained pasta; gently toss until combined with the sauce. Serve immediately topped with additional basil, olives, and some sprinkles of shredded cheese, if desired.

JEFF'S TIP Ricotta salata is a pressed, firmer, and saltier version of the creamy, more common ricotta cheese that comes in a tub. While very light and pliable once shredded, it doesn't melt into sauces, which is actually ideal for this dish as I like the cheese to stand out when combined with the marinara. If you can't find it at your local market in the cheese or deli section, an Italian market will very likely have it. But you can absolutely use grated Pecorino Romano or Parmesan in its place.

LEMON-PESTO ASPARAGUS PASTA

THE PASTA
1 tablespoon salt

1 pound casarecce

THE SAUCE
2 tablespoons extra-virgin olive oil

1½ pounds asparagus, tough bottoms trimmed and each stalk cut into thirds

1 teaspoon garlic powder

1 teaspoon seasoned salt

½ teaspoon black pepper

Grated zest and juice of 1 lemon

1 cup Pesto Sauce (page 50 or your favorite jarred brand—I like Costco's)

Grated Parmesan, for serving (optional)

As Stephen Sondheim once said, "Greens, greens, and nothing but greens!" In the original Broadway production of his musical *Into the Woods,* Bernadette Peters played the Witch who "raps" about every green vegetable in a garden and I memorized it when I was an 8-year-old kid. That is what inspired this musical theatre nerd to pen this recipe. Nowadays, one of my favorite veggies is asparagus sautéed in olive oil and seasoned simply with salt and pepper. Seriously, I could eat this springy, savory, and healthy treat as a meal in itself. But when tossed with pasta in a lemon-kissed pesto sauce? All bets of deliciousness are off because this one will win every time—just like the Witch's rampion (her champion, her favorite).

Prep Time: 10 min • Pasta Cook Time (casarecce): 8–12 min • Sauce Cook Time: 15–20 min • Total Time: 25–30 min • Serves: 4–6

1. Boil the Water: Fill an 8-quart pot halfway with tap water and bring to a rolling boil over high heat.

2. Start the Sauce: Heat the olive oil in a nonstick 4.5- to 5-quart sauté pan over medium-high heat. Once shimmering, after about 3 minutes, add the asparagus, garlic powder, seasoned salt, and pepper and stir until coated.

3. Reduce the heat to medium. Place a lid on the pot and let the asparagus cook and wilt for 10–12 minutes, removing the lid every few minutes to stir. After 10 minutes, taste the asparagus and make sure it's a chewy consistency you're happy with. If not, sauté it a few minutes more until it is.

TO HALVE Simply halve all the ingredients. However, the salted pasta water amount remains the same. The pasta, vegetable, and sauce cook times remain the same.

VEGGIE VARIATIONS

4. Cook the Pasta: When the asparagus is just about done, add the salt to the pot of boiling water and reduce the heat to medium. Add the pasta and stir. Set a timer to cook until al dente (per the package instructions), or to the shortest amount of time given. When done, drain the pasta in a colander in the sink without rinsing it.

5. While the pasta's cooking, return to the sauté pan, stir the lemon juice into the asparagus, and let simmer for 1 minute, when it practically evaporates. Turn the heat off. If the pasta isn't ready yet, cover the sauté pan with a lid until it is.

6. Just before adding the pasta to the sauté pan, add the pesto to the asparagus and give it a stir.

7. Marry It All: Add the cooked and drained pasta to the sauté pan and toss until combined with the sauce. Serve topped with lemon zest and Parmesan, if desired.

JEFF'S TIP

Want it more lemony? Taste the pasta once you add it to the sauce in Step 7 and if you want more lemon zing, squeeze in juice from up to 1 lemon.

5

SEA

Get ready to set sail on one tasty chapter. One of the joys of pasta is how it can feature some of the tastiest treasures of the sea. And pasta and seafood happen to get along swimmingly!

From a classic Puttanesca to a loaded Frutti di Mare, you're going to find that, as with all the recipes in this book, these dishes are as enjoyable to make as dipping your toes in the ocean. You'll quickly find there's no need to feel intimidated by cooking mollusks and other shellfish.

For more seafood recipes, check out the Stir-Fry and One-Pot chapters (pages 188 and 234).

(DF) Dairy-Free
(V) Vegetarian
(VN) Vegan
+ Compliant with Modifications

PASTA PUTTANESCA

THE PASTA
1 tablespoon salt

1 pound thin spaghetti

THE SAUCE
¼ cup extra-virgin olive oil

1 (2-ounce) can anchovy fillets (flat or rolled), with their oils (see Jeff's Tip)

2 large shallots, diced

6 cloves garlic, minced or pressed

3 cups Marinara Sauce (page 40 or use your favorite jarred brand)

1 cup black or kalamata olives, pitted and sliced

¼ cup capers, plus more for serving (optional)

Fresh oregano or parsley, for serving (optional)

This classic Italian pasta dish is yet another recipe that has countless minor variations depending on the kitchen it's made in. But one thing is a constant for any puttanesca: anchovies. Now, I get it: This is the one item that many of us refuse to put on our pizza. And when we order a Caesar salad, we are prone to say, "Hold the anchovies!" (By the way, they're usually almost always blended into the dressing.) But in this dish, they're sautéed alongside garlic and shallots in olive oil and then melt into an olive- and caper-filled tomato sauce. As a typical anti-anchovy eater, I assure you that the end result is completely magnificent (and not at all fishy).

Prep Time: 10 min • Pasta Cook Time (thin spaghetti): 6-9 min • Sauce Cook Time: 10 min • Total Time: 25 min • Serves: 4-6

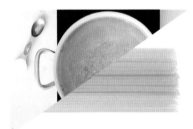

1. Boil the Water and Cook the Pasta: Fill an 8-quart pot halfway with tap water and bring to a rolling boil over high heat. Add the salt and reduce the heat to medium. Add the pasta and stir. Set a timer to cook until al dente (per the package instructions), or to the shortest amount of time given. When done, drain the pasta in a colander in the sink without rinsing it.

2. Make the Sauce: As soon as you add the pasta to the pot, heat the olive oil in a nonstick 4.5- to 5-quart sauté pan over medium heat. Once shimmering, add the anchovy fillets, shallots, and garlic. Sauté until the shallots are a bit translucent, the anchovies break apart, and the garlic is browned, 3 minutes.

3. Add the marinara sauce and combine with the anchovies, shallots, and garlic. Once bubbling, reduce the heat to medium-low and simmer for 3-5 minutes, stirring occasionally, until fragrant and lightly browned. If the sauce is done before the pasta, reduce the heat to low and cover the pan with a lid.

4. Marry It All: Turn the heat off. Add the cooked and drained pasta to the sauté pan along with the olives and capers (if using) and use tongs to toss to coat with the sauce. Serve topped with fresh oregano or parsley, and more capers or olives, if desired.

JEFF'S TIP

There are 5 or 6 anchovy fillets per 2-ounce can. By the way, if you are a big-time anchovy lover, feel free to double the amount.

TO HALVE Simply halve all the ingredients. However, the salted pasta water amount remains the same. The pasta and the sauce cook times also remain the same.

FRUTTI DI MARE

Frutti di mare translates as "fruit of the sea" in Italian and that could only mean one thing: the ultimate seafood pasta loaded with shellfish galore! This classic dish is rife with mollusks (mussels and clams), plus shrimp, scallops, and calamari in a wine- and marinara-based sauce (or see Jeff's Tips). I get my shrimp, scallops, and calamari from the frozen section of the seafood department of my market and simply place them in a colander in the sink and run them under cold water to thaw them in minutes. And I get mussels and clams fresh from a fish shop the day I make this dish. Of course, if one of these fruits of the sea isn't your style, you can leave it out.

THE PASTA
1 tablespoon salt

1 pound linguine fini/thin linguine

THE SAUCE
¼ cup extra-virgin olive oil

½ pound raw large or jumbo shrimp (tails on or off), peeled, deveined, and mixed by hand with a few sprinkles of garlic salt and pepper

½ pound scallops, mixed by hand with a few sprinkles of garlic salt and pepper

6 cloves garlic, minced or pressed

½ cup dry white wine (like a sauvignon blanc)

1 pound mussels (make sure they're tightly closed), scrubbed and beards removed

1 pound small clams (Manila or a smaller size; make sure they're tightly closed), scrubbed

4 cups Marinara Sauce (page 40 or use your favorite jarred brand)

½ pound calamari rings and/or tentacles

Juice of ½ lemon

Chopped fresh parsley (optional)

Prep Time: 10 min • Pasta Cook Time (linguine fini/thin linguine): 6–8 min • Seafood Cook Time: 8–10 min • Sauce Cook Time: 5 min • Total Time: 25–30 min • Serves: 4–6

1. Boil the Water: Fill an 8-quart pot halfway with tap water and bring to a rolling boil over high heat.

2. Cook the Shrimp and Scallops: Heat the oil in a nonstick 4.5- to 5-quart sauté pan over medium heat. Once shimmering, add the shrimp and scallops and cook on each side for about 1 minute, until the shrimp are curled and slightly opaque and the scallops are lightly browned (neither should be totally cooked, but rather just undercooked). Transfer to a bowl with a slotted spoon and set aside, leaving any remaining oil in the pan.

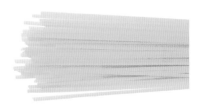

3. Cook the Pasta: Add the salt to the pot of boiling water and reduce the heat to medium. Add the pasta and stir. Set a timer to cook until al dente (per the package instructions), or to the shortest amount of time given. When done, drain the pasta in a colander in the sink without rinsing it.

Recipe Continues

4. Cook the Mussels and Clams: As soon as you add the pasta to the pot, return to the sauté pan, add the garlic, and sauté for 2 minutes, until lightly browned.

5. Add the wine, mussels, and clams. Cover the pan with a lid and simmer for 2–3 minutes, until the shells have opened. If any haven't, discard them.

6. Make the Sauce: Add the marinara to the sauté pan. Once bubbling, reduce the heat to medium-low, add the calamari, and simmer for 3 minutes.

7. Reduce the heat to low. Return the mostly cooked shrimp and scallops and simmer 1 minute longer, making sure the shrimp and scallops are cooked all the way through, but not overcooked. Turn the heat off.

8. Marry It All: Add the cooked and drained pasta to the sauté pan along with the lemon juice and use tongs to toss to coat with the sauce and seafood. Or, you can transfer the cooked and drained pasta to a large serving dish followed by the pan's contents and lemon juice, then toss to combine. Serve topped with chopped parsley, if desired.

JEFF'S TIPS

You can totally use a different sauce in place of the marinara! Try a vodka (page 47) or Sunday sauce (page 56). Of course, you can also use any jarred brand you love.

Want to use black squid ink pasta for this? Do it! It's a fabulous touch and goes nicely with the theme. You can find it at many Italian markets and online.

If you don't do wine, sub any broth of your choice in its place.

Make it fra diavolo (spicy) style by adding crushed red pepper flakes, cayenne pepper, or hot sauce to your liking when adding the shrimp and scallops to the sauce in Step 7.

TO HALVE Simply halve all the ingredients. However, the salted pasta water amount remains the same. The pasta and the sauce cook times also remain the same.

LOBSTER RAVIOLI

THE PASTA
1 tablespoon salt

24–30 ounces lobster ravioli (or any flavor you prefer)

THE MEAT
2 tablespoons (¼ stick) salted butter

2 tablespoons extra-virgin olive oil

1 pound thawed langostino meat or 2 thawed lobster tails, meat removed and diced into bite-size pieces

2 teaspoons Old Bay seasoning or garlic salt

THE SAUCE
2 large shallots, diced

½ cup brandy or sherry wine

1 cup heavy cream

1 (14.5-ounce) can diced tomatoes, with their juices

1 tablespoon all-purpose flour

2 teaspoons Old Bay seasoning or seasoned salt

1 teaspoon paprika

Lobster anything is always a treat. But when it's lobster-filled ravioli in a rich and creamy wine sauce loaded with additional lobster (or langostino meat), it's a party. This favorite may sound intimidating to make merely because the word "lobster" is in the title, but I assure you, it's one of the easiest, no-brainer meals you'll whip up! I get the ravioli from Costco, but any will do. Also, I prefer using langostino meat (which is from langoustines, which resemble large prawns), as it's usually cut popcorn-style at most markets (and Costco), sold either freshly refrigerated or frozen (see Jeff's Tips).

Prep Time: 10 min • Pasta Cook Time (ravioli): 4–5 min • Langostino/Lobster Meat Cook Time: 1–3 min • Sauce Cook Time: 10 min • Total Time: 25 min • Serves: 4–6

1. Boil the Water: Fill an 8-quart pot halfway with tap water and bring to a rolling boil over high heat.

2. Cook the Langostino or Lobster Meat: Heat the butter and olive oil in a nonstick 4.5- to 5-quart sauté pan over medium heat. Once the butter is melted, add the langostino or lobster meat and the Old Bay or garlic salt. Sauté for 1 minute if pre-cooked or 2–3 minutes if raw, until opaque and cooked, but not overcooked (we don't want it rubbery!). Transfer with a slotted spoon to a bowl and set aside, leaving the oil and butter in the pan.

3. Start the Sauce: Increase the heat to medium-high. Add the shallots to the sauté pan and sauté for 2 minutes, until softened.

Recipe Continues

4. Reduce the heat to medium. Add the brandy or sherry and simmer for 2 minutes as the alcohol burns off and it greatly reduces.

5. Cook the Pasta: Add the salt to the pot of boiling water and reduce the heat to medium. Add the pasta and stir. Set a timer to cook until al dente (per the package instructions), or to the shortest amount of time given. When done, drain the pasta in a colander in the sink without rinsing it.

6. While the pasta's cooking, return to the sauté pan and stir in the cream, tomatoes, flour, Old Bay or garlic salt, and paprika. Once bubbling, reduce the heat to medium-low and simmer for 3–5 minutes, stirring occasionally, until the sauce is perfectly thickened. Turn the heat off.

JEFF'S TIPS

If not using wine, sub in ½ cup lobster, garlic, or chicken broth.

Costco usually sells lobster tails and langostino meat in the seafood section, and frozen pre-cooked langostino meat in the frozen seafood section.

TO HALVE Simply halve all the ingredients. However, the salted pasta water amount remains the same. The pasta and the sauce cook times also remain the same.

7. Marry It All: Add the cooked and drained pasta to the sauce in the sauté pan along with the cooked langostino or lobster meat. Gently toss to coat with the sauce. Let rest for a few minutes in the pan before serving.

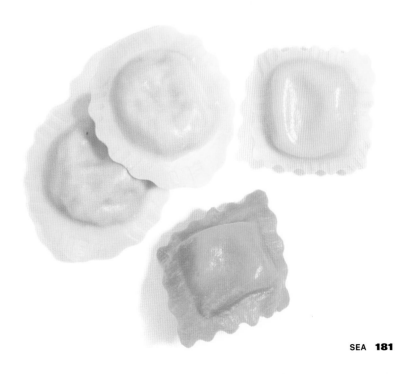

SASSY CRABBY SHELLS

THE PASTA
1 tablespoon salt

1 pound medium or large shells (not to be confused with jumbo shells)

THE SAUCE
3 cups Marinara Sauce (page 40 or use your favorite jarred brand)

¼ cup hot sauce (I use Frank's RedHot)

1 (5.2-ounce) package Boursin (any flavor) or ¾ cup Herb Cheese (page 28), cut into chunks

½–2 teaspoons crushed red pepper flakes, plus more for serving

½–2 teaspoons cayenne pepper

1 pound any type of canned crabmeat, drained

Grated Parmesan cheese, for serving (optional)

Let's get one thing clear, mmmkay? There is nothing wrong with using canned shellfish in cooking—especially if it's crabmeat because that stuff is 'spensive (that was me being sassy)! The sauce is remarkably easy—we're going to melt an herb cheese into a marinara sauce, then sass it up with pepper flakes and cayenne, and fortify it all with crabmeat. As for the choice of pasta? Shells, of course, to scoop it all up.

Prep Time: 5 min • Pasta Cook Time (large shells): 14 min • Sauce Cook Time: 10 min • Total Time: 20 min • Serves: 4-6

1. Boil the Water and Cook the Pasta: Fill an 8-quart pot halfway with tap water and bring to a rolling boil over high heat. Add the salt and reduce the heat to medium. Add the pasta and stir. Set a timer to cook until al dente (per the package instructions), or to the shortest amount of time given. When done, drain the pasta in a colander in the sink without rinsing it.

2. Make the Sauce: As soon as you add the pasta to the pot, combine the marinara and hot sauce in a nonstick 4.5- to 5-quart sauté pan and bring to a bubble over medium-high heat. Reduce the heat to medium-low, add the herb cheese, and stir until combined. Let simmer for 5 minutes.

3. Add the red pepper flakes and cayenne (start with ½ teaspoon of each) and stir into the sauce. Taste and adjust to how sassy you want it.

 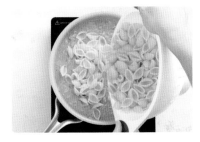

4. Add the crabmeat and stir into the sauce, then simmer for 1 minute. Turn the heat off. If the pasta isn't ready yet, cover the pan and let the sauce rest until it is.

5. Marry It All: Add the cooked and drained pasta to the sauté pan and toss to coat with the sauce. Serve topped with grated Parmesan and more red pepper flakes, if desired.

 This pasta is obviously on the spicier side (the name doesn't lie), but it doesn't have to be. Just leave out the hot sauce, red pepper flakes, and cayenne and it'll be a nice, mild crabby pasta.

TO HALVE Simply halve all the ingredients. However, the salted pasta water amount remains the same. The pasta and the sauce cook times also remain the same.

SHRIMP SCAMPI

RESERVE PASTA WATER!

THE PASTA
1 tablespoon salt

1 pound angel hair or capellini

THE SHRIMP
3 tablespoons extra-virgin olive oil

1½ pounds raw large or jumbo shrimp (tails on or off), peeled, deveined, and mixed by hand with 2 teaspoons seasoned salt

THE SAUCE
8 tablespoons (1 stick) salted butter

6 cloves garlic, minced or pressed

¼ cup dry white wine (like a sauvignon blanc)

Juice of 1 lemon

1 tablespoon dried parsley flakes

¼–½ cup grated Parmesan cheese, plus more for serving (optional)

Chopped fresh parsley, for serving

No seafood chapter in a pasta book is complete without a super simple, yet perfect, shrimp scampi. All it takes is some juicy, springy shrimp entwined in delicate angel hair with a little olive oil, butter, wine, and lemon juice to give you a tasty and gorgeous pasta that may just be the #1 go-to seafood pasta out there. If you don't do wine, check out Jeff's Tips for an easy sub.

Prep Time: 10 min • **Pasta Cook Time (angel hair or capellini): 2–4 min** • **Shrimp Cook Time: 3–4 min** • **Sauce Cook Time: 8 min** • **Total Time: 25 min** • **Serves: 4–6**

1. Boil the Water: Fill an 8-quart pot halfway with tap water and bring to a rolling boil over high heat.

2. Cook the Shrimp: Heat the oil in a nonstick 4.5- to 5-quart sauté pan over medium heat. Once shimmering, add the seasoned shrimp and cook on each side for 1½–2 minutes, until curled and opaque. Use a slotted spoon to transfer the shrimp to a bowl and set aside, leaving any remaining oil in the pan.

3. Start the Sauce: Melt the butter in the pan, add the garlic, and sauté for 2 minutes, until lightly browned. Then, add the wine, lemon juice, and parsley flakes. Stir and bring to a bubble.

4. Cook the Pasta: Add the salt to the pot of boiling water and reduce the heat to medium. Add the pasta and stir. Set a timer to cook until al dente (per the package instructions), or to the shortest amount of time given. When done, **reserve 1 cup of the pasta water** and then drain the pasta in a colander in the sink without rinsing it.

5. As soon as you add the pasta to the pot, return to the sauté pan. Reduce the heat to medium-low and simmer for 2–3 minutes, stirring occasionally, until the sauce is just slightly reduced.

6. Marry It All: Turn the heat off. Add the cooked and drained pasta to the sauté pan along with the cooked shrimp and Parmesan (if using, start with ¼ cup and work your way up). Using tongs, toss to combine. If you find you want it saucier, add ¼ cup of the pasta water at a time until the desired consistency is reached. Serve topped with additional grated Parmesan and fresh parsley, if desired.

JEFF'S TIPS

If you don't do wine, sub in chicken or garlic broth.

If you want it saucier, double the sauce ingredients, but only add an additional 4 tablespoons (½ stick) butter. Cook times remain the same.

TO HALVE Simply halve all the ingredients. However, the salted pasta water amount remains the same. The pasta and the sauce cook times also remain the same.

TEQUILA LIME SHRIMP PASTA

THE PASTA
1 tablespoon salt

1 pound spinach linguine or fettuccine

THE SHRIMP
3 tablespoons extra-virgin olive oil

1½ pounds raw shrimp (tails on or off), peeled, deveined, and mixed by hand with 2 teaspoons Cajun/Creole/Louisiana seasoning (I use Tony Chachere's) or seasoned salt

THE SAUCE
2 tablespoons (¼ stick) salted butter

2 large bell peppers (I use yellow and red), seeded and diced

3 cloves garlic, minced or pressed

½ cup tequila

½ cup chicken or garlic broth (e.g., made from Better Than Bouillon Roasted Garlic Base)

Juice of 2 limes

1 teaspoon dried oregano

1 teaspoon chili powder, plus more for serving

1 teaspoon Cajun/Creole/Louisiana seasoning (I use Tony Chachere's) or seasoned salt

1 teaspoon Old Bay seasoning (optional)

1 cup heavy cream

½ cup sour cream

¼ cup crumbled cotija cheese, plus more for serving (see Jeff's Tips)

Chopped fresh cilantro, for garnish (optional)

Maybe it's the perfectly cooked shrimp, maybe it's the vibrant spinach fettuccine, or maybe it's that tequila- and lime–infused creamy and cheesy sauce. Whatever the case, one taste of this delectable Tex-Mex–inspired pasta summons the Pee-Wee Herman dance, which I now do in his honor every time I make this (which is often).

Prep Time: 10 min • **Pasta Cook Time (spinach linguine or fettuccine): 10-12 min** • **Shrimp Cook Time: 3-4 min** • **Sauce Cook Time: 15 min** • **Total Time: 30 min** • **Serves: 4-6**

1. Boil the Water: Fill an 8-quart pot halfway with tap water and bring to a rolling boil over high heat.

2. Cook the Shrimp: Heat the oil in a nonstick 4.5- to 5-quart sauté pan over medium heat. Once shimmering, add the seasoned shrimp and cook on each side for 1½–2 minutes, until curled and opaque. Use a slotted spoon to transfer the shrimp to a bowl and set aside, leaving any remaining oil in the pan.

3. Start the Sauce: Increase the heat to medium-high and melt the butter in the pan. Add the bell peppers and garlic and sauté for 3-5 minutes, until softened.

4. Cook the Pasta: Add the salt to the pot of boiling water and reduce the heat to medium. Add the pasta and stir. Set a timer to cook until al dente (per the package instructions), or to the shortest amount of time given. When done, drain the pasta in a colander in the sink without rinsing it.

5. While the pasta's cooking, return to the sauté pan and add the tequila, broth, lime juice, oregano, chili powder, Cajun/Creole/Louisiana seasoning (or seasoned salt), and Old Bay (if using). Simmer for 2–3 minutes, until the sauce is just slightly reduced.

6. Add the cream. Once bubbling, reduce the heat to medium-low and allow it to simmer for 3–5 minutes, until slightly thickened. Stir the sour cream and cotija into the sauce. If the sauce is done before the pasta, reduce the heat to low and cover the pan with a lid.

7. Marry It All: Turn the heat off. Add the cooked and drained pasta to the sauté pan along with the shrimp and use tongs to toss to combine. Serve topped with fresh cilantro and additional chili powder and crumbled cotija, if desired.

 JEFF'S TIPS

If you're not into shrimp, the pasta tastes just as great without it. Skip the shrimp ingredients and Step 2.

If you don't do tequila, sub additional broth in its place.

If you can't find cotija cheese, Parmesan or Pecorino Romano will sub nicely!

TO HALVE Simply halve all the ingredients. However, the salted pasta water amount remains the same. The pasta and the sauce cook times also remain the same.

6

STIR-FRY

If you're even a smidge familiar with my favorite types of food, you'll know that Asian cuisine is right at the top of that list. Here I give you some of the best flavors of Asian-American noodle dishes in the best and simplest way I know how, making them nontraditional in terms of the cooking methods (no wok required!), but oh-so-delicious and authentic in flavor.

From my famous Asian Fusion Noodles to spicy Dan Dan Noodles to new things like Egg Roll Rotini, I hope you enjoy them as much as I do!

(DF) **Dairy-Free**

(V) **Vegetarian**

(VN) **Vegan**

+ **Compliant with Modifications**

ASIAN FUSION NOODLES

RESERVE PASTA WATER!

 DF V

THE NOODLES

2 pounds hokkien or thin udon noodles (see Jeff's Tips)

THE SAUCE

½ cup oyster sauce

½ cup hoisin sauce

2 tablespoons soy sauce, tamari, or coconut aminos

2 tablespoons minced or pressed fresh ginger (I use squeeze ginger)

1 tablespoon chili-garlic sauce or sriracha (optional)

¼ cup sesame oil

8–10 ounces shiitake or baby bella mushrooms, sliced

1 large red bell pepper, seeded and sliced into matchsticks

9 cloves garlic, minced or pressed

1 bunch scallions, thinly sliced, with some reserved for garnish

2 teaspoons dried tarragon

1 teaspoon garlic powder

2 tablespoons sesame seeds (I use a combo of white and black), plus more for garnish

This recipe is one of the most popular recipes in my arsenal to date. The sauce is filled with deep, sweet, and savory flavors from ingredients you can find in most supermarkets in the Asian section, along with a generous amount of garlic laced throughout the noodles. And to make matters easier, you can use spaghetti or any other long-form pasta (see Jeff's Tips)!

Prep Time: 15 min • Sauce Cook Time: 10 min • Noodle Cook Time (hokkien or thin udon): 2–4 min • Total Time: 25 min • Serves: 4–6

1. Boil the Water: Fill an 8-quart pot halfway with tap water and bring to a rolling boil over high heat.

2. Start the Sauce: Add the oyster sauce, hoisin sauce, soy sauce, ginger, and chili-garlic sauce (if using) to a bowl and whisk to combine. Set aside.

3. Heat the sesame oil in a nonstick 4.5- to 5-quart sauté pan over medium-high heat. Once shimmering, add the mushrooms, bell pepper, garlic, scallions, tarragon, and garlic powder. Sauté for 5 minutes, until the veggies soften a bit.

Recipe Continues

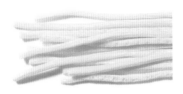

4. Cook the Noodles: Reduce the heat to medium under the pot of boiling water. Once it begins to die down, add the noodles and cook for 2–4 minutes, until pliable and heated through. When done, **reserve 1 cup of the pasta water** and then drain the noodles in a colander in the sink and rinse with cold water.

5. While the noodles are cooking, return to the sauté pan and add the sauce mixture from Step 2 to the pan.

6. Once bubbling, reduce the heat to medium-low and let simmer for 1 minute. Turn the heat off, cover with a lid, and wait for the noodles to be done if they aren't already.

7. Marry It All: Add the noodles and sesame seeds to the sauté pan and gently toss until fully coated in the sauce. If you want you want a thinner sauce, add the pasta water in ¼-cup increments and toss until you're happy. Top with additional scallions and sesame seeds, if desired, and serve.

JEFF'S TIPS

Hokkien, thin udon, and other Asian noodles of the thin variety can be found in any Asian market (and some larger supermarkets) either on the shelf or in the frozen or refrigerated section. Although I prefer them refrigerated or frozen (the Twin Marquis brand has one called "Plain Noodles"), Ka-Me brand noodles, which are already soft, are popular for the shelved ones. I suggest using 32–40 ounces for this recipe and just microwave them according to the package instructions. You can also use regular, fat udon noodles like in my Dan Dan Noodles (page 202).

If you don't feel like getting (or finding) hokkien or thin udon, use spaghetti or vermicelli and simply cook according to the package instructions. Start the pasta at the same time as specified in the recipe (Step 4), adding 1 tablespoon of salt to the water as well.

TO HALVE Simply halve all the ingredients. However, the noodle cooking water amount remains the same. The noodle and the sauce cook times also remain the same.

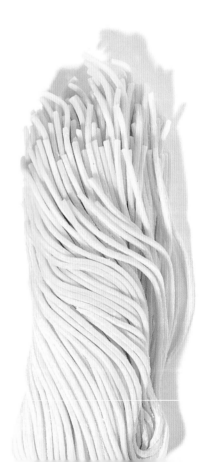

STEAK & NOODLE STIR-FRY

This recipe was a creation inspired by my love of spicy noodles and flank steak and is heavily influenced by Thai cuisine. It's sort of a combination of pad kee mao (aka drunken noodles) and pad see ew, where we create a beautiful, dark veggie-laden sauce filled with deep, rich flavors. This is a bowl of stir-fry at its finest and can be either spicy or mild. Either way, it warrants an icy soft drink on hand to wash it down.

THE NOODLES

1 pound wide or XL rice noodles or rice sticks (about as wide as fettuccine or pappardelle, but any will do; see Jeff's Tips)

THE SAUCE

½ cup oyster sauce

½ cup pad thai sauce (I like the Pantai brand), sweet soy sauce, or teriyaki sauce

¼ cup soy sauce, tamari, or coconut aminos

1–3 tablespoons Thai red curry paste, chili-garlic sauce, and/or sriracha (optional and to taste, see Jeff's Tips)

¼ cup sesame oil

1½ pounds skirt or flank steak, sliced into bite-size pieces and mixed by hand with a few sprinkles of garlic salt

1 white or yellow onion, sliced lengthwise into ½-inch-thick strips

2 large green or red bell peppers, seeded and thinly sliced into matchsticks

1 bunch scallions, sliced, with some reserved for garnish

⅓ cup loosely packed fresh Thai basil leaves or tarragon leaves

3 cloves garlic, minced or pressed

1–2 cups broccoli florets (optional)

1 cup snow peas (optional)

1 tablespoon minced or crushed fresh ginger (I use squeeze ginger)

1 teaspoon cornstarch + 1 teaspoon water

Prep Time: 15 min • **Sauce Cook Time: 15 min** • **Steak Cook Time: 3–7 min** •
Noodle Cook Time (wide or XL rice noodles or rice sticks): 4–8 min • **Total Time: 35–40 min** • **Serves: 4–6**

1. Boil the Water: Fill an 8-quart pot halfway with tap water and bring to a rolling boil over high heat.

2. Start the Sauce: In a bowl, whisk together the oyster sauce, pad thai sauce, soy sauce, and red curry paste (and/or any of its variants) to combine. Set aside.

3. Cook the Steak: Heat the oil in a nonstick 4.5- to 5-quart sauté pan over medium-high heat. Once shimmering, add the steak and sauté for 3–7 minutes, until fully cooked to your liking (130°F–160°F). Use a slotted spoon to transfer to a plate and set aside, keeping the juices and oil in the pan.

Recipe Continues

4. Add the onion, bell peppers, scallions, Thai basil or tarragon, garlic, broccoli (if using), and snow peas (if using) to the pan. Sauté for 5–8 minutes, until the veggies soften a bit. Add the ginger and sauté for 1 minute more.

5. Reduce the heat to medium and add the sauce mixture from Step 2.

6. In a small bowl, whisk the cornstarch and water to form a slurry.

7. Cook the Noodles: While bringing the sauce to a bubble, reduce the heat to medium under the pot of boiling water. Once it begins to die down, add the rice noodles and cook for 4–6 minutes, stirring frequently and taste-testing a noodle every 2 minutes to see where they stand. Once they're pleasant and soft to the bite, they're done. Drain the noodles in a colander in the sink, then rinse with cold water.

8. While the noodles are cooking, return to the sauté pan and stir the cornstarch slurry into the bubbling sauce. Simmer until thickened, 1–2 minutes. Turn the heat off and cover with a lid until the noodles are done cooking.

9. Marry It All: Add the noodles to the sauté pan along with the cooked steak and toss until fully coated. Top with additional Thai basil and scallion, if desired.

JEFF'S TIPS

Don't feel like getting rice noodles? Use any long-form noodle, such as linguine or fettuccine, and simply cook according to the package instructions. Just make sure to salt the water and to start cooking the pasta earlier, after the steak is done in Step 3 and before adding the veggies to the pan in Step 4. This will ensure the timing works out when the sauce is ready to be married to the pasta.

How spicy these noodles turn out depends on you. Start with 1 tablespoon of the Thai red curry paste (and/or any of its variants) and work your way up to 3 tablespoons if you so dare! And if you don't want it spicy at all, just leave this out.

If you want to sub sliced chicken or peeled shrimp for the steak, be my guest! Season it the same as the steak. Just make sure the protein you use is fully cooked in Step 3 before removing from the pan (about 5 minutes for chicken and 2 minutes for shrimp). Or use diced extra-firm tofu, or no protein at all.

TO HALVE Simply halve all the ingredients. However, the noodle cooking water amount remains the same. The noodle and the sauce cook times also remain the same.

SINGAPORE SPAGHETTI

If you've ever had Singapore noodles, found in many Chinese and Asian fusion restaurants, you'll know they are loaded with zesty, fragrant flavor and beautiful color. The key to making both happen is the use of curry powder. Here, you're going to achieve the joys of Singapore noodles with accessible ingredients found in most any market, done simply and using spaghetti for the noodles, as they provide a nice bite.

 DF **V+** *(if not using shrimp)*

THE PASTA

1 tablespoon salt

1 pound spaghetti or vermicelli

THE SAUCE

2 tablespoons oyster sauce

2 tablespoons soy sauce, tamari, or coconut aminos

1 tablespoon hoisin sauce

6 tablespoons chili oil, divided

1 white or yellow onion, sliced into ¼-inch-thick strips

1 large red bell pepper, seeded and sliced into matchsticks

2–3 jalapeño peppers, diced (keeping the ribs and seeds will make it spicier)

1- to 2-pound head napa cabbage, hard stalk sliced off and softer, ruffled outer layers of each leaf ripped up by hand (discard the tougher vein from each leaf)

8–10 ounces shiitake or baby bella mushrooms, sliced (optional)

¼ cup Shaoxing cooking wine or sherry wine (see Jeff's Tips)

3 cloves garlic, minced or pressed

2 tablespoons curry powder

2 teaspoons seasoned salt

2 large eggs, lightly beaten (see Jeff's Tips)

½ pound raw large or jumbo shrimp (tails on or off), peeled and deveined (optional)

Prep Time: 15 min • Pasta Cook Time (spaghetti or vermicelli): 5–10 min • Sauce Cook Time: 15 min • Shrimp Cook Time (optional): 2–3 min • Total Time: 35 min • Serves: 4–6

1. Boil the Water: Fill an 8-quart pot halfway with tap water and bring to a rolling boil over high heat.

2. Start the Sauce: In a bowl, whisk together the oyster sauce, soy sauce, and hoisin sauce to combine. Set aside.

3. Heat 4 tablespoons of the chili oil in a nonstick 4.5- to 5-quart sauté pan over medium-high heat. Once shimmering, add the onion, bell pepper, and jalapeño and sauté for 5 minutes, until the onion is translucent and the peppers soften a bit.

Recipe Continues

4. Add the remaining 2 tablespoons oil along with the cabbage and mushrooms (if using). Sauté for 3 minutes, until the cabbage has wilted down.

5. Cook the Pasta: Add the salt to the pot of boiling water and reduce the heat to medium. Add the pasta and stir. Set a timer to cook until al dente (per the package instructions), or to the shortest amount of time given. When done, drain the pasta in a colander in the sink without rinsing it.

6. While the pasta's cooking, return to the sauté pan and reduce the heat to medium. Add the wine, garlic, curry powder, and seasoned salt to the pan and stir to combine with all the veggies. Let simmer for 30–60 seconds.

7. Move the veggies over to one side of the pan and pour in the eggs. They will begin to cook immediately. Gently use a silicone spatula to fold the eggs frequently until scrambled. Once cooked, you can aggressively mix the scrambled eggs into the veggies so they break apart and combine.

8. Cook the Shrimp (optional): If using the shrimp, add them to the pan now and sauté until curled and opaque, 2–3 minutes.

9. Add the sauce mixture from Step 2 to the pan and stir until everything is coated and it begins to simmer, 1–2 minutes. (**NOTE:** If the pasta isn't done cooking by now, turn the heat off and cover with a lid.)

10. Marry It All: Turn the heat off. Add the pasta to the sauté pan and use tongs to toss until all is fully combined before serving.

 JEFF'S TIPS

If you don't wish to use the wine, sub ¼ cup broth of your choice instead.

If you want it eggier, add a third or even a fourth egg.

You can also use angel hair or capellini. But since those noodles cook more quickly than spaghetti, I'd suggest boiling them in between Steps 8 and 9 while cooking the shrimp or between Steps 9 and 10 if not adding shrimp.

TO HALVE Simply halve all the ingredients. However, the salted pasta water amount remains the same. The pasta and the sauce cook times also remain the same.

CHICKEN PAD THAI

I don't have the research to back me up on this, but I'm willing to bet that this quintessential noodle dish is the most popular item on Thai menus here in the States. This version is definitely my own approach to the dish, but the end results are right on the money. Just make sure you use tamarind paste/concentrate (see Jeff's Tips), which is tart by nature and the consistency of a very thick applesauce. It can be found online and at many Asian and Indian markets. Once combined with the other sauce ingredients, it becomes that perfect pad thai blend of sweet and savory. To save time, feel free to sub 1½ to 2 cups of a store-bought pad thai sauce (I like Pantai brand) instead of using the ingredients in Step 2.

THE NOODLES

1 pound medium or large rice noodles or rice sticks (about as wide as thin linguine or linguine, but any will do)

THE SAUCE

½ cup packed light or dark brown sugar

¼ cup fish sauce

2 tablespoons oyster sauce or soy sauce

1 tablespoon rice vinegar

Juice of ½ lime, plus 1 lime sliced into wedges for garnish

Tamarind paste or concentrate (see Jeff's Tips for amount)

1 teaspoon cornstarch

¼ cup sesame oil

1–2 pounds chicken breasts, sliced into ¼-inch-thick cutlets, lightly rubbed with some garlic salt, and cut into bite-size pieces

4–8 ounces extra-firm tofu, diced (optional)

1 large carrot, peeled and cut into matchsticks

1 bunch scallions, cut into 1-inch pieces

⅓ cup loosely packed fresh Thai basil leaves or tarragon leaves

3 cloves garlic, minced or pressed

2 large eggs, well beaten

½ cup dry-roasted peanuts, crushed, plus more for garnish

½–1 cup bean sprouts (fresh or drained from a can), optional

Chopped fresh cilantro, for garnish (optional)

Prep Time: 15 min ● **Chicken Cook Time: 5 min** ● **Sauce Cook Time: 15 min** ●
Noodle Cook Time (medium or large rice noodles or rice sticks): 4–6 min ● **Total Time: 35 min** ● **Serves: 4–6**

1. Boil the Water: Fill an 8-quart pot halfway with tap water and bring to a rolling boil over high heat.

2. Start the Sauce: In a bowl, whisk together the brown sugar, fish sauce, oyster or soy sauce, rice vinegar, and lime juice. Then, whisk in the tamarind, to taste, according to **Jeff's Tips**. Once happy with the flavor blend, whisk in the cornstarch. Set aside.

3. Cook the Chicken: Heat the oil in a nonstick 4.5- to 5-quart sauté pan over medium-high heat. Once shimmering, add the chicken and tofu (if using) and sauté for 5 minutes, or until the chicken is fully cooked (165°F). Use a slotted spoon to remove the chicken and tofu and set aside, keeping the oil in the pot.

Recipe Continues

4. Add the carrot, scallions, Thai basil (or tarragon), and garlic to the pan and sauté for 5–8 minutes, until the veggies soften a bit.

5. Reduce the heat to medium. Move the veggies over to one side of the pan and then pour in the eggs; they will begin to cook immediately. Gently use a silicone spatula to fold the eggs frequently until scrambled. Once cooked, you can begin to aggressively mix the scrambled eggs into the veggies so they break apart.

JEFF'S TIPS

If you want to sub sliced steak or peeled shrimp for the chicken, be my guest! Just make sure the protein you use is fully cooked in Step 3 before removing from the pan (about 5 minutes for chicken and 2 minutes for shrimp). Or use just the diced extra-firm tofu or no protein at all.

If you want it super saucy, double the ingredients in Step 2.

So here's the deal with sour tamarind concentrate or paste, which is a crucial ingredient for this recipe: The potency can vary greatly depending on the brand and variety used. After much trial and error, I found starting with 2 tablespoons of Tamican brand's Tamarind Paste Concentrate (the label specifically says this) is the right amount to balance out the other sweet and savory ingredients in this recipe. **NOW, A WARNING:** The Asian Kitchen TamiCAN brand is NOT the same as the similar-sounding TamiCON brand; they will yield very different results, potentially making the sauce too sour. Therefore, if using a different brand than Tamican, while mixing the sauce ingredients together in Step 2, add the tamarind after combining all the other ingredients and before the cornstarch. Whisk in 1 tablespoon of tamarind at a time, tasting the sauce along the way. You can then decide to keep adding more by the tablespoon until the sauce reaches your desired harmony of sweet & sour pad thai perfection.

6. Cook the Noodles: Reduce the heat to medium under the pot of boiling water. Once it begins to die down, add the rice noodles and cook for 4–6 minutes, stirring frequently and taste-testing a noodle every 2 minutes to see where they stand. Once they're pleasant and soft to the bite, they're done. Drain the noodles in a colander in the sink and rinse with cold water.

7. While the noodles are cooking, return to the sauté pan, add the sauce mixture from Step 2, and stir. Once bubbling, reduce the heat to medium-low and allow the sauce to simmer and thicken, about 2 minutes. Turn the heat off and cover with a lid until the noodles are done cooking.

8. Marry It All: Add the noodles to the pan along with the cooked chicken and tofu, peanuts, and bean sprouts (if using, start with ½ cup and you can add up to ½ cup more if you want). Toss until all is fully combined. Serve topped with additional peanuts, fresh cilantro (if using), and a lime wedge, if desired.

TO HALVE Simply halve all the ingredients. However, the noodle cooking water amount remains the same. The noodle and the sauce cook times also remain the same.

DAN DAN NOODLES

DF **VN**

THE NOODLES

2 pounds large udon (sanuki) noodles (**see** Jeff's Tips)

THE SAUCE

3 tablespoons sesame oil

6 cloves garlic, minced or pressed

5 ounces baby spinach

⅔ cup chili oil (I use spicy chili crisp by Lao Gan Ma)

¼ cup sweet and sour sauce or duck sauce

1–3 tablespoons chili-garlic sauce or sriracha

½–1 teaspoon crushed red pepper flakes (optional, add more or less to taste)

¼–½ cup smooth peanut butter (optional)

Frankly, my dear, I *do* give a Dan Dan! I just love this classic dish because of its spicy simplicity. Fat and chewy Japanese udon noodles are what I prefer, but Italian bucatini/perciatelli can also do the trick. They also taste great whether served hot or cold. The peanut butter is optional, but I love it in there as a really nice balance to the heat. And because everyone's spice level varies, check out Jeff's Tips for some options.

Prep Time: 10 min • **Sauce Cook Time: 8 min** • **Noodle Cook Time (large udon noodles): 1 min** •
Total Time: 20 min • **Serves: 4–6**

1. Boil the Water: Fill an 8-quart pot halfway with tap water and bring to a rolling boil over high heat.

2. Start the Sauce: Heat the sesame oil in a nonstick 4.5- to 5-quart sauté pan over medium heat. Add the garlic and sauté until lightly browned, 2–3 minutes.

3. Add the spinach and sauté until wilted, another 2–3 minutes. Turn the heat off and cover the pan with a lid while you cook the noodles.

4. Cook the Noodles: Reduce heat to medium under the pot of the boiling water. Once it begins to die down, add the udon noodles and cook for 1 minute, or until pliable and heated through. Drain the noodles in a colander in the sink, then rinse with cold water.

5. Marry It All: Add the cooked noodles to the sauté pan along with all the remaining sauce ingredients. Using tongs, toss until combined and serve.

JEFF'S TIPS

The udon noodles I use for these are sanuki and are found in the frozen section of Asian markets. Although I prefer them frozen, Ka-Me is a popular shelved brand with wet soft noodles that don't require boiling. Use about 2 pounds and skip the boiling. Just microwave them according to the package instructions and add to the pan in Step 5.

Don't feel like getting udon? Use any long-form noodle, such as bucatini or perciatelli, and simply cook according to the package instructions. Just make sure to salt the water with 1 tablespoon salt before cooking the pasta. Start the pasta at the same time specified in the recipe (Step 4).

You get to call the shots on the spice factor for these noodles. You can start with less and always add more to taste when tossing everything together.

TO HALVE Simply halve all the ingredients. However, the noodle cooking water amount remains the same. The noodle and the sauce cook times also remain the same.

EGG ROLL ROTINI

THE PASTA

1 tablespoon salt

1 pound rotini

THE SAUCE

¼ cup soy sauce, tamari, or coconut aminos

¼ cup oyster sauce

¼ cup hoisin sauce

¼ cup duck sauce or sweet and sour sauce, plus more for drizzling

¼ cup sesame oil

1 (12- to 14-ounce) bag shredded green cabbage or coleslaw mix

1 pound ground pork (see Jeff's Tips)

Wonton crisps or chow mein noodles, for serving

If you're familiar with my tales of eating, you'll know that Chinese food is at the very top of my favorites. And I am the type of person who cannot get through life without trying a cabbage-and-pork-stuffed deep-fried egg roll at every Chinese joint I see. Here, we are going to deconstruct the egg roll and do something absolutely (but deliciously) insane: Transform it into a pasta!

Prep Time: 10 min • Pasta Cook Time (rotini): 7–10 min • Sauce Cook Time: 10 min • Total Time: 25 min • Serves: 4–6

1. Boil the Water and Cook the Pasta: Fill an 8-quart pot halfway with tap water and bring to a boil over high heat. Add the salt and reduce the heat to medium. Add the pasta and stir. Set a timer to cook until al dente (per the package instructions), or to the shortest amount of time given. When done, drain the pasta in a colander in the sink without rinsing it.

2. Make the Sauce: As soon as you put the pasta in the water, whisk together the soy sauce, oyster sauce, hoisin sauce, and duck sauce in a bowl to combine. Set aside.

JEFF'S TIPS If pork isn't your style, feel free to sub any ground meat of your choice, including a plant-based one.

I think this is perfect as written but if you want this pasta super porky, cabbage-y and/or saucy, feel free to double those ingredients. Same cook times.

3. Heat the sesame oil in a nonstick 4.5- to 5-quart sauté pan over medium-high heat. Once shimmering, add the cabbage or coleslaw mix and sauté for 3 minutes, until slightly softened.

TO HALVE Simply halve all the ingredients. However, the salted pasta water amount remains the same. The pasta and the sauce cook times also remain the same.

4. Add the ground pork and sauté for 3–5 minutes, until crumbled and cooked.

5. Reduce the heat to medium. Add the sauce mixture to the pan and stir until fully combined with the meat and veggies, then simmer for 1 minute. (**NOTE:** If the pasta isn't done cooking yet, turn the heat off and cover the sauté pan with a lid.)

6. Marry It All: Turn the heat off. Add the cooked and drained pasta to the sauté pan and toss to coat with the sauce. Serve topped with wonton crisps or chow mein noodles and an additional drizzle of duck sauce, if desired.

7

AL FORNO

First, a quick lesson: The term "al forno" in Italian literally means "to the oven," and thus "baked." So, if you seek a pasta dish that has a baked finish, that means you're a lover of it al forno–style (which also means that plenty of cheese is likely making an appearance).

This chapter is quite fun and varied because not only is it about covering icons such as Lasagna (three ways!), Stuffed Shells or Manicotti, and Baked Ziti, but also things you may not have tried, such as Jewish Noodle Pudding (Kugel), Quiche Carbonara, and a Southern-Style Ravioli Lasagna! Even better is that these recipes are as comforting and delicious as they are simple and quick to make.

🟡	Dairy-Free
🟢	Vegetarian
🟣	Vegan
✛	Compliant with Modifications

LASAGNA

Perhaps the most popular, cherished (and messiest) al forno pasta of them all, lasagna has more variations than there are noodles in the world. This dish is essentially a pasta cake, where we take broad sheets of lasagna noodles and layer them with a meaty sauce and a ricotta-mozzarella-Parmesan cheese blend, repeat the layering, and then bake it all into foodie nirvana. My version is crazy easy and so super out-of-this-world that it may just become your new go-to—especially since I give you a second way to make it as individual roll-ups! See Jeff's Tip for that, as well as changing the sauce from a red to a pink or white, and a vegetarian option.

 (see Jeff's Tips)

THE PASTA
1 tablespoon salt

1 pound lasagna noodles (see Jeff's Tips)

THE CHEESE
3 cups ricotta cheese

5 cups (1¼ pounds) shredded mozzarella cheese, divided

1 cup grated Parmesan cheese, plus more for topping

3 large eggs

1 tablespoon dried parsley flakes

1 teaspoon salt

THE SAUCE
¼ cup extra-virgin olive oil

1 yellow onion, diced

6 cloves garlic, minced or pressed

2 pounds ground meat of your choice (I use 1 pound veal/pork/beef meatloaf mixture and 1 pound uncased sweet Italian sausage, but any will do)

6 cups Marinara Sauce (page 40 or your favorite brand), or see Jeff's Tips

---

Prep Time: 20 min • Pasta Cook Time (lasagna noodles): 8-12 min • Sauce Cook Time: 12 min •
Baking Time: 42-45 min • Total Time: 1 hour 20 min • Serves: 6-8

1. Preheat the Oven, Boil the Water, and Cook the Pasta: Preheat the oven to 375°F. Fill an 8-quart pot halfway with tap water and bring to a rolling boil over high heat. Add the salt and reduce the heat to medium. Add the pasta and stir. Set a timer to cook until al dente (per the package instructions), or to the shortest amount of time given. Stir often, making sure the noodles don't stick to each other. When done, drain the lasagna in a colander in the sink and **rinse under cold water until cool to the touch,** moving the noodles around to keep them slick and separated.

2. Make the Cheese Mixture: As soon as you start to cook the noodles, add the ricotta, 1 cup (4 ounces) of the shredded mozzarella, the Parmesan, eggs, parsley flakes, and salt to a large bowl. Stir until well combined and set aside.

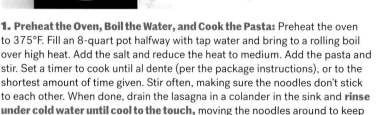

3. Make the Sauce: Heat the olive oil in a nonstick 4.5- to 5-quart sauté pan over medium-high heat. Add the onion and sauté for 2–3 minutes, until slightly softened. Add the garlic and meat and sauté for 3–4 minutes, until crumbled and browned. Leave the juices in the pan!

4. Add the marinara sauce and stir until combined into the onion and meat. Reduce the heat to medium and simmer for 5 minutes. Remove from the heat and wait for the noodles to be done and/or cooled to the touch if they aren't by now.

5. Assemble and Bake the Lasagna: We're going to make a three-layer lasagna. In a deep 9x13-inch casserole dish/pan or disposable tin of the same size and **approximately 3 inches deep** (seriously—your lasagna won't fit otherwise), ladle just enough sauce to lightly cover the bottom of the pan, about ¾ cup. Then, add a single layer of the cooked lasagna noodles (**see Jeff's Tips**). Gently spread one-third of the cheese mixture over the noodles (a silicone spatula works best). Next, evenly ladle 1¾ cups of the sauce over the cheese mixture. Then sprinkle 1 cup (4 ounces) of the shredded mozzarella on top of the sauce. Repeat the process twice more (noodles ➡ cheese mixture ➡ sauce ➡ mozzarella) with the final layer of mozzarella being 2 cups (8 ounces) instead of 1. Sprinkle with additional Parmesan, if desired.

Recipe Continues

6. Carefully place the pan on a baking sheet large enough to support it. (Trust me, it is going to make it so much easier to remove if you use a disposable tin, and it will catch any drippings. You can also do this in Step 5 prior to assembling.) Cover the pan with nonstick foil (leaving a little gap between it and the cheese to ensure it doesn't stick). Bake on the middle oven rack for 30 minutes. Remove the foil, increase the heat to 425°F, and bake for another 10 minutes. Turn on the broiler and broil for 2–5 minutes, until the cheese is bubbly-brown (keep an eye on it as all broilers vary).

7. Remove the lasagna from the oven (that baking sheet came in handy, eh?) and let rest on a trivet on the counter for 15 minutes to set before serving.

TO HALVE Simply halve all the ingredients. However, the salted pasta water amount remains the same. The pasta, sauce, and bake times also remain the same.

JEFF'S TIPS I have recipes for all the classic sauces in this book and you can use any you wish in place of the marinara, be it a meat-filled sauce such as Bolognese (page 44) or Sunday Sauce (page 56), or something meatless like Vodka (page 47) or Alfredo (page 42). (If using any of my sauce recipes here, just leave out the pasta steps in the original recipe!) Of course, you can also use any jarred sauce of your choosing.

Keep this vegetarian by using plant-based ground "meat" or simply keeping it meat-free.

Feel free to mix and match sauces for each layer if you really want to get inventive, like my Pasta Italia (page 68)!

You can break/rip/cut the noodles if need be to ensure they properly fit in the pan/dish you're using. And to save time and a little work, you can skip the boiling of the lasagna noodles and use oven-ready (aka no-boil) noodles instead.

To make lasagna roll-ups, which are a bit less messy to serve and have portions that are easier to dole out: Preheat the oven to 375°F and follow Steps 1–4 as written. Then, ladle in just enough sauce to coat the bottom of a deep 9x13-inch casserole dish/pan or deep disposable tin (about ¾ cup of sauce should do the trick). Prepare the lasagna rolls by laying each cooked noodle on a flat surface and using a silicone spatula (or any tool that spreads easily) to spread each noodle with about ¼ cup of the cheese mixture (not *too* much, but enough), sprinkle about ⅓ cup mozzarella on top, then roll it up like a jelly roll. Place in the casserole dish with the seam side down. Repeat until the pan is filled with roll-ups. Generously cover them with the remaining meat sauce followed by a generous amount of shredded mozzarella. From there, follow Steps 6–7 as written to complete this fabulous and fun dish!

BAKED ZITI

We're all familiar with baked ziti: tubes of pasta bathed in a rich meat and cheese sauce and baked for extra ooey-gooey amazingness. Well, this here baked ziti is the end-all, be-all. It's not only one of the easiest you'll ever make: The flavors are next level thanks to some herb cheese and a thick ricotta mixture melting into the meat sauce. I personally think it's just the right balance of cheese and sauce. Like my Lasagna (page 208), there's no shame in using a premade or your favorite jarred sauce here. In fact, I encourage it, to save even more time! Check out Jeff's Tips about changing up the sauce from a meat-filled red to any you wish.

 (see Jeff's Tips)

THE PASTA
1 tablespoon salt

1 pound ziti or ziti rigati

THE CHEESE
1 cup ricotta cheese

4 cups (1 pound) shredded mozzarella cheese, divided

½ cup grated Parmesan cheese

1 large egg

1½ teaspoons dried basil

1 teaspoon salt

THE SAUCE
¼ cup extra-virgin olive oil

1 large onion, diced

6 cloves garlic, minced or pressed

2 pounds ground meat of your choice (I like a veal/pork/beef meatloaf mixture, but any will do)

5 cups Marinara Sauce (page 40 or your favorite brand), or see Jeff's Tips

1 (5.2-ounce) package Boursin (any flavor) or ¾ cup Herb Cheese (page 28), cut into chunks

---

Prep Time: 10 min • Pasta Cook Time (ziti or ziti rigati): 7–11 min • Sauce Cook Time: 12 min • Baking Time: 7–10 min • Total Time: 35 min • Serves: 6–8

1. Preheat the Oven, Boil the Water, and Cook the Pasta: Preheat the oven to 425°F. Fill an 8-quart pot halfway with tap water and bring to a rolling boil over high heat. Add the salt and reduce the heat to medium. Add the pasta and stir. Set a timer to cook until al dente (per the package instructions), or to the shortest amount of time given. When done, drain the pasta in a colander in the sink without rinsing it.

2. Make the Cheese Mixture: As soon as you start to cook the pasta, add the ricotta, 2 cups (8 ounces) of the shredded mozzarella, the Parmesan, egg, dried basil, and salt to a large bowl. Stir until well combined (it will be thick) and set aside.

3. Make the Sauce: Heat the oil in a nonstick 4.5- to 5-quart sauté pan over medium-high heat. Add the onion and sauté for 2–3 minutes, until slightly softened. Add the garlic and meat and sauté for 3–4 minutes, until crumbled and browned. Leave the juices in the pan!

Recipe Continues

4. Add the marinara sauce and stir until combined into the onion and meat.

5. Reduce the heat to medium and simmer for 5 minutes. Stir in the cheese mixture and herb cheese until melded into the sauce. Turn the heat off, cover the pan, and wait for the pasta to be done if it isn't by now.

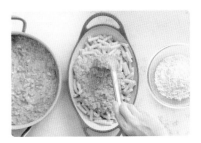

6. Assemble and Bake the Ziti: In a large and deep casserole dish/pan or disposable tin (about 9x13 and close to 3 inches deep), add the cooked and drained ziti and ladle the sauce over them. Gently toss to combine. (**NOTE:** If you have extra sauce, <u>see Jeff's Tips</u>.)

7. Carefully place the pan on a baking sheet large enough to support it and top with the remaining 2 cups (8 ounces) shredded mozzarella. Bake on the middle oven rack, uncovered, for 5 minutes. Then, set to broil and broil for another 2–5 minutes, until the cheese is bubbly-brown (keep an eye on it as all broilers vary).

8. Remove the pan from the oven (aren't you glad you used a baking sheet to support it?) and let rest on a trivet on the counter for 3–5 minutes to cool slightly before serving.

JEFF'S TIPS

I have recipes for all the classic sauces in this book and you can use any you wish in place of the marinara, be it a meat-filled sauce such as Bolognese (page 44) or Sunday Sauce (page 56), or something meatless such as Vodka (page 47) or Alfredo (page 42). (If using any of my sauce recipes here, just leave out the pasta steps in the original recipe while making it!) Of course, you can also use any jarred sauce of your choosing.

Keep this vegetarian by using a meat-free sauce or plant-based meat.

In Step 6, while ladling the sauce over the ziti in the casserole dish, you may find you have some leftover sauce depending on how deep the dish you use is (don't go any shallower than about 3 inches). If so, you can save it in the fridge for up to a week or freeze it in a container for up to 6 months!

TO HALVE Simply halve all the ingredients. However, the salted pasta water amount remains the same. The pasta, sauce, and bake times also remain the same.

EGGS FLORENTINE RIGATONI

 (See Jeff's Tips)

THE PASTA

1 tablespoon salt

1 pound mezzi or short rigatoni

THE SAUCE

8 tablespoons (1 stick) salted butter

¼ cup all-purpose flour (see Jeff's Tips for GF option)

4 cups half-and-half or whole milk

1 teaspoon seasoned salt

1 teaspoon garlic powder

½ teaspoon pepper

8 ounces spinach

4 cups (1 pound) shredded sharp white Cheddar cheese, divided

4 large eggs plus 2 large yolks, lightly beaten

½ cup bacon bits, plus more for topping (optional, see Jeff's Tips)

1 cup frozen peas, thawed (optional)

Every so often I create a dish that is so good, it's absolutely bonkers. This is one of those recipes. Here we are marrying three things: an eggy-meaty carbonara, eggs Florentine (which throws a spotlight on spinach), and a béchamel-style mac & cheese. The end result is something that can only be experienced to believe how good it is. As for the bacon (the carbonara part), I'm keeping it simple and less time-consuming by using store-bought bacon bits that work super well (and are far less greasy once baked), but you can definitely make your own ahead of time and crumble it (six to eight slices should do). And if you want this dish without meat and/or spinach, I've got you covered in Jeff's Tips.

Prep Time: 10 min • Pasta Cook Time (mezzi or short rigatoni): 10–14 min • Sauce Cook Time: 12 min • Baking Time: 12–15 min • Total Time: 40–45 min • Serves: 6–8

1. Preheat the Oven, Boil the Water, and Cook the Pasta: Preheat the oven to 375°F. Fill an 8-quart pot halfway with tap water and bring to a rolling boil over high heat. Add the salt and reduce the heat to medium. Add the pasta and stir. Set a timer to cook until al dente (per the package instructions), or to the shortest amount of time given. When done, drain the pasta in a colander in the sink without rinsing it.

2. Make the Sauce: As soon as you start to cook the pasta, melt the butter in a nonstick 4.5- to 5-quart sauté pan over medium heat. Add the flour and whisk until fragrantly nutty and a lightly browned roux has formed, about 1 minute.

3. Slowly pour the half-and-half or milk into the pan while whisking constantly. Once bubbling, continue to whisk for 3–5 minutes, until it thickens significantly into a béchamel (it should coat the back of spoon with no issues).

Recipe Continues

4. Reduce the heat to medium-low. Whisk in the seasoned salt, garlic powder, pepper, and spinach. The spinach will wilt quickly. (You now have a lovely Florentine-style béchamel sauce!)

5. Add 2 cups (8 ounces) of the shredded cheese and whisk into the béchamel until melded. (The béchamel will have transformed into a Mornay sauce!) If the pasta isn't ready yet, reduce the heat to low and keep whisking the sauce every so often until it the pasta is done.

6. Assemble and Bake the Pasta: Add the cooked and drained pasta to a large, deep casserole dish/pan or disposable tin (about 3 inches deep) and pour the Mornay sauce over it, tossing the pasta with it so it's all coated. Let rest for 5 minutes, until slightly cooled (this is so the eggs don't cook into it immediately).

7. Pour the beaten eggs and yolks, bacon bits, and peas (if using) over the pasta and toss until all is combined.

8. Carefully place the pan on a baking sheet large enough to support it. Top with the remaining 2 cups (8 ounces) shredded cheese and more bacon bits to your liking. Bake on the middle oven rack, uncovered, for 10 minutes. Then, set the oven to broil and broil for another 2–5 minutes, until the cheese is bubbly-brown (keep an eye on it as all ovens vary).

9. Remove from the oven (that baking sheet came in handy, eh?) and rest on a trivet on the counter for 3–5 minutes to cool slightly before serving.

JEFF'S TIPS

For the bacon bits, I use the soft and chewy kind, like from Hormel or Oscar Meyer (and Costco sells them in large bags). Just don't use the fake-tasting crunchy kind used in some salads.

Want it vegetarian? Leave out the bacon bits.

Don't want spinach? Leave it out and you have Carbonara Mac & Cheese!

To make the sauce gluten-free, omit the flour and mix 2 tablespoons cornstarch and 2 tablespoons cold water in a small bowl to form a slurry. Set aside. Begin the sauce by placing both the butter and the half-and-half or milk in the pan and heating it up. Once the butter's melted into the half-and-half or milk and comes to a bubble in Step 3, stir in the slurry and it will thicken perfectly! Continue the recipe from there as written.

TO HALVE Simply halve all the ingredients. However, the salted pasta water amount remains the same. The pasta, sauce, and bake times also remain the same.

FRIED OR TOASTED RAVIOLI

(if using cheese ravioli)

THE PASTA

Salt

1 (10-ounce) package refrigerated ravioli of your choice (**see Jeff's Tips**)

THE COATING

½ cup all-purpose flour

2 large eggs

2 tablespoons heavy cream or half-and-half

1 cup seasoned or Italian breadcrumbs

½ cup grated Parmesan cheese

1 teaspoon seasoned salt

Extra-virgin olive, vegetable, or canola oil for baking or frying

THE ACCOMPANIMENT

1 cup pasta sauce (any kind), warmed

When I was in St. Louis on one of my book tours, I asked my audience what food the city was known for (apart from BBQ, of course). They unanimously said, "Toasted ravioli!" Of course, I had to try it. This deliciously crispy and cheesy treat is essentially a creamy mozzarella stick, but in the form of ravioli and it is the BOMB. Here, I give you three ways to make it: baked in the oven (or a convection toaster oven), air fried, or shallow fried. Although not technically "al forno," I personally think deep fried is the best simply for that rich and crisped outer edge, but all the methods give great results.

Prep Time: 10 min • Pasta Cook Time (ravioli): 4–5 min •
Frying/Toasting Time: 10–20 min (depending on method) • Total Time: 25–35 min • Serves: 4–6

1. Preheat, Boil the Water, and Cook the Pasta: If frying, prepare to heat the oil in a sauté pan as detailed in Step 4. Or, preheat the oven or convection oven to 400°F or the air fryer to 375°F. Fill an 8-quart pot halfway with tap water and bring to a rolling boil over high heat. Add the salt and reduce the heat to medium. Add the ravioli and stir. Set a timer to cook until al dente (per the package instructions), or to the shortest amount of time given. When done, drain the ravioli in a colander in the sink without rinsing them.

2. Set Up Three Stations:

a. Place the flour in a shallow bowl.

b. Whisk together the eggs and cream in a large bowl.

c. Combine the breadcrumbs, Parmesan, and seasoned salt in a shallow bowl and mix together with a fork.

3. Coat the Ravioli: Place the cooked ravioli in the flour (Station A) and turn to coat on both sides. Dip in the egg mixture (Station B) to coat both sides; then turn in the breadcrumb mixture (Station C), making sure the breadcrumbs are coating each side. The ravioli should be thickly coated with breadcrumbs. If not, coat in the egg and breadcrumbs again.

Recipe Continues

JEFF'S TIPS

While you can use any ravioli, I suggest a cheese-filled one for this. The ooey gooey center will give you the best results.

For a pretty, Instagrammable finishing touch, feel free to sprinkle some dried or fresh chopped parsley and more Parmesan on the fried or toasted ravioli before serving.

TO HALVE Simply halve all the ingredients. However, the salted pasta water amount remains the same. The pasta cook time and bake/fry times and oil amount (if frying) also remain the same.

4. TO SHALLOW FRY

Once the ravioli are boiled and just before breading them add ½ inch oil to either a nonstick 4.5- to 5-quart sauté pan or a large Dutch oven. (You can also use a deep fryer—just fill with oil to the line your model specifies.) Heat over medium-high heat until the temperature reaches 360°F.

Once the oil is heated, in batches (and careful not to overcrowd the pan), gently place the coated ravioli in the oil (use tongs or a spider). Fry for 2–3 minutes, flipping every 30 seconds or so, until golden brown. Remove to a wire rack and enjoy with a dipping sauce of your choice.

5. TO BAKE IN OVEN OR CONVECTION TOASTER OVEN

Use a mister and mist some oil over the breaded ravioli before toasting—it will enhance the experience!

Once the oven is heated, line a large baking sheet with parchment paper. Place the coated ravioli in a single layer on the sheet. Bake, flipping the ravioli midway through with tongs, for 15–20 minutes, until golden brown (keep an eye on them as all ovens vary). Transfer to a plate and enjoy with a dipping sauce of your choice.

6. TO AIR FRY

Use a mister to mist oil all over the breaded ravioli before toasting—it will enhance the experience!

Once the air fryer is heated, spray the bottom of the basket with nonstick cooking spray. In batches, carefully place the coated ravioli in a single layer and air fry, flipping the ravioli midway through with tongs, for 3–5 minutes, or until golden brown. Transfer to a plate and enjoy with a dipping sauce of your choice.

STUFFED SHELLS OR MANICOTTI

THE PASTA
1 tablespoon salt

12 ounces jumbo shells or 8 ounces manicotti

THE CHEESE
3 cups ricotta cheese

1 cup grated Parmesan cheese, plus more for topping

3 large eggs

10 ounces frozen chopped spinach, thawed and squeezed dry (see Jeff's Tips)

1 teaspoon salt

1–2 cups (4–8 ounces) shredded mozzarella cheese

THE SAUCE
4–5 cups Vodka Sauce (page 47) or Marinara Sauce (page 40), or use your favorite brand (or see Jeff's Tips), divided, and either at room temperature or microwaved for 1–2 minutes so it's warm or hot

This dish is one of my all-time go-to favorites. There's just something super satisfying about stuffing big, fat pieces of pasta with spinach-flecked ricotta and then draping some sauce on top, loading it with more cheese, and then baking it. This is a universal recipe for stuffing shells or manicotti so it's the same rules for whichever you choose. Bonus: Portion control is easier to manage this way (although I've been guilty of having more than my share as it's so good). Vodka or marinara are my sauces of choice for this (with zero preheating required since this is a baked dish), but you can use any kind you want (including your favorite jarred brand), be it meaty or veggie-friendly (see Jeff's Tips).

Prep Time: 15 min • **Pasta Cook Time (jumbo shells or manicotti): 7–9 min** • **Baking Time: 40 min** • **Total Time: 1 hour** • **Serves: 6–8**

1. Preheat the Oven, Boil the Water, and Cook the Pasta: Preheat the oven to 375°F. Fill an 8-quart pot halfway with tap water and bring to a rolling boil over high heat. Add the salt and reduce the heat to medium. Add the pasta and stir. Set a timer to cook until al dente or for baking (per the package instructions), or for the shortest amount of time the package suggests. When done, drain the pasta in a colander in the sink and rinse under cold water until cool to the touch.

2. Make the Cheese Mixture: As soon as you start to cook the pasta, add the ricotta, Parmesan, eggs, spinach, and salt to a large bowl and stir until well combined. Set aside.

3. Assemble and Bake the Shells or Manicotti: Evenly spoon the cheese mixture into the cooked jumbo shells. For manicotti, place a large piping bag in a tall glass, spoon in the cheese mixture, and cut off a wide enough tip at the bottom. Evenly pipe the mixture into each cooked pasta tube.

TO HALVE Simply halve all the ingredients. However, the salted pasta water amount remains the same. The pasta, sauce, and bake times also remain the same.

JEFF'S TIP If spinach isn't your thing in the cheese mixture, leave it out or replace with 2 tablespoons dried basil or parsley flakes.

4. Once each piece of pasta is stuffed, spread 3 cups of the sauce on the bottom of a 9x13-inch casserole dish/pan or disposable tin. Nestle the stuffed shells or manicotti in the sauce in one even layer.

5. Top the stuffed pasta with the remaining 1–2 cups sauce, followed by 1–2 cups (4–8 ounces) of the shredded mozzarella—you get to decide how saucy and cheesy you want the top to be. Sprinkle with additional Parmesan, if desired.

6. Carefully place the pan on a baking sheet large enough to support it. Cover the pan with nonstick foil (leaving a little gap between it and the cheese to ensure it doesn't stick). Bake on the middle oven rack for 25 minutes. Remove the foil, increase the heat to 425°F, and bake for another 10 minutes. Turn on the broiler and broil for 2–5 minutes, until the cheese is bubbly-brown (keep an eye on it as all broilers vary).

7. Remove from the oven (that baking sheet will help), place on a trivet on the counter, and serve topped with additional Parmesan, if desired.

 JEFF'S TIPS You can use any sauce from any recipe in this book in place of the marinara or vodka—just skip the pasta steps. Of course, you can also use any jarred sauce of your choosing.

I generally leave the package of frozen chopped spinach out on the counter overnight or in the fridge to thaw. The next day, I wrap the spinach in two sheets of paper towels and squeeze over the sink to get all the water out so it becomes nice and dry. But if you don't have the time, simply place it in a fine-mesh strainer and run cold water over it until it's thawed. From there, dry it out as previously stated.

PEPPERONI PIZZA PASTA

THE PASTA

1 tablespoon salt

1 pound wagon wheel or mini wagon wheel pasta

THE PIZZA

4 cups pizza sauce or Marinara Sauce (page 40 or your favorite jarred brand), microwaved or heated in a saucepan for 2–4 minutes so it's hot

1 (6- to 8-ounce) package sliced pepperoni: three-quarters diced, one-quarter kept as whole slices

4 cups (1 pound) shredded mozzarella cheese, divided (see Jeff's Tips)

If you ever wanted to try pepperoni pizza in pasta form, you've just met your favorite new guilty pleasure. I originally developed this dish for the Instant Pot in my *Super Shortcut* cookbook. And with just five of the simplest ingredients, you'll be shocked at how quick and easy it is to make while truly emulating a perfect slice. Sharing photos of it will make your friends drool. To pay homage to pizza, I like using wagon wheel pasta, but you can use any pasta (and sauce) you wish.

Prep Time: 5 min • **Pasta Cook Time (wagon wheels or mini wheels): 6–7 min** • **Baking Time: 10–13 min**
Total Time: 25–30 min • **Serves: 6–8**

1. Preheat the Oven, Boil the Water, and Cook the Pasta: Preheat the oven to 425°F. Fill an 8-quart pot halfway with tap water and bring to a rolling boil over high heat. Add the salt and reduce the heat to medium. Add the pasta and stir. Set a timer to cook until al dente (per the package instructions), or to the shortest amount of time given. When done, drain the pasta in a colander in the sink without rinsing it.

2. Assemble and Bake the Pasta: In a large, deep casserole dish/pan or disposable tin (about 2–3 inches deep), combine the cooked and drained pasta, the heated sauce, the diced pepperoni, and 2 cups (8 ounces) of the mozzarella (**see Jeff's Tips**). Toss until all is combined (the cheese will likely stretch while tossing with the hot pasta and sauce).

3. Top with the remaining 2 cups (8 ounces) shredded mozzarella followed by the whole slices of pepperoni.

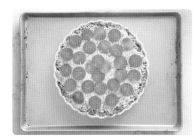

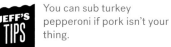

JEFF'S TIPS You can sub turkey pepperoni if pork isn't your thing.

If you want this pepperoni pizza pasta "extra cheese"-style, add up to 2 cups (8 ounces) more shredded mozzarella in Step 2 when combining with the pasta and sauce in the casserole dish.

4. Carefully place the pan on a baking sheet large enough to support it. Bake on the middle oven rack, uncovered, for 8 minutes. Then, set to broil and broil for another 2–5 minutes, until the pepperoni begins to crisp and the cheese is bubbly-brown (keep an eye on it as all broilers vary).

5. Remove from the oven (the baking sheet makes this so easy) and place on a trivet on the counter. Serve immediately alongside some buttery breadsticks or garlic knots, if desired.

TO HALVE Simply halve all the ingredients. However, the salted pasta water amount remains the same. The pasta and bake times also remain the same.

QUICHE CARBONARA

 (if not using bacon)

THE PASTA

1 tablespoon salt

1 pound spaghetti rigati (or any long pasta you prefer)

THE SAUCE

12 large eggs (yes, a whole dozen)

1 cup heavy cream or half-and-half

1 tablespoon garlic salt

8 tablespoons (1 stick) salted butter, cut into 8 pats

2 cups grated Parmesan cheese

½ cup bacon bits (the soft chewy kind, not the crunchy fake ones used for salad)

The idea of pasta being served quiche-style is like using plant-based meat for the first time: It may sound questionable but, in the end, it earns a huge "WOW" factor. With the optional bacon, this is essentially a creamy carbonara baked into a giant pasta-style pancake (or pastacake) of sorts. What's more, the simple recipe can be served for breakfast, lunch, or dinner. The idea is for the lower layer to be more quiche-like and the upper layer to be more creamy, so you get the best of both worlds—see Jeff's Tips on how to serve it upside-down!

Prep Time: 5 min • **Pasta Cook Time (spaghetti rigati): 6 min** • **Sauté Time: 3 min** • **Baking Time: 20 min** • **Total Time: 40 min** • **Serves: 6–8**

1. Preheat the Oven, Boil the Water, and Cook the Pasta: Preheat the oven to 375°F. Fill an 8-quart pot halfway with tap water and bring to a rolling boil over high heat. Add the salt and reduce the heat to medium. Add the pasta and stir. Set a timer to cook until al dente (per the package instructions), or to the shortest amount of time given. When done, drain the pasta in a colander in the sink without rinsing it.

2. Make the Sauce: Just before the pasta's done cooking, whisk together the eggs, cream, and garlic salt in a large mixing bowl.

3. Add the cooked and drained pasta to the egg mixture, along with the butter, Parmesan, and bacon bits. Toss with tongs until the butter is melted into the pasta and all is well combined.

4. Assemble and Bake the Pasta:
Transfer the coated pasta to a 4.5- to 5-quart nonstick, oven-safe sauté pan or a round enameled cast-iron pan. Place over medium heat and smooth down the pasta with a spatula so it's in an evenly distributed layer. From there, *do not stir* while the bottom cooks, as we want the bottom to firm up just a bit. Let this cook for 3 minutes.

5. Transfer the pan to the oven's center rack and bake for about 20 minutes, or until the top begins to get a bit crispy with a slightly golden-brown hue. When done, let rest on a trivet on the counter for 5 minutes to set before serving.

6. Use a silicone spatula to loosen the pasta quiche from the edges for easy removal from the pan (**see Jeff's Tips**). Slice like a quiche and serve.

JEFF'S TIPS

For easiest removal, after loosening the sides of the quiche from the edges of the pan, invert a serving platter with a diameter larger than the pan over it. Using mitts, carefully flip the pan and platter and the pancake will fall right out onto the platter, upside-down. This not only makes it easy to serve like a quiche, but also looks fantastic and photo-worthy!

Do you have some leftover meatballs (frozen or refrigerated, page 54) on hand? Feel free to add about 1 cup of roughly cut-up leftover thawed meatballs in Step 3 when tossing the pasta with the sauce.

Want it vegetarian? Skip the bacon.

While already creamy, you can also feel free to add warmed marinara sauce (page 40) to drizzle over a plated portion of the pasta.

TO HALVE Simply halve all the ingredients and use a nonstick 10-inch oven-safe sauté pan in place of the larger sauté pan. However, the salted pasta water amount remains the same. The pasta, sauce prep, and bake times also remain the same.

CHICKEN TETRAZZINI

THE PASTA
1 tablespoon salt

1 pound spaghetti

THE TETRAZZINI
1½ pounds rotisserie chicken meat (or the meat of 1 whole rotisserie chicken), ripped into bite-size pieces

2 (10.5-ounce) cans any condensed "cream of" soup (I use 1 can each of Campbell's Cream of Chicken and Cream of Mushroom)

1 (16-ounce) container sour cream

1 cup chicken broth

8 tablespoons (1 stick) salted butter, melted

2 teaspoons Italian seasoning

1 teaspoon seasoned salt

1 teaspoon garlic powder

½ teaspoon black pepper

2 cups (8 ounces) shredded Cheddar or Mexican cheese blend (I like a mix with some white and some yellow)

2 tablespoons grated Parmesan cheese, plus more for serving

The story goes that this Italian-American dish was born in San Francisco at the turn of the 20th century. It's since been widely adapted by home cooks and become one of those dishes you turn to when you just want something super comforting and filling—but don't feel like doing much work to get there. Now, I'm breaking my own rules a bit by using canned soup, but seeing that's how tetrazzini is commonly made, I'm going that route here. Plus, this is one of the few recipes where canned soup makes the dish what it is. I make it even easier, quicker, and tastier by using a rotisserie chicken that requires no sautéing whatsoever.

Prep Time: 15 min • **Pasta Cook Time (spaghetti): 9–10 min** • **Baking Time: 45 min** • **Total Time: 1 hour 15 min** • **Serves: 6–8**

1. Preheat the Oven, Boil the Water, and Cook the Pasta: Preheat the oven to 375°F. Fill an 8-quart pot halfway with tap water and bring to a rolling boil over high heat. Add the salt and reduce the heat to medium. Add the pasta and stir. Set a timer to cook until al dente (per the package instructions), or to the shortest amount of time given. When done, drain the pasta in a colander in the sink without rinsing it.

2. Make the Sauce: Just before the pasta's done cooking, combine the chicken meat, canned soup, sour cream, broth, melted butter, Italian seasoning, seasoned salt, garlic powder, and pepper in a very large mixing bowl. Stir until combined.

3. Assemble and Bake the Tetrazzini: Add the cooked and drained pasta to the mixing bowl with the sauce. Toss everything together until the pasta is coated.

 JEFF'S TIP To give this tetrazzini a glorious French onion or ranch flair, add a 1-ounce packet of one of these powdered dip mixes in Step 2.

TO HALVE Simply halve all the ingredients. However, the salted pasta water amount remains the same. The pasta, sauce prep, and bake times also remain the same.

4. Transfer the coated pasta to a deep 9x13-inch casserole dish/pan or disposable tin.

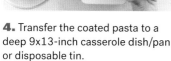

5. Carefully place the pan on a baking sheet large enough to support it. Top with the shredded cheese and Parmesan. Cover the pan with nonstick foil (leaving a little gap between it and the cheese so it doesn't stick). Bake on the middle oven rack for 30 minutes. Remove the foil, increase the heat to 425°F, and bake for another 10 minutes. Turn on the broiler and broil for 2–5 minutes, until the cheese is bubbly-brown (keep an eye on it as all broilers vary).

6. Remove from the oven (the baking sheet will help) and let rest on a trivet on the counter for 5 minutes to set. Serve topped with additional Parmesan, if desired.

SOUTHERN-STYLE RAVIOLI LASAGNA

Once upon a snowy day in the North, while cooped up in a tiny apartment in Astoria, Queens, my partner, Richard, who hails from Alabama, came up with an amazing lasagna filled with flavors from his homeland, including the Holy Trinity (pepper, onion, celery), andouille sausage, and some spice (which is optional)! Since we already have a lasagna recipe in this book, I changed it up and used ravioli in place of noodles, and it works just as well. But if you want a lasagna-noodle classic, check out Jeff's Tips.

 (see Jeff's Tips)

THE PASTA

1 tablespoon salt

1 (20- to 24-ounce) package large refrigerated ravioli of your choice (you'll need about 30 ravioli total), or see Jeff's Tips

THE SAUCE

¼ cup extra-virgin olive oil

1 large red or yellow bell pepper, seeded and diced

1 large red onion, diced

3 ribs celery, diced

1 pound ground meat of your choice (I like a veal/pork/beef meatloaf mixture, but any will do)

1 pound andouille or smoked sausage, sliced into ½-inch-thick disks and quartered

5 cups Marinara Sauce (page 40 or use your favorite brand), or see Jeff's Tips

2 teaspoons Cajun/ Creole/Louisiana seasoning (I use Tony Chachere's)

1–2 tablespoons hot sauce of your choice (I use Crystal), optional

THE CHEESE

2 cups ricotta cheese (a 15-ounce container is fine)

3 cups (12 ounces) shredded sharp Cheddar cheese, divided

3 cups (12 ounces) shredded Monterey Jack, pepper Jack, or Colby Jack cheese, divided

1 cup grated Parmesan cheese

2 large eggs

1 tablespoon dried basil

2 teaspoons Cajun/ Creole/Louisiana seasoning (I use Tony Chachere's) or seasoned salt

½–2 teaspoons cayenne pepper (optional)

½–2 teaspoons crushed red pepper flakes (optional)

Prep Time: 20 min • **Pasta Cook Time (ravioli): 4–5 min** • **Sauce Cook Time: 15 min** • **Baking Time: 42–45 min** • **Total Time: 1 hour 25 min** • **Serves: 6–8**

1. Preheat the Oven and Boil the Water: Preheat the oven to 375°F. Fill an 8-quart pot halfway with tap water and bring to a rolling boil over high heat.

2. Make the Sauce: Heat the oil in a nonstick 4.5- to 5-quart sauté pan over medium-high heat. Once shimmering, add the pepper, onion, and celery and sauté for 3–5 minutes, until slightly softened.

3. Add the meat and sausage and sauté 3–5 minutes longer, until the meat is crumbled and browned. Leave the juices in the pan!

Recipe Continues

4. Add the marinara sauce, Cajun/Creole/Louisiana seasoning, and hot sauce (if using, and you can do it to taste) and stir until combined with the meat and veggies. Reduce the heat to medium and simmer for 5 minutes. Remove from the heat and cover the pan with a lid.

5. Cook the Pasta: Add the salt to the pot of boiling water and reduce the heat to medium. Add the ravioli and stir. Set a timer to cook until al dente (per the package instructions), or to the shortest amount of time given. When done, drain the ravioli in a colander in the sink without rinsing them.

6. Make the Cheese Mixture: As soon as you begin to cook the ravioli, add the ricotta, 1 cup (4 ounces) of each shredded cheese, the Parmesan, eggs, basil, Creole seasoning, cayenne (if using), and red pepper flakes (if using) to a large mixing bowl. Stir until well combined and set aside.

7. Assemble and Bake the Lasagna: We're going to make a two-layer lasagna. In a deep 9x13-inch casserole dish/pan or disposable tin of the same size and **approximately 3 inches deep** (seriously—this won't fit otherwise), ladle just enough sauce to lightly cover the bottom of the pan. Add a single layer of the cooked ravioli (you should have about 15 per layer). Then, take half of the cheese mixture and place dollops in the crevices of the ravioli. Ladle about half the sauce over this layer and then top with 1 cup (4 ounces) of each shredded cheese. Repeat the process once more (ravioli ➡ cheese mixture ➡ sauce ➡ shredded cheese) and you're done!

8. Carefully place the pan on a baking sheet large enough to support it. (Trust me, this is going to make it so much easier to remove if using a disposable tin, and it will catch any drippings.) Cover the pan with foil (leaving a little gap between it and the cheese so it doesn't stick). Bake on the middle oven rack for 30 minutes. Remove the foil, increase the heat to 425°F, and bake for another 10 minutes. Turn on the broiler and broil for 2–5 minutes, until the cheese is bubbly-brown (keep an eye on it as all broilers vary).

9. Remove the ravioli lasagna from the oven (the baking sheet makes it so much easier) and let rest on a trivet on the counter for 5 minutes to set before serving.

 JEFF'S TIPS If you wish to use lasagna noodles instead of the ravioli, that's perfectly fine! Use 1 pound of noodles (which is usually a whole box). Just cook them according to the package instructions and layer them as described in the recipe on page 208. However, since the noodles will create three layers instead of two, use 1 cup (4 ounces) of shredded cheese for the first two layers and 2 cups (8 ounces) for the top.

I have recipes for all the classic sauces in this book and you can use any you wish in place of the marinara, be it a meat-filled sauce such as Bolognese (page 44) or Sunday Sauce (page 56), or something meatless like Vodka (page 47) or Alfredo (page 42). (If using any of my sauce recipes here, just leave out the pasta step in its original recipe!) Of course, you can also use any jarred sauce of your choosing.

Make this vegetarian by using a meat-free sauce or plant-based meat.

 **TO HALVE** Simply halve all the ingredients. However, the salted pasta water amount remains the same. The pasta, sauce, and bake times also remain the same.

JEWISH NOODLE PUDDING (KUGEL)

THE PASTA
1 tablespoon salt

1 pound (16 ounces) wide egg noodles (use these for this specific recipe)

THE JEWNICORN FILLING
1 (8-ounce) brick of cream cheese, at room temperature

6 large eggs, at room temperature

1 cup white sugar

1 (16-ounce) tub cottage cheese

1 (16-ounce) tub sour cream

8 tablespoons (1 stick) salted butter, melted

¼ cup pure maple syrup

2 teaspoons vanilla extract

THE CRUST
2 cups graham cracker crumbs (see Jeff's Tips)

8 tablespoons (1 stick) salted butter, melted

½ cup white sugar

A Jewish-style noodle pudding, or what is commonly called kugel amongst my Jewish peers, is the quintessential side dish that can also double as a dessert. The reason is that it's essentially a cheesecake filling, which I'm calling the Jewnicorn filling because it's magical. (I personally think the secret is the combo of white sugar and pure maple syrup.) The filling is tossed with egg noodles and then topped with a buttery, sugary graham cracker crust. Think of it as a Jewish cheesecake filled with noodles. My sister Amanda is known for making this version at our gatherings and we're both proud to share the recipe with you.

Prep Time: 10 min • Pasta Cook Time (wide egg noodles): 6–11 min • Jewnicorn Filling Time: 5 min • Baking Time: 1 hour • Total Time: 1 hour 20 min • Serves: 6–8

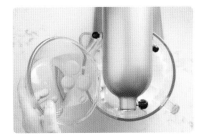

1. Preheat the Oven, Boil the Water, and Cook the Pasta: Preheat the oven to 350°F. Fill an 8-quart pot halfway with tap water and bring to a rolling boil over high heat. Add the salt and reduce the heat to medium. Add the egg noodles and stir. Set a timer to cook until al dente (per the package instructions), or to the shortest amount of time given. When done, rinse the noodles under cold water until cooled.

2. Make the Jewnicorn Filling: As soon as you begin to cook the noodles, add the softened cream cheese and eggs to a stand mixer or to a large mixing bowl ready for a hand mixer. Blend on a medium-low setting until the cream cheese and eggs are mostly blended, 30–60 seconds. (**NOTE:** After mixing, there will be small chunks of cream cheese present in the egg but that's how it should be. Don't overmix here as there is still more mixing to be done in the next few steps.)

3. Add the sugar and blend on medium-low until combined, 15–30 seconds.

Recipe Continues

4. Add the cottage cheese, sour cream, melted butter, maple syrup, and vanilla extract. Blend on low until creamy and combined, about 30 seconds. Set aside.

5. Prepare the Crust: In a large bowl, combine all the crust ingredients and mix with a fork until combined. Set aside.

6. Assemble and Bake the Kugel: In a 9x13-inch casserole dish/pan (preferably glass), add the cooked and drained noodles, pour the Jewnicorn filling over them, and toss the noodles until fully combined.

7. Smooth out the noodles so they're even in the dish and distribute the graham cracker topping to blanket the top. Carefully place the casserole dish, uncovered, on a baking sheet large enough to support it. Bake on the center rack of the oven for 1 hour, until the top is golden brown (check on it a few minutes before as all ovens vary).

8. Remove from the oven and let rest on a trivet on the counter for 5–10 minutes to set before serving.

 JEFF'S TIPS

I usually buy graham cracker crumbs in the baking section of the market, but if you can't find those, 16 whole crackers ground up in a food processor will equal about 2 cups.

Want raisins in your kugel? Mix 1 cup regular or golden ones into the Jewnicorn filling at the end of Step 4.

TO HALVE Simply halve all the ingredients. However, the salted pasta water amount remains the same. The pasta, filling prep, and bake times also remain the same.

8

ONE POT

In this chapter you're going to get a huge variety of one-pot pastas. Give your colanders a rest because there's no draining here! This is also the one chapter where we will disregard the box's instructions for cook time. You'll go for how long I tell you to.

For these recipes, I suggest using an 8-quart pot (the same pot I use to boil pasta in for all the other chapters). One rule, though: Pastas other than regular, whole wheat, or gluten-free won't work well with this method as they'll become mush. So, while pastas made of lentils, chickpeas, and the like are welcomed in every other chapter of this book, avoid them in this one.

Oh! And one more thing: As an added bonus, I give all my Instant Pot lovers alternate instructions for making these recipes in one as well.

DF **Dairy-Free**

Ⓥ **Vegetarian**

VN **Vegan**

✦ **Compliant with Modifications**

PHILLY CHEESESTEAK PASTA

4 tablespoons (½ stick) salted butter, divided

1½–2 pounds flank or skirt steak, sliced into ¼-inch-thick strips, then into bite-size pieces, and mixed by hand with a few sprinkles of garlic salt

1 large Vidalia (sweet) onion, sliced into thin strands

2 large green bell peppers, seeded and sliced into ¼-inch-thick strips

1 pound baby bella or white mushrooms, sliced (optional)

3 **or** 4 cups beef or chicken broth (**3 cups for Instant Pot and 4 cups for stovetop**)

1 teaspoon Italian seasoning

1 pound campanelle (or see Jeff's Tips)

1 (5.2-ounce) package Boursin (any flavor) or ¾ cup Herb Cheese (page 28), cut into chunks

2–4 cups (8 ounces–1 pound) shredded provolone or mozzarella cheese (or a blend of the two)

Cheez Whiz, warmed, for topping (optional, see Jeff's Tips)

The Philly cheesesteak is arguably the most beloved item in the American sandwich repertoire. Now, can you imagine transforming it into a pasta done in one pot with little work required? Well, you no longer need to imagine, because this recipe does just that for you! It's loaded with steak and cheese and is the ultimate pasta of brotherly love. As there is very much a clean divide on adding a Cheez Whiz finish, I make it totally optional. Of course, serving it on a plate or in a bowl works great. But if you want to be as insane as I am, serve it in a hoagie roll as the hero shot suggests.

Pasta: Campanelle • **Prep Time: 10 min** • **Sauté Time: 10–15 min** • **Stovetop Cook Time: 5 min for boiling; 10 min for cooking** • **Instant Pot Cook Time: 10–15 min for pressure building; 6 min for cooking** • **Resting Time: 5 min** • **Total Time: 40–51 min** • **Serves: 4–6**

1. Melt 2 tablespoons of the butter in a nonstick 8-quart pot over medium-high heat (or hit Sauté and Adjust to the High or More setting on the Instant Pot). Add the steak and sauté for 3–7 minutes, until cooked to your liking (130°F–160°F). Use a slotted spoon to transfer to a bowl and set aside, keeping the juices and oil in the pot.

2. Add the remaining 2 tablespoons butter and the onion, peppers, and mushrooms (if using) and sauté for 5–8 minutes, until the veggies are a bit softened and the mushrooms are browned.

3. Add some of the broth and deglaze (scrape) the bottom of the pan to get up anything that may have been browned onto it, then add the rest of the broth followed by the Italian seasoning and stir well.

JEFF'S TIPS

You can use any short-form pasta you wish for this, be it ziti rigati, penne, mezze penne, bow ties, or medium shells, to name a few (see page 31 in the Pasta Glossary for more ideas). Same cook times for all.

You can also totally add Cheez Whiz to the finished pasta in Step 5 when combining the other cheeses.

4. Cook the Pasta:

a. Stovetop: Increase the heat to high. Once boiling, add the pasta to the pot and stir, then lower the heat to medium or medium-low so the boil is gentle. Cover the pot with a lid and cook for 10 minutes, stirring every few minutes to make sure the pasta cooks evenly and doesn't stick to the bottom of the pot. When most of the broth has been absorbed by the pasta and it's fully cooked, remove the lid and reduce the heat to low. There should still be some liquid left and that's what we want!

b. Instant Pot: Add the pasta to the pot but *do not stir*. Simply smooth it out so it's mostly submerged. Secure the lid, move the valve to the sealing position, and hit Cancel followed by Pressure Cook or Manual for 6 minutes at High Pressure. Quick release when done. There will still be some liquid left and that's what we want!

5. Return the cooked steak to the pot and add the herb cheese and shredded cheese and stir until combined. Turn the heat off. Allow the pasta to rest for 5 minutes, stirring once or twice, as the sauce will thicken significantly in this time.

6. Give it all a final stir and serve with a few drizzles of Cheez Whiz (and in a hoagie), if desired.

TO HALVE Halve all the ingredients but reduce the broth to 2 cups for the Instant Pot and 3 cups for stovetop. Cook times remain the same.

ROTISSERIE CHICKEN MUSHROOM PASTA

 (see Jeff's Tips)

4 tablespoons (½ stick) salted butter

1 pound baby bella or white mushrooms, sliced

2 large shallots, diced

½ cup dry white wine (like a pinot grigio)

3½ *or* 4½ cups mushroom or garlic broth (e.g., made from Better Than Bouillon Mushroom or Roasted Garlic Base; 3½ cups for Instant Pot and 4½ cups for stovetop)

2 teaspoons dried thyme

1 pound penne rigate

5 ounces spinach (optional)

1–1½ pounds rotisserie chicken meat (or the meat of 1 whole rotisserie chicken), ripped into bite-size pieces

1 (5.2-ounce) package Boursin (any flavor) or ¾ cup Herb Cheese (page 28), cut into chunks

½ cup grated Parmesan cheese

White or black truffle oil or extra-virgin olive oil, for drizzling (optional)

I absolutely love rotisserie chickens from the market or Costco for a few reasons: They're usually cheaper than raw unseasoned chicken, they're already cooked for you, and they're loaded with flavor. This simple pasta dish has you adding some of that succulent meat to a mushroom-loaded pasta in a wine and Parmesan cream sauce. Get ready for one serious taste trip, folks!

Pasta: Penne rigate • **Prep Time: 10 min** • **Sauté Time: 10 min** • **Stovetop Cook Time: 5 min for boiling; 10 min for cooking** • **Instant Pot Cook Time: 10–15 min for pressure building; 6 min for cooking** • **Total Time: 35–41 min** • **Serves: 4–6**

1. Melt the butter in a nonstick 8-quart pot over medium-high heat (or hit Sauté and Adjust to the High or More setting on the Instant Pot). Add the mushrooms and shallots and sauté for 5 minutes, until the shallots are a bit softened and the mushrooms are browned.

2. Add the wine and deglaze (scrape) the bottom of the pot to get up anything that may have been browned onto it, then add the broth and thyme. Stir well.

JEFF'S TIPS

If you don't wish to use the wine, simply sub ½ cup broth in its place.

Leaving out the chicken will keep this vegetarian and make it a wonderfully creamy mushroom pasta! If you want to double the mushrooms, go for it! Just add another 4 tablespoons (½ stick) salted butter in Step 1 and sauté a few minutes longer until browned.

TO HALVE Halve all the ingredients but reduce the broth to 2½ cups for the Instant Pot and 3½ cups for stovetop. Cook times remain the same.

3. Cook the Pasta:

a. Stovetop: Increase the heat to high. Once boiling, add the pasta to the pot and stir. Top with the spinach, if using, then lower the heat to medium or medium-low so the boil is gentle. Cover the pot with a lid and cook for 10 minutes, stirring every few minutes to make sure the pasta cooks evenly and doesn't stick to the bottom of the pot. When most of the broth has been absorbed by the pasta and it's fully cooked, remove the lid and reduce the heat to low. There should still be some liquid left and that's what we want!

b. Instant Pot: Add the pasta to the pot but *do not stir*. Simply smooth it out so it's mostly submerged. If using, top with the spinach. Secure the lid, move the valve to the sealing position, and hit Cancel followed by Pressure Cook or Manual for 6 minutes at High Pressure. Quick release when done. There will still be some liquid left and that's what we want!

4. Add the rotisserie chicken to the pot as well as the herb cheese and Parmesan and stir until combined. Turn the heat off and serve with a few drizzles of truffle oil, if desired.

AMERICAN GOULASH

 DF **VN+** (see Jeff's Tips)

3 tablespoons extra-virgin olive oil

1 large yellow onion, diced (see Jeff's Tips)

1 large green bell pepper, diced (see Jeff's Tips)

1½ pounds ground beef or meatloaf mixture (veal/pork/beef, see Jeff's Tips)

3 cloves garlic, minced or pressed

3 *or* 3½ cups beef or chicken broth (**3 cups for Instant Pot and 3½ cups for stovetop**)

3–4 cups Marinara Sauce (page 40 or your favorite jarred brand), divided

1 pound elbow or large elbow macaroni (or any short-form pasta you prefer)

It was a big debate on what to call this one because it has so many names: American goulash (that's what won), American chop suey, Johnny Marzetti, slumgullion, Beefaroni, and hot dish. Whatever you know it as, it's all the same thing: macaroni in a tomato sauce loaded with meat and, usually, bell peppers and onions (see Jeff's Tips). I included a recipe in my *Simple Comforts* Instant Pot cookbook under the American Chop Suey name, but I simply couldn't leave it out of this book as it's a quick, easy, and delicious beloved classic. To give it a chili-flavored finish, stir in 1–2 tablespoons Better Than Bouillon Chili Base at the end of Step 5.

Pasta: Elbow macaroni • **Prep Time: 10 min** • **Sauté Time: 10 min** • **Stovetop Cook Time: 5 min for boiling; 10 min for cooking** • **Instant Pot Cook Time: 10–15 min for pressure building; 5 min for cooking** • **Total Time: 35–40 min** • **Serves: 4–6**

1. Heat the olive oil in a nonstick 8-quart pot over medium-high heat (or hit Sauté and Adjust to the High or More setting on the Instant Pot). Once shimmering, add the onion and pepper and sauté for 3–5 minutes, until the veggies are a bit softened.

2. Add the meat and garlic and sauté for another 3–5 minutes, until the meat is crumbled and lightly browned. Leave the juices in the pot as they'll add rich flavor to the sauce!

3. Add some of the broth and deglaze (scrape) the bottom of the pot to get up anything that may have been browned onto it, then add the rest of the broth and 1½ cups of the marinara sauce and stir well.

TO HALVE Halve all the ingredients but reduce the broth to 2 cups for the Instant Pot and 2½ cups for stovetop. Cook times remain the same.

4. Cook the Pasta:

a. Stovetop: Increase the heat to high. Once boiling, add the pasta to the pot and stir, then lower the heat to medium or medium-low so the boil is gentle. Cover the pot with a lid and cook for 10 minutes, stirring every few minutes to make sure the pasta cooks evenly and doesn't stick to the bottom of the pot. When most of the broth has been absorbed by the pasta and it's fully cooked, remove the lid, and reduce the heat to low.

b. Instant Pot: Add the pasta to the pot but *do not stir*. Simply smooth it out so it's mostly submerged. Secure the lid, move the valve to the sealing position, and hit Cancel followed by Pressure Cook or Manual for 5 minutes at High Pressure. Quick release when done. There will still be some liquid left and that's what we want!

5. Add the remaining marinara sauce (start with 1½ cups and work your way up to 2½ if you want it super saucy) and stir until warmed and combined. Turn the heat off and serve.

JEFF'S TIPS

Don't want onion or pepper? Leave them out and, after heating the olive oil, just start with Step 2.

To keep this vegetarian or vegan, omit the meat or use a plant-based version and use a vegetarian or vegan-friendly broth.

The marinara already provides a nice savory punch, but if you wish to season the ground meat, add 1–2 teaspoons garlic salt while sautéing the meat and garlic in Step 2. You can also always add some garlic salt to taste after stirring in the remaining marinara just before serving in Step 5.

LINGUINE WITH WHITE CLAM SAUCE

- ¼ cup extra-virgin olive oil
- 4 tablespoons (½ stick) salted butter
- 1 large shallot, diced
- 3 cloves garlic, minced or pressed
- ¼ cup dry white wine (like a sauvignon blanc)
- 2½ *or* 3½ cups chicken or garlic broth (e.g., made from Better Than Bouillon Roasted Garlic Base; **2½ cups for Instant Pot and 3½ cups for stovetop**)
- Juice of ½ lemon
- 3 (6.5-ounce) cans chopped clams, drained, juices reserved
- 1½ teaspoons dried basil
- 1½ teaspoons dried oregano
- 1 teaspoon Old Bay seasoning
- ½ teaspoon black pepper
- 1 pound linguine
- ½ cup grated Parmesan cheese, plus more for serving
- Freshly chopped parsley, for garnish (optional)

This recipe of mine is so popular, I obviously had to include it in this book. I am a lover of this dish, but the one thing I don't really enjoy is being served a plate of linguine in a watery sauce. I like it a bit thicker and with more substance. And that's how I designed this recipe—just make sure you're a little patient at the end and let the pasta rest for a few minutes as that's when it comes together. And as for whole clams in addition to the chopped canned clams (the juices from the canned clams are key to the sauce), check out Jeff's Tip. Wham. Bam. Thank you, Clam.

Pasta: Linguine • Prep Time: 10 min • Sauté Time: 5 min • Stovetop Cook Time: 5 min for boiling; 10 min for cooking • Instant Pot Cook Time: 10–15 min for pressure building; 6 min for cooking • Resting Time: 5–10 min • Total Time: 35–46 min • Serves: 4–6

1. Heat the oil and butter in a nonstick 8-quart pot over medium heat (or hit Sauté and Adjust to the High or More setting on the Instant Pot). Once the butter has melted, add the shallot and garlic and sauté for 2 minutes, until softened.

2. Add the wine and deglaze (scrape) the bottom of the pot to get up anything that may have been browned onto it, then add the broth, lemon juice, clam juice (but *not* the clams), basil, oregano, Old Bay, and pepper. Stir until well combined.

JEFF'S TIP

If you wish to add whole fresh clams, go with 1 pound of a smaller kind like Manila—just make sure they're scrubbed and all closed before cooking. However, I only advise doing this for the stovetop method because pressure cooking will overcook the clams given how long the pasta will take to cook. In Step 3a, add the clams to the pot 8 minutes into the pasta cooking, then cover with a lid and keep an eye on it. Once the clams have opened (2 minutes should do the trick), use a slotted spoon to transfer them to a bowl (and discard any that are still sealed shut). Then, add the steamed clams on top of the finished pasta in Step 5 before garnishing.

3. Cook the Pasta:

a. Stovetop: Increase the heat to high. Once boiling, add the pasta to the pot and stir until the linguine is limber and fully submerged in the broth, then lower the heat to medium or medium-low so the boil is gentle. Cover the pot with a lid and cook for 10 minutes, stirring every few minutes to make sure the pasta cooks evenly and doesn't stick to the bottom of the pot (or each other). When most of the broth has been absorbed by the pasta and it's fully cooked, remove the lid and reduce the heat to low. There should still be some liquid left and that's what we want!

b. Instant Pot: Break the pasta so it fits in the pot, then layer in a crisscross fashion but *do not stir*. Simply smooth it out so it's mostly submerged. Secure the lid, move the valve to the sealing position, and hit Cancel followed by Pressure Cook or Manual for 6 minutes at High Pressure. Quick release when done. There will still be some liquid left and that's what we want!

4. Stir in the clams and Parmesan and turn the heat off. Allow the pasta to rest for 5–10 minutes, stirring once or twice, as the sauce will thicken significantly in this time.

5. Give it all a final stir and serve topped with additional Parmesan and some freshly chopped parsley, if desired.

TO HALVE Halve all the ingredients but reduce the broth to 2 cups for the Instant Pot and 3 cups for stovetop. Cook times remain the same.

CHICKEN POT PIE PASTA

This dish is an adaption of my mega-popular Cockadoodle Noodles, which is already sort of a chicken pot pie casserole to begin with. But this time, I'm using scoopy and curly campanelle instead of egg noodles. The end result is a one-pot meal to write home about, and I can assure you it'll quickly become a favorite! To bring it home, feel free to bake up the optional store-bought puff pastry to place on top of each serving and give it that lovely crust finish!

2 tablespoons (¼ stick) salted butter

1 large shallot, diced

3½ **or** 4½ cups chicken broth (**3½ cups for Instant Pot and 4½ cups for stovetop**)

2 teaspoons seasoned salt, divided

1½ teaspoons Italian seasoning

1 teaspoon garlic powder

1 teaspoon onion powder

1 pound campanelle

24 ounces frozen veggie mix (I use corn, carrots, peas, and green beans)

1–1½ pounds rotisserie chicken meat (or the meat of 1 whole rotisserie chicken), ripped into bite-size pieces

2 cups (8 ounces) shredded cheese blend of your choice (I like Colby or Cheddar Jack)

½ cup grated Parmesan cheese

½ cup heavy cream or half-and-half

¼ cup ranch dressing (not the dry mix, but actual dressing)

1 (5.2-ounce) package Boursin (any flavor) or ¾ cup Herb Cheese (page 28), cut into chunks

Puff pastry sheets (found in the freezer section), thawed, sliced into 1-inch squares, and baked according to package instructions (optional)

Pasta: Campanelle • **Prep Time: 10 min** • **Sauté Time: 5 min** • **Stovetop Cook Time: 5 min for boiling; 10 min for cooking** • **Instant Pot Cook Time: 10–15 min for pressure building; 6 min for cooking** • **Total Time: 30–36 min** • **Serves: 4–6**

1. Melt the butter in a nonstick 8-quart pot over medium heat (or hit Sauté and Adjust to the High or More setting on the Instant Pot). Add the shallot and sauté for 2 minutes, until softened.

2. Add the broth, 1 teaspoon of the seasoned salt, the Italian seasoning, garlic powder, and onion powder. Stir until well combined.

JEFF'S TIPS

If you want this pot pie pasta buffalo or spicy-style, add ¼–½ cup buffalo or hot sauce of your choice (I like Frank's RedHot) in Step 4.

As for the optional puff pastry, you can get creative and fun! Take a thawed sheet, place the bowls you're serving the pasta in upside-down on top of the dough, and cut rounds with the diameter just slightly larger than the bowl. Bake the rounds. Then place the puff pastry right on top of each bowl and dig into the pasta through it! Another fun idea is to use a cookie cutter (or if you're crafty like Andy, my food stylist, use a knife) and cut shapes freehand out of the dough before baking and then placing on the finished pasta!

3. Cook the Pasta:

a. Stovetop: Increase the heat to high. Once boiling, add the pasta to the pot and stir. Top with the frozen veggies then lower the heat to medium or medium-low so the boil is gentle. Cover the pot with a lid and cook for 10 minutes, stirring every few minutes to make sure the pasta cooks evenly and doesn't stick to the bottom of the pot. When most of the broth has been absorbed by the pasta and it's fully cooked, remove the lid and reduce the heat to low. There should still be some liquid left and that's what we want!

b. Instant Pot: Add the pasta to the pot but *do not stir*. Simply smooth it out so it's mostly submerged. Top with the frozen veggies. Secure the lid, move the valve to the sealing position, and hit Cancel followed by Pressure Cook or Manual for 6 minutes at High Pressure. Quick release when done. There will still be some liquid left and that's what we want!

4. Add the chicken, shredded cheese, Parmesan, cream, ranch dressing, herb cheese, and remaining 1 teaspoon seasoned salt. Stir until combined and turn the heat off. If you like, serve topped with puff pastry squares (**see Jeff's Tips**).

TO HALVE Halve all the ingredients, but reduce the broth to 2½ cups for the Instant Pot and 3½ cups for stovetop. Cook times remain the same.

RED BEANS & ORZO

It always happens. I write a cookbook, shoot it, finalize it, and then create a recipe that I smack myself for not having done earlier to include in said book. In the case of my green *Super Shortcut* book, it was my version of Red Beans & Rice. But given that this is a pasta book, I'm swapping out the rice for orzo, which is a rice-shaped pasta and works just as great. This dish is super quick, simple, and provides a huge flavor payoff. And given its name, although it's red beans we use, feel free to use any bean you prefer—be it cannellini, pinto, pink, or black!

3 tablespoons extra-virgin olive oil

1 medium red or yellow onion, diced

1 large green or red bell pepper, seeded and diced

3 ribs celery, diced

6 cloves garlic, minced or pressed

About 14 ounces smoked sausage (andouille and kielbasa work well), sliced into ¼-inch-thick disks and then quartered

3 *or* 4 cups beef, chicken, ham, or chipotle broth (e.g., made from Better Than Bouillon Ham or Smoky Chipotle Base; **3 cups for Instant Pot and 4 cups for stovetop**)

1 tablespoon Cajun/Creole/Louisiana seasoning (I use Tony Chachere's)

2 teaspoons Italian seasoning

1 pound orzo

2 (15.5-ounce) cans red kidney beans, with their juices

1–2 tablespoons hot sauce (I use Frank's RedHot), plus more for serving (optional)

Pasta: Orzo • **Prep Time: 10 min** • **Sauté Time: 10 min** • **Stovetop Cook Time: 5 min for boiling; 10 min for cooking** • **Instant Pot Cook Time: 10–15 min for pressure building; 2 min for cooking** • **Total Time: 32–37 min** • **Serves: 4–6**

1. Heat the olive oil in a nonstick 8-quart pot over medium-high heat (or hit Sauté and Adjust to the High or More setting on the Instant Pot). Once shimmering, add the onion, pepper, and celery (aka the Holy Trinity) and sauté for 3 minutes, until softened.

2. Add the garlic and sausage and sauté for 3 minutes longer.

3. Add the broth, Cajun/Creole/Louisiana seasoning, and Italian seasoning. Stir until well combined.

4. Cook the Pasta:

a. Stovetop: Increase the heat to high. Once boiling, add the pasta to the pot and stir, then lower the heat to medium or medium-low so the boil is gentle. Cover the pot with a lid and cook for 10 minutes, stirring every few minutes to make sure the pasta cooks evenly and doesn't stick to the bottom of the pot. When most of the broth has been absorbed by the pasta and it's fully cooked, remove the lid and reduce the heat to low. There should still be some liquid left and that's what we want!

b. Instant Pot: Add the orzo to the pot but *do not stir*. Simply smooth it out so it's mostly submerged. Secure the lid, move the valve to the sealing position, and hit Cancel followed by Pressure Cook or Manual for 2 minutes at High Pressure. Quick release when done. There will still be some liquid left and that's what we want!

5. Add the beans and their juices, stir until combined, and turn the heat off. If you want hot sauce, start with 1 tablespoon, stir, and then add more to taste. Serve topped with additional hot sauce, if desired.

JEFF'S TIP Not into smoked sausage or want to keep this vegetarian or vegan? Leave out the sausage. You can also use a plant-based one. Just don't exceed 1 pound if using the Instant Pot, so it doesn't have issues coming to pressure.

TO HALVE Halve all the ingredients but reduce the broth to 2 cups for the Instant Pot and 3 cups for stovetop. Cook times remain the same.

TACO TWIRLS

This fiesta of a creation goes by the name Rotini Ranchero in my first (orange) Instant Pot book and was so mega-popular, I simply had to put it in this one for the stovetop (while also giving the Instant Pot version again). It's essentially the best of a cheesy, beefy taco in a pasta, using rotini to give it its twirly, alliterative new name. Of course, we load it up with some suggested fixin's at the end.

 (see Jeff's Tips)

3 tablespoons extra-virgin olive oil

1 medium yellow onion, diced

1 pound ground meat of your choice (I use beef or turkey depending on my mood)

1 (about 1-ounce) packet taco seasoning

3 *or* 4 cups beef or chicken broth (**3 cups for Instant Pot and 4 cups for stovetop**)

2 cups red salsa of your choice

1 pound rotini

10 ounces frozen corn (optional)

2 cups (8 ounces) shredded Mexican cheese blend, plus more for serving

½ cup crumbled cotija cheese, plus more for serving

1 (7- to 8-ounce) can diced green chiles (optional)

OPTIONAL TOPPINGS

Sliced jalapeños

Black olives, pitted and sliced

Sour cream

Guacamole

Freshly diced tomatoes

Tortilla chips or strips

Fritos

Pasta: Rotini • **Prep Time: 10 min** • **Sauté Time: 10 min** • **Stovetop Cook Time: 5 min for boiling; 10 min for cooking** • **Instant Pot Cook Time: 10–15 min for pressure building; 5 min for cooking** • **Total Time: 35–40 min** • **Serves: 4–6**

1. Heat the olive oil in a nonstick 8-quart pot over medium-high heat (or hit Sauté and Adjust to the High or More setting on the Instant Pot). Once shimmering, add the onion and sauté for 2–3 minutes, until a bit softened.

2. Add the meat and sauté another 2–3 minutes, until the meat is crumbled and lightly browned. Stir in the taco seasoning. Leave the juices in the pot as they'll add rich flavor to the sauce!

3. Add some of the broth and deglaze (scrape) the bottom of the pot to get up anything that may have been browned onto it, then add the rest of the broth and the salsa and stir well.

TO HALVE Halve all the ingredients but reduce the broth to 2 cups for the Instant Pot and 3 cups for stovetop. Cook times remain the same.

4. Cook the Pasta:

a. Stovetop: Increase the heat to high. Once boiling, add the pasta to the pot and stir. Top with the frozen corn (if using), then lower the heat to medium or medium-low so the boil is gentle. Cover the pot with a lid and cook for 10 minutes, stirring every few minutes to make sure the pasta cooks evenly and doesn't stick to the bottom of the pot. When most of the broth has been absorbed by the pasta and it's fully cooked, remove the lid and reduce the heat to low. There should still be some liquid left and that's what we want!

b. Instant Pot: Add the pasta to the pot but *do not stir*. Simply smooth it out so it's mostly submerged. Top with the corn (if using). Secure the lid, move the valve to the sealing position, and hit Cancel followed by Pressure Cook or Manual for 5 minutes at High Pressure. Quick release when done. There will still be some liquid left and that's what we want!

5. Stir in the cheeses and green chiles (if using) until all is combined into the pasta. Turn the heat off.

6. Serve topped with any of the optional toppings and additional cheese, if desired.

JEFF'S TIPS

To make this vegetarian, omit the meat or use a plant-based version and use a vegetarian-friendly broth.

If you can't find crumbled cotija cheese, grated Parmesan will work as well.

CHICKEN CORDON BLEU MACARONI

4 tablespoons (½ stick) salted butter

1½ pounds boneless, skinless chicken breasts and/or thighs, cut into bite-size pieces

3 or 4 cups chicken broth (**3 cups for Instant Pot and 4 cups for stovetop**)

2 teaspoons garlic powder

1 teaspoon onion powder

1 teaspoon seasoned salt

1 teaspoon dried thyme

1 pound large elbow macaroni

2 cups (8 ounces) shredded Swiss, Gruyère, or mozzarella cheese, plus more for serving

1 (5.2-ounce) package Boursin (any flavor) or ¾ cup Herb Cheese (page 28), cut into chunks

1 tablespoon Dijon mustard (optional)

½ pound ham of your choice, cut into ¼-inch cubes (**see Jeff's Tips**)

Crushed Ritz crackers, for topping (optional)

A French chicken cordon bleu consists of breaded chicken fillets stuffed with ham and cheese. I don't need to say more because I'm sure your mouth is watering like mine was when I wrote those words. Given this is a one-pot recipe, we'll forego breading the chicken and change that up with a simple (and optional) sprinkling of crushed buttery Ritz crackers at the end, which works beautifully.

Pasta: Large elbow macaroni • **Prep Time: 10 min** • **Sauté Time: 5 min** • **Stovetop Cook Time: 5 min for boiling; 10 min for cooking** • **Instant Pot Cook Time: 10–15 min for pressure building; 6 min for cooking** • **Total Time: 30–36 min** • **Serves: 4–6**

1. Melt the butter in a nonstick 8-quart pot over medium-high heat (or hit Sauté and Adjust to the High or More setting on the Instant Pot). Add the chicken and sauté until pinkish-white in color, 3–5 minutes.

2. Add some of the broth and deglaze (scrape) the bottom of the pot to get up anything that may have been browned onto it, then add the rest of the broth followed by the garlic powder, onion powder, seasoned salt, and thyme. Stir well.

JEFF'S TIPS

For easy dicing, ask the deli counter to slice the ham into one thick slice that weighs ½ pound.

For a creamier finish, feel free to add ¼–½ cup milk, half-and-half, or heavy cream while mixing everything together in Step 4.

TO HALVE Halve all the ingredients but reduce the broth to 2 cups for the Instant Pot and 3 cups for stovetop. Cook times remain the same.

3. Cook the Pasta:

a. Stovetop: Increase the heat to high. Once boiling, add the pasta to the pot and stir, then lower the heat to medium or medium-low so the boil is gentle. Cover the pot with a lid and cook for 10 minutes, stirring every few minutes to make sure the pasta cooks evenly and doesn't stick to the bottom of the pot. When most of the broth has been absorbed by the pasta and it's fully cooked, remove the lid and reduce the heat to low. There should still be some liquid left and that's what we want!

b. Instant Pot: Add the pasta to the pot but *do not stir*. Simply smooth it out so it's mostly submerged. Secure the lid, move the valve to the sealing position, and hit Cancel followed by Pressure Cook or Manual for 6 minutes at High Pressure. Quick release when done. There will still be some liquid left and that's what we want!

4. Add the shredded cheese, herb cheese, and Dijon (if using) and stir until the cheese is melted and it becomes a rich sauce. Turn the heat off and stir the ham into the pasta.

5. Serve topped with crushed Ritz crackers and additional cheese, if desired.

SAUSAGE STARS

2 tablespoons (¼ stick) salted butter

2 large shallots, diced

3 cloves garlic, minced or pressed

2 pounds Italian sausage (sweet, hot, or a mix), casings removed

½ cup dry white wine (like a sauvignon blanc)

3 *or* 4 cups chicken broth (**3 cups for Instant Pot and 4 cups for stovetop**)

1 pound stelline or stars

5 ounces spinach

1 (5.2-ounce) package Boursin (any flavor) or ¾ cup Herb Cheese (page 28), cut into chunks

½ cup grated Parmesan cheese, plus more for serving

½–1 cup Marinara Sauce (page 40 or your favorite jarred brand), at room temperature (optional and to taste)

1–2 teaspoons crushed red pepper flakes (optional)

Oh, how I just love this recipe! Cooking with Italian sausages is a gift because the juices they release provide so much flavor to a dish—especially when it's a pasta featuring adorable stars or stelline (although ditalini, tubetti, mini farfalle, mini/small shells, and acini di pepe also work great). This is a meaty, creamy, dreamy dish where a little white wine also lends a nice undertone of flavor. As for the finishing touch, I give you the option to add a kiss of marinara and/or some crushed red pepper flakes for a spicy sparkle, both of which I do.

Pasta: Stelline or stars (see Jeff's Tips) • **Prep Time: 10 min** • **Sauté Time: 10 min** • **Stovetop Cook Time: 5 min for boiling; 10 min for cooking** • **Instant Pot Cook Time: 10–15 min for pressure building; 6 min for cooking** • **Total Time: 35–41 min** • **Serves: 4–6**

1. Melt the butter in a nonstick 8-quart pot over medium-high heat (or hit Sauté and Adjust to the High or More setting on the Instant Pot). Add the shallots and garlic and sauté for 2 minutes.

2. Add the sausage and sauté until crumbled and lightly browned, 3–5 minutes.

3. Add the wine and deglaze (scrape) the bottom of the pot to get up anything that may have been browned onto it, then add the broth.

JEFF'S TIPS

About the pasta stars: Stelline is what I 100% suggest, due to the one-pot nature, as they're substantial for their smaller size and can hold their own. Because pastina (very tiny stars) are so delicate, I don't suggest them here as the pasta will be too soupy and mushy. If you can't find stars or stelline, just use one of the others suggested in the headnote (same cook times).

If you want to omit the wine, just add an additional ½ cup broth in its place.

While Italian sausage works best here, feel free to use any type of sausage you wish. A raw, uncooked sausage versus a precooked one is preferred as it will release juices that will seep into the finished pasta.

4. Cook the Pasta:

a. Stovetop: Increase the heat to high. Once boiling, add the pasta to the pot and stir. Top with the spinach, then lower the heat to medium or medium-low so the boil is gentle. Cover the pot with a lid and cook for 10 minutes, stirring every few minutes to make sure the pasta cooks evenly and doesn't stick to the bottom of the pot. When most of the broth has been absorbed by the pasta and it's fully cooked, remove the lid and reduce the heat to low. There should still be some liquid left and that's what we want!

b. Instant Pot: Add the pasta to the pot but *do not stir*. Simply smooth it out so it's mostly submerged. Top with the spinach. Secure the lid, move the valve to the sealing position, and hit Cancel followed by Pressure Cook or Manual for 6 minutes at High Pressure. Quick release when done. There will still be some liquid left and that's what we want!

5. Add the herb cheese, Parmesan, marinara (if using; start with ½ cup and work your way up to 1 cup, if desired), and red pepper flakes (if using). Stir until the cheese is melded into the pasta. Turn the heat off.

6. Serve topped with additional Parmesan, if desired.

TO HALVE Halve all the ingredients but reduce the broth to 2 cups for the Instant Pot and 3 cups for stovetop. Cook times remain the same.

SAUSAGE, BEAN & ESCAROLE ORECCHIETTE

 DF (see Jeff's Tips)

V (see Jeff's Tips)

VN (see Jeff's Tips)

3 tablespoons extra-virgin olive oil

2 pounds Italian sausage (sweet, hot, or a mix), casings removed

1 bunch escarole, tougher white bottoms discarded, roughly chopped

6 cloves garlic, minced or pressed

3 *or* 4 cups chicken broth (**3 cups for Instant Pot and 4 cups for stovetop**)

1 teaspoon black pepper

1 pound orecchiette

2 (15.5-ounce) cans cannellini, navy, or great northern beans (either with their juices or drained, see Jeff's Tips)

½–1 cup grated Parmesan cheese, plus more for serving

Inspired by an Italian-style bean and escarole soup, this pasta dish (like any in this book, especially in this chapter) is deceptively simple in its preparation, but deep and complex in its flavors. The homage to the classic soup is the slightly brothy sauce. It's also quite stunning to look at as the goodies in the sauce pool into the orecchiette. The sausage provides excellent flavor, but to make it dairy-free, vegetarian, and/or vegan, check out Jeff's Tips.

Pasta: Orecchiette • Prep Time: 10 min • Sauté Time: 5 min • Stovetop Cook Time: 5 min for boiling; 10 min for cooking • Instant Pot Cook Time: 10–15 min for pressure building; 6 min for cooking • Resting Time: 5 min • Total Time: 35–41 min • Serves: 4–6

1. Heat the olive oil in a nonstick 8-quart pot over medium-high heat (or hit Sauté and Adjust to the High or More setting on the Instant Pot). Once shimmering, add the sausage and sauté for 2–3 minutes, until crumbled and browned. Leave the juices in the pot as they'll add rich flavor to the sauce!

2. Add the escarole and garlic and sauté until the escarole is wilted, 1–2 minutes. The escarole will quickly cook down.

3. Add some of the broth and deglaze (scrape) the bottom of the pot to get up anything that may have been browned onto it, then add the rest of the broth and the pepper and stir well.

JEFF'S TIPS

The juices from the cans of beans add extra flavor and creaminess to the pasta. I suggest starting with the juices from one can. See how you like the consistency, then decide if you'd like to also add the juices from the second can.

To make this vegetarian, omit the meat or use a plant-based version and use a vegetarian-friendly broth.

TO HALVE Halve all the ingredients but reduce the broth to 2 cups for the Instant Pot and 3 cups for stovetop. Cook times remain the same.

To make this dairy-free, omit the Parmesan. The sauce will still come together nicely, but allow it a few extra minutes to rest in Step 5. Doing this, as well as the previous tip, will also make the dish vegan.

4. Cook the Pasta:

a. Stovetop: Increase the heat to high. Once boiling, add the pasta to the pot and stir, then lower the heat to medium or medium-low so the boil is gentle. Cover the pot with a lid and cook for 10 minutes, stirring every few minutes to make sure the pasta cooks evenly and doesn't stick to the bottom of the pot. When most of the broth has been absorbed by the pasta and it's fully cooked, remove the lid and reduce the heat to low. There should still be some liquid left and that's what we want!

b. Instant Pot: Add the pasta to the pot but *do not stir*. Simply smooth it out so it's mostly submerged. Secure the lid, move the valve to the sealing position, and hit Cancel followed by Pressure Cook or Manual for 6 minutes at High Pressure. Quick release when done. There will still be some liquid left and that's what we want!

5. Add the beans and Parmesan (start with ½ cup) and stir until combined into the pasta. Turn the heat off. Allow the pasta to rest for 5 minutes, stirring once or twice, as the sauce will thicken a bit in this time, but still have a rich, brothy edge to it.

6. Give it all a final stir and serve topped with additional Parmesan, if desired.

BLOODY MARY PASTA

Picture a savory and zesty Bloody Mary just loaded with all the fixin's. This meal of a drink has so much flavor and decor going on that it only seems natural to transform it into a stunning pasta. But not to worry, we're keeping this Mary a virgin and skipping the vodka (it isn't necessary in this case). And seeing as the Bloody Mary is the staple before-noon cocktail, it's perfectly acceptable to serve this pasta before then as well. But if you want to get all Blanche Devereaux at the Rusty Anchor and make it a little sexy, check out Jeff's Tips.

 (see Jeff's Tips)

2 tablespoons (¼ stick) salted butter

1 large red or yellow bell pepper, seeded and diced

1 large red onion, diced

2 ribs celery, diced

1½–2 pounds andouille or smoked sausage, sliced into ½-inch-thick disks and quartered

Juice of 1 lemon

4 *or* 5 cups of your favorite Bloody Mary mix (**4 cups for Instant Pot and 5 cups for stovetop, see Jeff's Tips**)

1 pound cavatappi or cellentani

1 (about 14-ounce) bag frozen pearl onions (optional)

2 cups (8 ounces) shredded Cheddar cheese blend

OPTIONAL FIXIN'S

½ pound thawed frozen shrimp (tails on or off), peeled and deveined

½ pound precooked crabmeat (either fancy refrigerated lump crab or a shelved canned one is fine)

1–2 cups frozen sliced okra, thawed under water

2–4 tablespoons horseradish of your choice (I like Gold's, usually near the dairy in the refrigerated section of your market)

¼–½ cup bacon bits or crumbled bacon

¼–½ cup sliced green olives with pimentos

Up to 1 tablespoon Worcestershire sauce

A few dashes hot sauce of your choice

Pasta: Cavatappi or cellentani • Prep Time: 10–15 min • Sauté Time: 10 min •
Stovetop Cook Time: 5 min for boiling; 10–15 min for cooking • Instant Pot Cook Time: 10–15 min for
pressure building; 6 min for cooking • Total Time: 35–51 min • Serves: 4–6

1. Melt the butter in a nonstick 8-quart pot over medium-high heat (or hit Sauté and Adjust to the High or More setting on the Instant Pot). Add the Holy Trinity (that is, the pepper, onion, and celery) and sauté for 3–5 minutes, until slightly softened.

2. Add the sausage and sauté another 2–3 minutes.

TO HALVE Halve all the ingredients but reduce the Bloody Mary mix to 2 cups for the Instant Pot and 3 cups for stovetop. Cook times remain the same.

3. Add the lemon juice and deglaze (scrape) the bottom of the pot to get up anything that may have been browned onto it, then add the Bloody Mary mix and stir well.

4. Cook the Pasta:

a. Stovetop: Increase the heat to high. Once boiling, add the pasta to the pot and stir. Top with the frozen pearl onions (if using), then lower the heat to medium or medium-low so the boil is gentle. Cover the pot with a lid and cook for 10–15 minutes, stirring every few minutes to make sure the pasta cooks evenly and doesn't stick to the bottom of the pot. When most of the broth has been absorbed by the pasta and it's fully cooked, remove the lid and turn the heat to low. There should still be some liquid left and that's what we want!

b. Instant Pot: Add the pasta to the pot and top with the pearl onions (if using) but *do not stir*. Simply smooth it out so it's mostly submerged. Secure the lid, move the valve to the sealing position, and hit Cancel followed by Pressure Cook or Manual for 6 minutes at High Pressure. Quick release when done. There will still be some liquid left and that's what we want!

5. Add the cheese and stir until melded into the sauce.

6. Add any of the optional fixin's to your delight. Basically, the way you garnish your Bloody Mary is the way you should garnish this pasta! (**NOTE:** If using the raw shrimp, be sure to cook and stir it in the sauce for 2–3 minutes, until curled and opaque. No need to increase the pot's heat—the heat of the pasta alone will ensure this.) When ready to serve, turn the heat off and enjoy the party.

JEFF'S TIPS

Make sure you use a thinner Bloody Mary mix for this. Some brand suggestions are Zing Zang, Master of Mixes, and Mr & Mrs T. Alternatively, you can keep this pasta on the mild side if you sub a flavorful vegetable juice such as V8 for the Bloody Mary mix.

Want it vegetarian? Use a plant-based sausage or omit it.

Thawing frozen shrimp is quick and easy! Simply put in a colander in the sink and run COLD water over the shrimp (hot will begin to cook them) for 5 minutes or so, mixing them up by hand often, until fully thawed. You can do this while the pasta cooks in Step 4. Also, if your shrimp have tails that you want discarded before adding to the pasta, they'll pull right off after thawing.

The Blanche Devereaux reference got you here, didn't it? Feel free to add ¼ cup of a spicy-flavored vodka in Step 3 when adding the lemon juice and let simmer for 1 minute before adding the Bloody Mary mix.

9

SOUPER ZUPPA

"Zuppa" means "soup" in Italian and, since there are quite a few soups in the universe that feature pasta (and because I love soup), it felt only right to give this book a chapter focused on making some astounding pasta soups—both classics and my own creations.

Using just one pot as our vessel, these pasta-filled soups inspired by global flavors are so outrageously delicious and simple to make you may never make any others again.

Because pasta continues to absorb liquid around it, these soups are all meant to be served soon after cooking. If you plan on leftovers and don't want the pasta to absorb all your broth when chilling in the fridge, boil your tiny pasta separately from the soup and then dole the desired amount in a soup bowl followed by a few ladles of soup.

DF Dairy-Free
V Vegetarian
VN Vegan
♦ Compliant with Modifications

TORTELLINI IN BRODO

 (if using non-dairy tortellini)

 (if using non-meat tortellini and vegetable broth)

8 cups chicken broth (see Jeff's Tips)

Parmesan cheese rind, any size (optional, see Jeff's Tips)

20–24 ounces tortellini (or mini ravioli) of your choice

½ cup grated Parmesan cheese, plus more for serving (optional)

1–2 teaspoons seasoned salt (see Jeff's Tips)

1–2 teaspoons black pepper (freshly ground, if possible), plus more for topping

Translated as "tortellini in broth," this soup isn't only an Italian classic, it's one of the simplest and most comforting recipes of all time. Featuring tortellini (or feel free to use mini ravioli) in a light chicken broth, this recipe is easy *and* economical, since we're simply using refrigerated or frozen pasta from the store.

Prep Time: 5 min • Cook Time: 15 min (includes cooking tortellini in the soup) • Total Time: 20 min • Serves: 4–6

1. Bring the broth to a boil in an 8-quart nonstick soup pot over high heat. Add the Parmesan rind (if using).

2. Add the tortellini, reduce the heat to medium, and cook until al dente (according to package instructions), or the shortest amount of time given. Be sure to stir occasionally—especially so the rind doesn't stick to the bottom of the pot. Once the tortellini are cooked, reduce the heat to low.

3. Stir in the grated Parmesan, if using. Then taste the soup and add seasoned salt and pepper to taste.

 JEFF'S TIPS

The Parmesan rind isn't necessary here but will add a richer depth of flavor. If you already have grated Parmesan on hand, that's perfectly fine—you don't need to seek out a wedge of Parmesan with a rind. But if you have a hunk of Parmesan in the fridge with the rind on it, this is the perfect opportunity to use it.

4. Remove from the heat. Ladle the soup into bowls and top with additional pepper and Parmesan, if desired. If any cheese settled to the bottom of the pot, use a spatula to scrape some off and add it to each bowl for a nice flourish of cheese pull in your bowl.

TO HALVE Simply halve the recipe. Cook times remain the same.

While chicken broth is the norm for this soup, feel free to use any kind of broth you want—especially to make it vegetarian.

You can absolutely feel free to add more salt or even any other seasonings you love here. I personally love a few pinches of Tony Chachere's Cajun/Creole/Louisiana seasoning.

ITALIAN & JEWISH WEDDING SOUP

As I stated in the introduction to this book, I have a saying about Jews and Italians: "Same behavior, different savior." Italian wedding soup combines mini meatballs in a lush and vibrant broth loaded with veggies and pasta pearls known as acini di pepe. But if you want to make it Jewish-style, I've got you covered by replacing the mini meatballs with mini matzo balls (aka Jewish dumplings) and the acini di pepe with pastina. And if you want this to be an interfaith wedding soup, halve the meatballs and matzo balls ingredients and add them both in Step 5!

Prep Time: 25 min • Chill Time (Jewish-style only): 30 min • Cook Time: 30 min (includes cooking acini di pepe or pastina in the soup) • Total Time: 1–1½ hours • Serves: 4–6

 (if going Jewish-Style)

 (if going Jewish-Style)

ITALIAN-STYLE MINI MEATBALLS

1 pound Italian sausage (sweet, hot, or a mix), casings removed (see Jeff's Tips)

½ pound ground beef (the less lean the better)

½ cup grated Parmesan cheese

⅓ cup breadcrumbs

6 cloves garlic, minced or pressed

2 tablespoons dried parsley

2 teaspoons seasoned salt

1 teaspoon black pepper

1 teaspoon dried oregano

⅓ cup whole milk

1 large egg, lightly beaten

JEWISH-STYLE MINI MATZO BALLS

⅓ cup vegetable oil or schmaltz (rendered chicken fat, see page 167)

4 large eggs

1½ teaspoons kosher or seasoned salt

1 teaspoon white or black pepper

½ teaspoon ground ginger

¼ cup ginger ale or seltzer

1–1½ cups matzo meal (NOT to be confused with matzo ball mix)

THE SOUP

2 tablespoons extra-virgin olive oil

2 large shallots, diced

2 medium carrots, peeled and diced

3 ribs celery, diced, leafy green tops reserved

3 cloves garlic, minced or pressed

Leaves from 1 bunch fresh basil, stemmed

1 cup sherry wine (or see Jeff's Tips)

7 cups chicken or garlic broth (e.g., made from Better Than Bouillon Roasted Garlic Base)

1½ teaspoons Italian seasoning

1½ teaspoons dried oregano

1½ teaspoons garlic powder

¼–½ cup acini di pepe (peppercorn-shaped) or pastina or stelline (star-shaped) pasta, see Jeff's Tips

8 ounces spinach

JEFF'S TIPS

For the meatballs, any kind of sausage and/or ground meat can work here—be it chicken or plant-based.

If wine isn't your thing, feel free to add another cup of broth in its place in Step 3 when deglazing.

For the pasta, ¼ to ½ cup may not seem like much when uncooked, but trust me it's plentiful! Use ¼ cup if you want less in your soup (there will still be plenty) and no more than ½ cup if you want a substantial amount.

Contrary to popular belief, pastina is still available from a few major brands—both in markets and online. But if you can't find it, acini di pepe or any other tiny pasta from the chart on page 35 will work fine.

If you went Jewish-style, feel free to add some pre-cooked shredded rotisserie chicken at the very end in Step 6 just before serving!

The meatballs will be fully cooked by the end of Step 5. But if you aren't adding the pasta directly to the soup in Step 6, you may need to cook your matzo balls longer, about an additional 5 minutes.

TO HALVE Simply halve the recipe. Cook times remain the same.

Recipe Continues

1. Choose Your Wedding:

a. Italian Wedding: In a large mixing bowl with clean hands, mix together all the mini meatball ingredients until well combined. Roll into balls about the size of a pinball and set on a plate. (**Optional for browned meatballs:** In the soup pot that you'll use later, heat an additional 2 tablespoons extra-virgin olive oil over high heat. Once shimmering, add the meatballs, in batches if necessary, and sear on all sides until lightly browned. Remove the meatballs and set aside on a plate.)

b. Jewish Wedding: In a large mixing bowl, combine the oil or schmaltz, eggs, salt, pepper, ginger, and ginger ale. Mixing with a dinner fork, add the matzo meal: Start with 1 cup and add more until it thickens to the point where it looks like thick oatmeal (you'll likely add ¼ cup to ½ cup additional matzo meal). Your fork should be able to comb through it, but thickly and with a little friction. Refrigerate the matzo ball mixture, uncovered, for 30 minutes to firm up. Roll into balls about the size of a pinball and set on a plate.

2. For the Soup: Heat the olive oil in an 8-quart nonstick soup pot over medium-high heat. (**NOTE:** If you browned the meatballs in Step 1a, you can use the same pot without rinsing it.) Once shimmering, add the shallots, carrots, and diced celery (save the tops) and sauté for 5 minutes, until fragrant and just slightly softened (they get softer as the recipe progresses). Add the garlic and basil leaves and sauté for 1 minute longer.

3. Add the sherry and deglaze (scrape) the bottom of the pot to remove any browned bits. Allow the veggies to simmer for 1 minute.

4. Add the broth, Italian seasoning, oregano, and garlic powder and stir.

5. Add the meatballs or matzo balls (or both). Bring the broth to a boil and reduce the heat to medium-low. Cover with a lid and simmer for 10 minutes (whether using meatballs or matzo balls), stirring occasionally. (**NOTE:** Matzo balls will float and expand in size when cooked.)

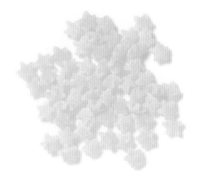

6. Uncover, add the spinach, pasta, and leafy green tops from the celery and stir.

7. Cook the pasta according to the package instructions, stirring occasionally. When done to your liking, turn the heat off, ladle the soup into bowls, and enjoy the wedding!

BEER CHEESE & SHELLS SOUP

When we were kids, I remember my friend making boxed macaroni and cheese (the stuff with the powdered cheese mix) and doctoring it up with extra milk and cheese until it was so saucy, it practically became a soup. She is an amazing cook and cooked full-on amazing meals for her family when she was probably too young to be doing so and I always marveled at it. I felt that this memory was the perfect opportunity to combine the likes of my rich beer cheese soup with some pasta shells and make what can only be known as a new pasta soup classic: Beer Cheese & Shells Soup! But if you don't do beer, I've got you covered in Jeff's Tips. And while I call for small shells, you can also use pipette pasta for a nice, scoopy situation.

 (if using garlic broth)

8 tablespoons (1 stick) salted butter

2 shallots, diced

2 large carrots, peeled and diced

1 red bell pepper, diced

6 cloves garlic, minced or pressed

1 tablespoon dried thyme, plus more for topping

1 cup beer (a lager or pale ale works best, or see Jeff's Tips)

6 cups chicken or garlic broth (e.g., made from Better Than Bouillon Roasted Garlic Base)

1½ cups small shells or pipette pasta (see Jeff's Tips)

1 cup heavy cream or half-and-half

4 cups (1 pound) aged sharp Cheddar cheese (see Jeff's Tips)

1 (5.2-ounce) package Boursin (any flavor) or ¾ cup Herb Cheese (page 28), cut into chunks

OPTIONAL SEASONINGS

1 tablespoon Worcestershire sauce

1 tablespoon hot or buffalo wing sauce (or more to taste)

1 teaspoon Old Bay seasoning

1 teaspoon liquid smoke

¼ teaspoon nutmeg

Prep Time: 15 min • Cook Time: 30 min (includes cooking small shells in the soup) • Total Time: 45 min • Serves: 4–6

1. Melt the butter in an 8-quart nonstick soup pot over medium-high heat. Add the shallots, carrots, bell pepper, garlic, and thyme and sauté for 5–8 minutes, until softened and fragrant.

2. Add the beer, stir, and let simmer for 1 minute.

3. Add the broth and stir. Once bubbling, cover with a lid and let bubble over medium-high heat for 10 minutes, or until the carrots are soft enough to sink your teeth into without crunching.

Recipe Continues

4. Remove the lid, take an immersion blender (mind the cord hitting the hot stove), and blend directly in the pot until pureed. (**NOTE:** You can also puree the soup in a blender in batches, but that's way messier and more time-consuming.)

5. Reduce the heat to medium. Add the pasta to the soup and, using the package's suggested timing, cook the pasta until it's to your liking, stirring occasionally.

6. Once the pasta's cooked to your liking, add the cream and cheeses and gently stir until they're fully melded into the pasta soup.

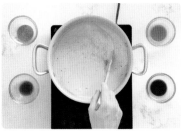

7. If you want any of the optional seasonings, stir them in now. Reduce the heat to low and let the soup rest for 5 minutes as the pasta continues to absorb and cook into the soup, giving itself more of a presence.

8. Turn the heat off. Ladle the soup into bowls and top with additional thyme, if desired.

JEFF'S TIPS

If not using beer, add another cup of broth in Step 3.

If you want even more pasta, add 2 cups instead of 1½ in Step 5. But remember, the more pasta you add now, the more it will absorb the soup as it rests! To that point, if you want it to be more of a super saucy soup-like pasta, add the entire 1-pound box of pasta.

As for the cheese, even though I usually hate grating, a block of a decent aged Cheddar works wonders for this soup. However, you can absolutely use 4 cups (1 pound) of a bagged shredded Cheddar (or any melty cheese blend) as well.

A hot pretzel also goes nicely with this for dunking! You can find them in the frozen section of most markets, then prepare according the package instructions.

TO HALVE Simply halve the recipe. Cook times remain the same.

LAZY LASAGNA SOUP

Lasagna in soup form? Yes, please! You're about to experience one of my favorite soups. Not only is this essentially the laziest version of lasagna you'll ever make, but it's also "souper" satisfying to slurp it from a spoon. What I love about my take on this soup is that you get to control how much cheese goes into it, as the cheesy part gets integrated directly in your bowl upon serving. To give it that true lasagna look in the pasta department, I strongly suggest you use either mafalda or mafaldine, broken into bite-size pieces.

 DF (see Jeff's Tips)

V (if using plant-based meat)

3 tablespoons extra-virgin olive oil

1½ pounds ground meat (any combo will work, see Jeff's Tips)

1 heaping tablespoon tomato paste

1½ teaspoons Italian seasoning

1½ teaspoons dried oregano

Leaves from 1 bunch fresh basil, stemmed

4 cups beef, chicken, or vegetable broth

3 cups Marinara Sauce (page 40 or your favorite jarred brand)

½ cup heavy cream or half-and-half (optional but suggested)

6 ounces mafalda (my preference) or radiatore; or mafaldine/lasagna noodles broken into bite-size pieces

THE CHEESE DOLLOPS

1½ cups (6 ounces) shredded mozzarella cheese

1 cup ricotta cheese

½ cup grated Parmesan cheese

1 tablespoon dried parsley flakes

½ teaspoon salt

¼ cup heavy cream or half-and-half

Prep Time: 10 min • Cook Time: 25 min (includes cooking mafalda in the soup) • Total Time: 35 min • Serves: 4–6

1. Heat the oil in an 8-quart nonstick soup pot over medium-high heat. Once shimmering, add the meat and sauté for 3–5 minutes, until browned and crumbled. (**NOTE:** Do *not* drain the pot of the meat's juices—it adds loads of flavor to the soup!)

2. Add the tomato paste, Italian seasoning, oregano, and basil leaves and sauté for 1 minute.

3. Add the broth, marinara sauce, and cream (if using) and stir. Once bubbling, reduce the heat to medium and let simmer for 5 minutes, stirring occasionally.

4. Add the pasta to the soup and, using the package's suggested timing, cook the pasta until it's to your liking, stirring occasionally.

5. Meanwhile, in a medium bowl, combine all the cheese dollop ingredients, pouring the cream over everything at the end. Set aside.

6. Once the pasta's cooked to your liking, turn the heat off. Ladle the finished soup into bowls and add a generous dollop of the cheese mixture to each before swirling it in to combine. (This will also add an amazing savory touch.) Or, feel free to add all of the cheese dollop mixture directly to the pot of soup, stir to combine, and serve.

JEFF'S TIPS For the meat, I personally love using a meatloaf mixture here. (It's ground veal, beef, and pork—many markets have it prepackaged in the meat section.) But you can absolutely use Italian sausage meat (uncased) or a plant-based variety.

To keep this dairy-free (although some may view it sacrilegious to lasagna), omit the cheese dollop. But since that supplies the soup with a savory element, you may want to add some salt to the finished soup, to taste, in Step 4 once the pasta is done cooking.

TO HALVE Simply halve the recipe. Cook times remain the same.

SAUSAGE, SPINACH & GNOCCHI SOUP

4 tablespoons (½ stick) salted butter, divided

2 pounds uncooked sausage of your choice (**see Jeff's Tips**), casings removed

½ cup all-purpose flour (**see Jeff's Tips** for GF option)

1 cup sherry wine or dry white wine (like a sauvignon blanc, **see Jeff's Tips**)

6 cups chicken or garlic broth (e.g., made from Better Than Bouillon Roasted Garlic Base)

2 teaspoons Italian seasoning

1 teaspoon seasoned salt

1 teaspoon black pepper

1–2 pounds gnocchi of your choice (**see Jeff's Tips**)

8 ounces spinach

1 cup heavy cream or half-and-half

1 (5.2-ounce) package Boursin (any flavor) or ¾ cup Herb Cheese (page 28), cut into chunks

Two of the most popular soups in my Instant Pot cookbooks are Sausage & Spinach and Chicken Gnocchi Soups (if you've tried them, you'll know how legit they are). Both employ rich and creamy perfectly seasoned broths. And so I simply had to make a version that combined the two for the stovetop. It's a winning and seriously comforting pasta soup that's worth a spot in this book, and in your home. It goes great with crusty Italian or French bread, especially after a day of skiing, shoveling your driveway, or if you're just curled up on the couch on a chilly evening with your favorite show on the tube.

Prep Time: 10 min • Cook Time: 25 min (includes cooking gnocchi in the soup) • Total Time: 35 min • Serves: 4–6

1. Melt 2 tablespoons of the butter in an 8-quart nonstick soup pot over medium-high heat. Add the sausage and sauté until browned and crumbled, 3–5 minutes.

2. Add the remaining 2 tablespoons butter. Once melted, add the flour and stir until the buttery sausage is coated in it. This will form your sausage roux!

3. Add the wine, broth, Italian seasoning, seasoned salt, and pepper and stir. Once bubbling, reduce the heat to medium and simmer for 5 minutes, stirring occasionally as the broth thickens.

4. Add the gnocchi and spinach. Gently stir and the spinach will immediately wilt into the soup. Let simmer until the gnocchi are cooked through, about 3 minutes.

5. Stir in the cream and herb cheese until melded into the soup, then bring to a gentle simmer and cook for 1 minute.

6. Turn off the heat and ladle the soup into bowls. This soup goes best with comfy clothes.

 JEFF'S TIPS

For the sausage, feel free to use any uncooked variety you enjoy—be it Italian sweet, Italian hot, chicken, or plant-based. Just make sure you use 2 pounds. I will say that the red oils from a hot Italian sausage will give this soup a gorgeous color to really make it pop!

Don't do wine? Sub another cup of broth in its place in Step 3.

Gnocchi are usually found in the market at room temp near the deli, or frozen in the freezer section, but I strongly suggest using the shelved type in an air-sealed bag as they're the most supple once cooked. You can also use ravioli or tortellini from your market's refrigerated or freezer sections. Just cook according to the package instructions in Step 4.

To make this gluten-free, omit the flour and mix ¼ cup cornstarch and ¼ cup cold water in a small bowl to form a slurry. Stir the slurry into the soup in Step 5 and it will thicken perfectly! Also, use gluten-free gnocchi.

I give you a range for the amount of gnocchi in case you want it really loaded. Start with 1 pound in Step 4 and you can always add up to 1 pound more!

TO HALVE Simply halve the recipe. Cook times remain the same.

STEWPID CHICKEN NOODLE SOUP

8 cups chicken broth

8 ounces baby carrots, sliced into ¼-inch-thick disks (I use half a 16-ounce bag)

3 ribs celery, sliced into ¼-inch pieces, with leafy green tops

1 loosely packed cup fresh dill leaves

½ loosely packed cup fresh parsley leaves (or 1 tablespoon dried parsley flakes), plus more for garnish

1 teaspoon Italian seasoning

1 teaspoon lemon pepper seasoning

3 bay leaves (optional)

6 ounces egg noodles (I use wide, see Jeff's Tips)

1½ pounds rotisserie chicken meat (or 1 whole large rotisserie chicken or see Jeff's Tips), ripped into bite-size pieces

1½ teaspoons seasoned salt, plus more to taste

1 teaspoon black pepper, plus more to taste

Did this title grab your attention? That's because I sometimes feel stupid and want to give my brain a break. That's when this soup happens. It's your classic chicken noodle soup (or Jewish penicillin), but you don't have to be "on" when you're making it. We're going to make things stupid simple here by heating up chicken broth, tossing in some basic veggies and seasonings, pre-cooked rotisserie chicken, and then noodles. And that's all, folks. This may just be the easiest and fastest homemade chicken soup you've ever had. It's so good, it's "stew"pid. See Jeff's Tips to give it an optional creamy finish.

Prep Time: 10 min • **Cook Time: 25 min (includes cooking egg noodles in the soup)** • **Total Time: 35 min** • **Serves: 4–6**

1. Bring the broth to a boil in an 8-quart nonstick soup pot over high heat.

2. Once boiling, add the carrots, celery, dill, parsley, Italian seasoning, lemon pepper, and bay leaves (if using) and stir. Reduce the heat to medium-high, cover with a lid, and cook for 10 minutes. This will ensure your veggies soften.

3. Remove the lid and if you used the bay leaves (they create a nice flavor tone), discard them. Reduce the heat to medium and add the egg noodles (or **see Jeff's Tips**) and, using the package's suggested timing, cook the pasta until it's to your liking, stirring occasionally.

4. Once the noodles are cooked to your liking, add the chicken meat, seasoned salt, and pepper. Stir well and taste the soup. If you want more seasoning, add more seasoned salt and pepper to your heart's content (though I don't think you'll need more as this is Goldilocks "just right").

5. Turn the heat off, ladle the soup into bowls, and top with additional parsley, if desired.

JEFF'S TIPS I wouldn't go above 6 ounces egg noodles in the soup, as dry noodles are deceptive in size compared to how big they get once cooked. To that point, just be mindful that when you boil noodles in the soup, your leftovers will continue to absorb the soup while in the fridge. If you'd rather that not happen, simply prepare the noodles separately, according to the package instructions, and add as much as you want to each bowl when serving the soup.

In lieu of a whole rotisserie chicken, you can also use cold rotisserie chicken meat that they often sell at Costco (it's what I often use).

You can also use rings for the pasta, which many kids seem to love. Follow the same guidelines above.

Want to give this Chicken Noodle Soup a creamy touch? Add ½–1 cup heavy cream or half-and-half in Step 3 after adding the egg noodles. To make it *really* creamy, decadent, and rich, add a (5.2-ounce) package of Boursin or ¾ cup Herb Cheese (page 28) in the same moment.

TO HALVE Simply halve the recipe. Cook times remain the same.

MINESTRONE

 DF **VN**

Perhaps the mother of all vegetable soups, a healthy and hearty minestrone sets itself apart from the rest with one core ingredient added to that savory pot of fresh greens in a rich tomato base. Given the theme of the book, you guessed it: pasta, pasta, pasta! I have found that my new favorite way to make minestrone is to use a one-and-done Marinara Sauce (page 40, or your favorite jarred brand) for the tomato component. And if you want it white-style (meaning rich and creamy), check out Jeff's Tip on page 275.

¼ cup extra-virgin olive oil

1 medium Spanish or yellow onion, diced

2 large carrots, peeled and sliced into ¼- to ½-inch-thick disks and then into quarters

3 ribs celery, sliced into ¼-inch pieces, leafy green tops reserved

1 zucchini, sliced into ¼- to ½-inch-thick disks and then into quarters

1 (10- to 14-ounce) bag frozen cut green beans, thawed (you can quickly do this under cold water in the sink)

6 cups vegetable broth

2 cups Marinara Sauce (page 40 or your favorite jarred brand)

2 (15.5-ounce) cans beans of your choice (I use one cannellini and one red kidney), drained

2 teaspoons seasoned salt

1 teaspoon dried oregano

1 teaspoon dried basil

1 teaspoon black pepper, plus more for topping

1 teaspoon dried thyme

1 cup pennettine (ditalini, pipette pasta, or small shells also work, see Jeff's Tips)

5 ounces spinach

Grated Parmesan, for serving (optional)

Prep Time: 15 min • Cook Time: 30 min (includes cooking pennettine in the soup) • Total Time: 45 min • Serves: 4–6

1. Heat the olive oil in an 8-quart nonstick soup pot over medium-high heat. Once shimmering, add the onion, carrots, celery, zucchini, and green beans and sauté for 5–8 minutes, until softened.

2. Add the broth, marinara sauce, beans, seasoned salt, oregano, basil, pepper, and thyme and stir. Once bubbling, cover with a lid and let bubble over medium-high heat for 10 minutes, or until the carrots are soft enough to sink your teeth into without crunching.

3. Remove the lid and reduce the heat to medium. Add the pasta and spinach and, using the package's suggested timing, cook the pasta until it's to your liking, stirring occasionally.

 JEFF'S TIPS

For a lightning-fast cheat, you can forego all the fresh veggies and add about 32 ounces of a frozen vegetable mix from the freezer section of your market. If you do this, omit the olive oil as well, skip Step 1 (apart from heating the pot, of course), and add the frozen veggies in Step 2 along with the other ingredients.

If you use alphabets or child-friendly shapes for the pasta, you just may turn your kids on to eating their veggies!

4. Once the pasta's cooked to your liking, add the leafy green tops from the celery and stir.

5. Ladle the soup into bowls. Top with Parmesan and additional pepper, if desired.

JEFF'S TIP To make this a rich and creamy white minestrone soup, skip the marinara sauce in Step 2 and add ¾ cup herb cheese (page 28, or a 5.2-ounce package of Boursin), 1 cup heavy cream, and ½ cup grated Parmesan in Step 4. Stir until the dairy is melded into the soup.

TO HALVE Simply halve the recipe. Cook times remain the same.

AVGOLEMON-OS

DF **V•** (if using garlic broth)

6 cups chicken or garlic broth (e.g., made from Better Than Bouillon Roasted Garlic Base)

1 cup pasta rings or orzo

3–6 large eggs (see Jeff's Tips)

Juice of 2–3 lemons (see Jeff's Tips)

OPTIONAL FINISHES
Up to 2 cups shredded rotisserie chicken meat

Up to 1 cup crumbled feta or blue cheese

Pronounced "ahv-go-LEM-oh-no," this Greek egg-lemon-orzo soup is as easy to make as it is soothing to the soul: It requires only four simple ingredients. Orzo is the typical pasta used (and definitely can be here), but when I caught a glimpse of an O-shaped pasta made by Ronzoni simply called "rings," I knew I had a great play on words for an amazingly simple soup. Feel free to zhuzh it up at the end with some crumbled feta, blue cheese, and/or rotisserie chicken! Check out Avgolemono Angel Hair (page 149) for a pasta-fied version of this soup!

Prep Time: 5 min • Cook Time: 20 min (includes cooking pasta rings or orzo in the soup) • Total Time: 25 min • Serves: 4–6

1. Bring the broth to a boil in an 8-quart nonstick soup pot over high heat.

2. Add the pasta, reduce the heat to medium and, using the package's suggested timing, cook the pasta until it's to your liking, stirring occasionally.

3. Just before the pasta's done cooking, whisk together the eggs and lemon juice in a large Pyrex measuring cup or heatproof bowl.

4. Add 1 cup of the broth from the pot to the egg mixture and whisk together so the mixture is tempered.

5. Pour the tempered egg-lemon mixture into the soup pot and stir for 2 minutes, until cooked through.

6. Taste the soup. Feel free to add the chicken now and any additional lemon juice (**see Jeff's Tips**), if desired. Reduce the heat to low and let the soup rest for 5 minutes as the pasta continues to absorb and cook into the soup, giving itself more of a presence. Turn the heat off.

7. Ladle the soup into bowls and top with the crumbled cheese, if desired.

The eggs have a range because it will alter how thick your soup is. If you want it thinner, use 3 eggs. If you want it thicker, use up to 6. Everything else in the recipe remains the same.

It's up to you how lemony you want the soup. Start with the juice of 2 lemons for the egg mixture and then feel free to add up to 1 more in Step 4 after giving it a taste.

If you want more pasta, add up to 1 cup more rings in Step 2. But remember, the more pasta you add now, the more it will absorb the soup as it rests! To that point, if you want it to be more of a super saucy soup-like pasta, add the entire 1-pound box of pasta.

TO HALVE Simply halve the recipe. Cook times remain the same

SPICY DUMPLING SOUP

When I was walking around Italy after eating pasta and pizza for seven days straight, it was inevitable I'd also be on the hunt for Chinese restaurants. When I came across them, I noticed the restaurants advertised their dumplings as "Ravioli Cinesi." And it makes total sense, as an Asian-style dumpling is a filling wrapped by a dough, like ravioli. And although a dumpling isn't technically a pasta, I deem this recipe entirely appropriate for this book given its relationship to Italian ravioli. Besides, this is one of my most popular soups from my blog—bar none. Many who've made it said it has joined the ranks of their all-time favorite recipes. It's very spicy as written (like, enough to clear the sinuses), but I've got you covered on how to tone it down or keep it totally mild, if that's your game.

  (if using non-meat dumplings and vegetable broth)

½ cup chili oil (see Jeff's Tips), divided

10 ounces sliced shiitake mushrooms (you can also use up to 1 pound sliced white or baby bella mushrooms; or see Jeff's Tips if you don't do mushrooms)

1 tablespoon minced or crushed fresh ginger (I use squeeze ginger)

¼ cup rice vinegar

7 cups chicken, beef, or vegetable broth

¼ cup low-sodium soy sauce, tamari, or coconut aminos

1 teaspoon white pepper (optional)

1 (16-ounce) can bamboo shoots, drained (optional)

8 ounces spinach

3 tablespoons cornstarch + 3 tablespoons cold water (see Jeff's Tips)

1½ pounds frozen dumplings, wontons, or potstickers with filling of your choice (you can find these in the frozen section at most markets, Asian markets, and Costco—any size will do), see Jeff's Tips

⅓ cup chili-garlic sauce or sriracha (both are usually in the same section of your market)

2 tablespoons sesame oil

2 tablespoons hoisin sauce

1 bunch scallions, sliced, some reserved for garnish

2 tablespoons sesame seeds (optional, I use half black and half white for color)

Prep Time: 15 min • Cook Time: 25 min (includes cooking frozen dumplings or wontons in the soup) • Total Time: 40 min • Serves: 4–6

1. Heat ¼ cup of the chili oil in an 8-quart nonstick soup pot over medium-high heat. Add the mushrooms and ginger and sauté for 3 minutes, until the mushrooms are nice and colorful.

2. Add the rice vinegar and deglaze (scrape) the bottom of any browned bits, about 1 minute.

3. Add the broth, soy sauce, white pepper (if using), bamboo shoots (if using), and spinach and stir. Once bubbling, cover the pot with a lid, reduce the heat to medium, and simmer for 5 minutes.

Recipe Continues

4. Meanwhile, make a slurry by mixing together the cornstarch and water in a bowl. Set aside.

5. Remove the lid from the pot and add the frozen dumplings or wontons. Simmer for 5 minutes or so, until cooked.

6. Stir in the cornstarch slurry and the soup will thicken up perfectly. Reduce the heat to low.

7. Add the remaining ¼ cup chili oil, the chili-garlic sauce or sriracha, sesame oil, hoisin sauce, scallions, and sesame seeds (if using) and stir, then gently simmer for 5 minutes more.

8. Turn the heat off. Ladle the soup and desired amount of dumplings into bowls and top with reserved scallions and sesame seeds, if desired.

 Simply halve the recipe. Cook times remain the same.

This recipe, as written, is going to give you a 4 out of 5 in terms of spice factor (aka VERY SPICY). It is a pretty serious soup and the perfect remedy to a cold night or spicy craving! But since that's not everyone's bag, I'm providing some options to make this friendly for all:

MILD: If you *don't* want this soup spicy at all, leave out the chili oil, white pepper, and chili-garlic sauce (or sriracha). Simply use 4 tablespoons (¼ cup) sesame oil in Step 1 to sauté the mushrooms. (And still use 2 tablespoons sesame oil in Step 7, and omit the chili oil there.)

MEDIUM-SPICY: If you still want the soup spicy but prefer it *less* spicy, reduce the chili oil and chili-garlic sauce (or sriracha). Follow Steps 1 through 3 as is but taste the soup after adding the slurry in Step 6. If you feel you want more spice but not super intense, start with an additional 1 tablespoon chili oil and 1 tablespoon chili-garlic sauce (or sriracha). From there, continue to add more of each spice by the tablespoon.

If you don't want mushrooms, just leave them out. Skip Step 1's sautéing and start by setting the pot over high heat and combining Steps 2 and 3. You'll also add the first ¼ cup of chili oil, the ginger, and the rice vinegar here. (And if you don't want it spicy at all, omit the chili oil, white pepper, and chili-garlic sauce or sriracha altogether).

The 3:3 cornstarch slurry makes for a nice, thick soup. But should you wish it to be thinner, you can start with 1:1 or 2:2 of the slurry instead.

Want to be unconventional and make this soup extra wild? Use a mini ravioli or tortellini of your choice in place of the dumplings (I'd suggest a meat-based one). Same 5-minute cook time in Step 5.

The longer the dumplings sit in the soup, the more they'll absorb the broth. This won't be an issue if serving the full pot at once. But if you plan on having leftovers, you can always add 1–2 cups more broth when reheating as well as additional chili oil and/or chili-garlic sauce to compensate for the additional liquid. You can also add the exact amount of dumplings you wish to eat right away and have them bubble after adding the slurry in Step 6 for about 5 minutes until they're cooked. From there, store the remaining dumpling-free soup for leftovers with no worries about absorption!

PASTA E FAGIOLI

 (if not using pancetta)

2 tablespoons extra-virgin olive oil

8 ounces pancetta or thick-cut bacon, diced (optional, **see Jeff's Tips**)

1 medium yellow onion, diced

½ cup sherry or dry white wine (like a sauvignon blanc; optional, **see Jeff's Tips**)

4 cups chicken, ham, or garlic broth (e.g., made from Better Than Bouillon Ham or Roasted Garlic Base)

1 (15-ounce) can tomato sauce (not the same as jarred pasta sauce)

2 (14.5-ounce) cans stewed tomatoes, drained

2 (15.5-ounce) cans cannellini beans, one can drained

2 (15.5-ounce) cans red kidney beans, one can drained

1½ cups mini farfalle or farfalline

1 cup grated Parmesan cheese, plus more for serving

1–2 teaspoons liquid smoke (optional)

In case you've never had it before, pasta e fagioli (often pronounced "fah-ZOOL" or "fah-JOOL") is a soup that features a small pasta in a rich and, in my case, optionally hammy tomato-based broth loaded with beans. It's so *soooo* good. The pasta most commonly used is little tubes such as ditalini or tubettini, but I'm going for a mini farfalle, also known as farfalline. Whichever pasta you choose, this version is as simple as it gets with one pot to get it all done.

Prep Time: 10 min • **Cook Time: 30 min (includes cooking mini farfalle/farfalline in the soup)** • **Total Time: 40 min** • **Serves: 4–6**

1. Heat the olive oil in an 8-quart nonstick soup pot over medium-high heat. Once shimmering, add the pancetta (if using) and sauté until it's just between being cooked and crisped, about 5 minutes. Remove the pancetta with a slotted spoon and place in a paper towel–lined bowl.

2. Add the onion to the pot and sauté in the existing oil for 5 minutes, until softened. Add the sherry and deglaze (scrape) the bottom of the pot.

3. Add the broth, tomato sauce, stewed tomatoes, and 1 undrained can of each bean (*with* their juices) and stir. Once bubbling, reduce the heat to medium, cover the pot with a lid, and simmer for 5 minutes.

Recipe Continues

4. Remove the lid. Take an immersion blender (mind the cord hitting the hot stove) and blend directly in the pot until pureed. (**NOTE:** You can also blend the soup in a blender in batches, but that's way messier and more time-consuming.)

5. Increase the heat to medium-high. Once bubbling, add the pasta along with the remaining 2 cans of (drained) beans and reduce the heat to medium. Using the package's suggested timing, cook the pasta until it's to your liking, stirring occasionally.

6. Once the pasta's cooked to your liking, reduce the heat to low. If using pancetta, return it to the pot, then add the Parmesan and stir until blended into the soup. Taste the soup and decide if you want to add the liquid smoke for a little extra smoky flavor (start with 1 teaspoon and work your way up). Let the soup rest for 5 minutes as the pasta continues to absorb and cook into the soup, giving itself more of a presence.

7. Turn the heat off. Ladle the soup into bowls and top with additional Parmesan, if desired.

JEFF'S TIPS

If not using the pancetta or bacon, start with Step 2 with the olive oil in the pot over medium-high heat. Once shimmering, add the onion and follow the rest of the recipe as written.

If not using the sherry, simply add ½ cup more broth in Step 2 when deglazing the pot.

The more the pasta sits in the soup, the more it will absorb the broth around it, eventually turning the soup into a soupy-sauced pasta dish (which can also be quite amazing, to be honest). Therefore, if you plan on having leftovers, cook the pasta separately according to the package instructions and only add it when serving.

TO HALVE Simply halve the recipe. Cook times remain the same.

10

PASTA SALADS

As a cool-down chapter, it only made sense to bring down the curtain with some mind-blowingly fantastic pasta salads, loaded with color and culture.

Unlike the previous chapters featuring hot pastas, here we actually *want* to rinse our cooked pasta under cold water to cool it down before adding all the goodies.

These chilled delights carry their own personalities and are all perfect to make ahead of time for family dinners, picnics, barbecues, or any gathering when you want to impress.

Ⓓⓕ **Dairy-Free**

Ⓥ **Vegetarian**

Ⓥⓝ **Vegan**

+ **Compliant with Modifications**

JEFFREY'S RIDICULOUS MACARONI SALAD

THE PASTA

1 tablespoon salt

1 pound elbow or large elbow macaroni

THE DRESSING

2 cups mayonnaise (see Jeff's Tips)

1 cup sour cream

1 cup Thousand Island or ranch salad dressing (use whichever you like more, or ½ cup of each)

1½ tablespoons white vinegar, red wine vinegar, or apple cider vinegar

1 tablespoon Worcestershire sauce

1 tablespoon Dijon mustard, plus more to taste (optional)

1 teaspoon garlic or celery salt

1 teaspoon black pepper

1 teaspoon white sugar

OPTIONAL MIX-INS

1 (16-ounce) jar bread-and-butter or dill pickles (I like using Vlasic stacks for easy slicing), drained and diced

1 (10-ounce) jar sweet relish

½–1 cup pitted black olives, drained and diced

2–3 scallions, chopped

1 small red bell pepper, seeded and diced

1 cup shredded carrots (I save time and use pre-shredded from a bag)

2–3 ribs celery, diced

8 ounces Colby Jack (or any) cheese, diced

½ pound ham (any kind), sliced ½ inch thick by the deli, diced

What can be said about a macaroni salad? For me, it's the star of the show at any grilling gathering—and my version is a party so ridiculously loaded with goodies, it looks like edible confetti. The genius thing is that the mix-ins are all customizable so you are in full control of what goes into (and what stays out of) your macaroni salad. The dressing for my over-the-top version also provides you with the most important aspect: making sure it's not too vinegar-heavy and has no bitter aftertaste!

Prep Time: 10–20 min • Pasta Cook Time (elbow or large elbow macaroni): 6–8 min • Total Time: 20–35 min • Serves: 4–6

1. Boil the Water and Cook the Pasta: Fill an 8-quart pot halfway with tap water and bring to a rolling boil over high heat. Add the salt and reduce the heat to medium. Add the pasta and stir. Set a timer to cook until al dente (per the package instructions), or to the shortest amount of time given. When done, drain the pasta in a colander in the sink and **run cold water over it for 2–3 minutes**, shaking it around until it's no longer hot at all (not even warm). It should be cool to the touch. (**NOTE:** To make sure the pasta doesn't dry out or stick, rinse and shake it around every so often while you finish the recipe.)

2. Make the Dressing: As the pasta continues to rest and cool, combine all the dressing ingredients in a generously large bowl and stir until combined. (**NOTE:** You can do this while the pasta's cooking as well.)

3. Assemble the Pasta Salad: Add the drained and cooled pasta to the bowl with the dressing and your choice of mix-ins.

4. Toss to coat the pasta with everything until well combined. Serve immediately, or cover with a lid or plastic wrap and chill in the fridge for 2–3 hours. It will keep well in the fridge for up to 5–7 days.

 JEFF'S TIPS There are interesting flavors of mayo available these days—feel free to use one of those varieties instead of plain.

If, after chilling, you find you want more dressing because some may have gotten absorbed by the pasta, simply add more mayo, sour cream, and/or dressing and mix into the macaroni salad until it's the desired consistency.

TO HALVE Simply halve all the ingredients. However, the salted pasta water amount remains the same. The pasta cook time and assembly also remain the same.

SESAME PEANUT NOODLES

THE PASTA

1 tablespoon salt

1 pound linguine fini or thin linguine

THE DRESSING

½ cup peanut butter (smooth or chunky)

½ cup chicken or garlic broth, at room temperature (see Jeff's Tip)

½ cup sesame oil

¼ cup low-sodium soy sauce, tamari, or coconut aminos

2 tablespoons hoisin sauce

2 tablespoons honey

1 tablespoon minced or grated fresh ginger (I use squeeze ginger)

½–1 cup roasted peanuts, crushed

1 bunch scallions, sliced

2 tablespoons sesame seeds (I use a mix of white and black)

If I'm at the market's deli counter for a pasta salad to satisfy all my sweet and savory cravings, it's usually sesame peanut noodles that I reach for. Sitting on the couch, watching reruns of *Mama's Family*, slurping 'em up. Well, even better than the deli, my sesame noodles are so good and peanut buttery that they can be considered a dessert! I prefer linguine over rice noodles here because they're more supple and pasta salad–friendly and work much better when refrigerated.

Prep Time: 15 min • **Pasta Cook Time (linguine fini or thin linguine): 6–8 min** • **Total Time: 25 min** • **Serves: 4–6**

1. Boil the Water and Cook the Pasta: Fill an 8-quart pot halfway with tap water and bring to a rolling boil over high heat. Add the salt and reduce the heat to medium. Add the pasta and stir. Set a timer to cook until al dente (per the package instructions), or to the shortest amount of time given. When done, drain the pasta in a colander in the sink and **run cold water over it for 2–3 minutes**, shaking it around until it's no longer hot at all (not even warm). It should be cool to the touch. (**NOTE:** To make sure the pasta doesn't dry out or stick, rinse and shake it around every so often while you finish the recipe.)

2. Make the Dressing: As the pasta continues to rest and cool, microwave the peanut butter in a small microwave-safe bowl for 30 seconds, until it almost becomes liquid. Transfer to a generously large mixing or serving bowl, add all the remaining dressing ingredients, and stir until combined. (**NOTE:** You can do this while the pasta's cooking as well.)

JEFF'S TIP If you want a thicker sauce, leave out the broth when making the dressing in Step 2.

TO HALVE Simply halve all the ingredients. However, the salted pasta water amount remains the same. The pasta cook time and assembly also remain the same.

3. Assemble the Pasta Salad: Add the drained and cooled pasta to the bowl with the dressing.

4. Toss to coat the pasta with everything until well combined. Serve immediately or cover with a lid or plastic wrap and chill in the fridge for 2–3 hours. It will keep well in the fridge for up to 5–7 days.

PICKLEBALL PASTA SALAD

THE PASTA

1 tablespoon salt

1 pound racchette

THE DRESSING

2 cups (1–2 bunches depending on their size) packed fresh basil leaves, stemmed, plus more for garnish

1 cup extra-virgin olive oil

1 cup grated Parmesan cheese, plus more for serving

4 cloves garlic, roughly chopped

½ cup of one of the following: pine nuts, raw sunflower seeds, raw almonds, raw cashews

1 cup diced dill pickles plus ½ cup of their juice from the jar (I prefer the refrigerated Claussen brand), plus more for tossing into the finished pasta salad, if desired (see Jeff's Tips)

THE SALAD

10 ounces frozen peas, thawed (do this quickly by placing in a colander and running hot water over for 45 seconds)

1 pound mini (pearl) mozzarella balls (also known as ciliegini in the cheese section)

Okay, I know some of you came to this recipe because you're genuinely curious about the idea, while others came here to see what I was smoking and to make fun of it. The inspiration behind this pasta salad comes from finding an adorable pasta called racchette, which are shaped like tennis racquets. When I saw them at the market, I immediately grabbed a box because the idea of a tennis-inspired pasta was too good to pass up. Or, in this case, pickleball. That's right. This is a pesto-inspired sauce where we add a handful of pickles and their juice to make the flavor something super curious, crisp, cool, and completely delicious. Then, we toss in some peas and mozzarella pearls that not only counter the dish with sweetness and creaminess, but "serve" as the balls to those racquets. If it doesn't sound like your game, that's cool. There are a ton of other options in the book for you to ace. But if you're willing to give it a go, you may have just won your match point.

Prep Time: 10 min • Pasta Cook Time (racchette): 9 min • Total Time: 25 min • Serves: 4–6

1. Boil the Water and Cook the Pasta: Fill an 8-quart pot halfway with tap water and bring to a rolling boil over high heat. Add the salt and reduce the heat to medium. Add the pasta and stir. Set a timer to cook until al dente (per the package instructions), or to the shortest amount of time given. When done, drain the pasta in a colander in the sink and **run cold water over it for 2–3 minutes**, shaking it around until it's no longer hot at all (not even warm). It should be cool to the touch. (**NOTE:** To make sure the pasta doesn't dry out or stick, rinse and shake it around every so often while you finish the recipe.)

2. Make the Dressing: As the pasta continues to rest and cool, pulse the basil, olive oil, Parmesan, garlic, nuts, and pickles and pickle juice in a food processor or blender until pureed. (**NOTE:** You can do this while the pasta's cooking as well.)

3. Assemble the Pasta Salad:
Transfer the drained and cooled pasta to a generously large bowl and add the peas, mozzarella balls, pickle pesto sauce, and additional diced pickles (if desired).

4. Toss to coat the pasta with everything until well combined. Serve in your court immediately or cover with a lid or plastic wrap and chill in the fridge for 2–3 hours. It will keep well in the fridge for up to 5–7 days.

JEFF'S TIPS

If you want to experiment a bit more with the flavor and make it a pickleball party, try using a different variety of pickle such as bread-and-butter pickles, spicy pickles, full sour kosher pickles, sweet baby gherkins, or cornichons. You can also add more to taste when blending in Step 2.

For an extra touch, feel free to add a few tablespoons (to taste) of sweet relish in Step 4 once tossing everything together.

TO HALVE Simply halve all the ingredients. However, the salted pasta water amount remains the same. The pasta cook time and assembly also remain the same.

LA SCALA PASTA SALAD

THE PASTA
1 tablespoon salt

1 pound ditalini

THE SALAD
1 medium red onion, diced

1 (16-ounce) jar sliced banana peppers (or whole pepperoncini), drained

1 (16-ounce) jar roasted red peppers, drained and diced

2 (15.5-ounce) cans chickpeas (garbanzo beans), drained

1 pound provolone cheese, diced

8–12 ounces dry salami, soppressata, and/or pepperoni, sliced thin and diced

2 cups creamy Italian salad dressing (see Jeff's Tips)

Picture the best of an Italian hero: salami, pepperoni, red onion, banana peppers, and roasted red peppers. Oh yeah—add creamy Italian dressing, of course. Now picture it as the ultimate pasta salad and it will be one you can't refuse. This salad was inspired by my Godfather Pasta (which is served hot and cheesy in the yellow *Simple Comforts* Instant Pot cookbook) as well as the famed Joe Allen La Scala salad in NYC (also known as "the meat salad," as my friend Alex would say). It's truly a loaded charcuterie board in pasta salad form.

Prep Time: 15 min • **Pasta Cook Time (ditalini): 8-10 min** • **Total Time: 30 min** • **Serves: 4-6**

1. Boil the Water and Cook the Pasta: Fill an 8-quart pot halfway with tap water and bring to a rolling boil over high heat. Add the salt and reduce the heat to medium. Add the pasta and stir. Set a timer to cook until al dente (per the package instructions), or to the shortest amount of time given. When done, drain the pasta in a colander in the sink and **run cold water over it for 2–3 minutes**, shaking it around until it's no longer hot at all (not even warm). It should be cool to the touch. (**NOTE:** To make sure the pasta doesn't dry out or stick, rinse and shake it around every so often while you finish the recipe.)

2. Assemble the Pasta Salad: Transfer the drained and cooled pasta to a generously large bowl.

3. Add all the remaining ingredients on top of the pasta, with the Italian dressing being the last thing you pour on top.

4. Toss to coat the pasta with everything until well combined. Serve immediately or cover with a lid or plastic wrap and chill in the for fridge 2–3 hours. It will keep well in the fridge for up to 5–7 days.

JEFF'S TIPS

If there's any ingredient I call for that isn't your style, simply leave it out. And if there's one you don't see that you'd enjoy, add it. And if you want even more of one ingredient, simply add more!

I actually love using either Olive Garden's Signature Italian Dressing or any other store-bought creamy Italian for this to save time. But if you want to go all out and make your own amazingly creamy Italian dressing, who am I to not help you out? Add all of the following ingredients to a large bottle, jar, or salad dressing shaker. Stir with a spoon to get a mixture going, then cover with a lid and shake until combined. This will be the right amount for the pasta salad:

1 cup mayonnaise

¾ cup extra-virgin olive oil

½ cup white wine vinegar or rice vinegar

Juice of ½ lemon

2 tablespoons Dijon mustard

6 cloves garlic, minced or pressed (2 tablespoons)

1½ teaspoons Italian seasoning

1½ teaspoons white sugar

1 teaspoon dried basil

1 teaspoon dried thyme

½ cup grated Parmesan or Pecorino Romano cheese

TO HALVE Simply halve all the ingredients. However, the salted pasta water amount remains the same. The pasta cook time and assembly also remain the same.

PERUVIAN-STYLE CHICKEN PASTA SALAD

 (if you don't add chicken)

THE PASTA

1 tablespoon salt

1 pound tri-color rotini

THE DRESSING

1 cup mayonnaise (see Jeff's Tips)

½ cup crumbled cotija or grated Parmesan cheese

¼ cup extra-virgin olive oil

2 bunches fresh cilantro, stemmed

3 cloves garlic, minced or pressed

Juice of 1 lime

2 jalapeño peppers, roughly chopped (optional, and see Jeff's Tips)

2 teaspoons white vinegar

1–2 pounds rotisserie chicken meat

Queens, New York, is basically the melting pot food capital of the United States. People from all over the world live there, making for rich and varied cuisines that put a trip to Epcot to shame. I first discovered aji, an often green cilantro- and mayo–based Peruvian sauce commonly served with rotisserie chicken, at a place across from my first apartment. Once I took my own shot at making aji, it dawned on me how well it would work as a pasta salad dressing. To make things even easier and more economical, we're tossing rotisserie chicken meat in at the end. For the cilantro-sensitive, see Jeff's Tips on how to give it the Argentinean chimichurri treatment!

Prep Time: 15 min • Pasta Cook Time (tri-color rotini): 7–10 min • Total Time: 30 min • Serves: 4–6

1. Boil the Water and Cook the Pasta: Fill an 8-quart pot halfway with tap water and bring to a rolling boil over high heat. Add the salt and reduce the heat to medium. Add the pasta and stir. Set a timer to cook until al dente (per the package instructions), or to the shortest amount of time given. When done, drain the pasta in a colander in the sink and **run cold water over it for 2–3 minutes**, shaking it around until it's no longer hot at all (not even warm). It should be cool to the touch. (**NOTE:** To make sure the pasta doesn't dry out or stick, rinse and shake it around every so often while you finish the recipe.)

2. Make the Dressing: As the pasta continues to rest and cool, pulse all the dressing ingredients (but not the chicken) in a food processor or blender until pureed. (**NOTE:** You can do this while the pasta's cooking as well.)

3. Assemble the Pasta Salad:
Transfer the drained and cooled pasta to a generously large bowl.

4. Top the pasta with the chicken, followed by the dressing.

5. Toss to coat until everything is well combined. Serve immediately or cover with a lid or plastic wrap and chill in the fridge 2–3 hours. It will keep well in the fridge for up to 5–7 days.

JEFF'S TIPS

If you want it super saucy, double all of the dressing ingredients.

If you're not into mayonnaise, use sour cream instead.

If you're using jalapeños, removing their seeds and ribs will keep them on the milder side. But if you keep them intact before blending, it will definitely conjure a spicier finish. You can also keep the seeds and ribs from just one pepper or just use one pepper without the seeds. Your call!

If you're not into cilantro and think it tastes/smells like soap for whatever reason, you can sub with 1 bunch of fresh parsley leaves. The flavor profile will be totally different from aji, but it'll still work! In fact, this will make the dressing reminiscent of a creamy-style Argentinean chimichurri.

TO HALVE Simply halve all the ingredients. However, the salted pasta water amount remains the same. The pasta cook time and assembly also remain the same.

SANTORINI SALAD

THE PASTA
1 tablespoon salt

1 pound orzo

THE SALAD
1 (10- to 14-ounce) jar sun-dried tomatoes, roughly chopped

1 medium red onion, diced

1 medium cucumber, diced

1 small red bell pepper, seeded and diced

1 (15-ounce) can chickpeas (garbanzo beans), drained and rinsed

½–1 cup kalamata olives, pitted and diced (if you want more, add more)

1½ cups crumbled feta cheese

2 cups Greek salad dressing (see Jeff's Tip)

I think that if there's a pasta salad out there that will transport you to the Mediterranean without having to actually go there, it's this one. Inspired by a classic Greek salad and aptly named after Greece's too-beautiful-for-words Santorini, this cool and crisp pasta salad brings you the bold and refreshing flavors of that gorgeous island with every forkful.

Prep Time: 15 min • Pasta Cook Time (orzo): 9 min • Total Time: 30 min • Serves: 4–6

1. Boil the Water and Cook the Pasta: Fill an 8-quart pot halfway with tap water and bring to a rolling boil over high heat. Add the salt and reduce the heat to medium. Add the pasta and stir. Set a timer to cook until al dente (per the package instructions), or to the shortest amount of time given. When done, drain the pasta in a fine-mesh strainer in the sink and **run cold water over it for 2–3 minutes**, shaking it around until it's no longer hot at all (not even warm). It should be cool to the touch. (**NOTE:** To make sure the pasta doesn't dry out or stick, rinse and shake it around every so often while you finish the recipe.)

2. Assemble the Pasta Salad: Transfer the drained and cooled pasta to a generously large bowl.

TO HALVE Simply halve all the ingredients. However, the salted pasta water amount remains the same. The pasta cook time and assembly also remain the same.

3. Add all the remaining ingredients on top of the pasta, with the Greek dressing being the last thing you pour on top.

4. Toss to coat the pasta with everything until well combined. Serve now or cover with a lid or plastic wrap and chill in the fridge for 2–3 hours. It will keep well in the fridge for up to 5–7 days.

JEFF'S TIP

I use Ken's Steakhouse Greek Dressing in a pinch, but if you don't mind a few more ingredients and moments of your time, here's a way to make your own amazingness. Simply combine the following in a bowl and whisk together or store in a salad dressing shaker:

1 cup extra-virgin olive oil
½ cup red wine vinegar
3 cloves garlic, minced or pressed
1 tablespoon lemon juice
2 teaspoons dried oregano
2 teaspoons salt
1 teaspoon Dijon mustard (optional)
1 teaspoon black pepper

CAPRESE PASTA SALAD

V (if using cheese tortellini)

THE PASTA

1 tablespoon salt

24–30 ounces tortellini of your choice

THE SALAD

20 ounces (about 2 pints) cherry tomatoes (I like using a multi-colored variety), halved

1 pound mini (pearl) mozzarella balls (also known as "ciliegini" in the cheese section)

2 bunches fresh basil, stemmed and chopped, some reserved for garnish

¼ cup balsamic vinegar

¼ cup balsamic glaze, plus more for serving

1 cup extra-virgin olive oil

Salt, to taste

Freshly ground black pepper, to taste

If there's anything my other half, Richard, loves, it's a caprese salad. And I know he's not the only one. It's quite simple, really: a bed of juicy tomatoes topped with sliced fresh mozzarella and basil and then drizzled with olive oil and balsamic vinegar and topped with a few grinds of salt and pepper. But make no mistake, these flavors are complex. And they've now found new life in a pasta salad. I like using a heartier, cheese-stuffed tortellini or mini ravioli for this dish, but you can just as well use any short-form pasta you choose from the Pasta Glossary (page 31).

Prep Time: 15 min • Pasta Cook Time (tortellini): 2–4 min • Total Time: 25 min • Serves: 4–6

1. Boil the Water and Cook the Pasta: Fill an 8-quart pot halfway with tap water and bring to a rolling boil over high heat. Add the salt and reduce the heat to medium. Add the pasta and stir. Set a timer to cook until al dente (per the package instructions), or to the shortest amount of time given. When done, drain the pasta in a colander in the sink and **run cold water over it for 2–3 minutes**, shaking it around until it's no longer hot at all (not even warm). It should be cool to the touch. (**NOTE:** To make sure the pasta doesn't dry out or stick, rinse and shake it around every so often while you finish the recipe.)

2. Assemble the Pasta Salad: Transfer the drained and cooled pasta to a generously large bowl.

JEFF'S TIP

I know that the whole "to taste" thing can be a burden to some because they like to know exactly how much of something to put into a dish (and I get it because I'm usually like that too). As a result, you don't see that too often in this book. But for this recipe, it's truly best to add S&P to taste. A good general rule regarding Step 5 is to start out with ½ teaspoon each salt and pepper, then work your way up from there, in ½-teaspoon increments, until it's perfect for you.

TO HALVE Simply halve all the ingredients. However, the salted pasta water amount remains the same. The pasta cook time and assembly also remain the same.

3. Add the tomatoes, mozzarella, basil, balsamic vinegar, and balsamic glaze on top of the pasta. Pour the olive oil over it all.

4. Gently toss to coat the pasta with everything until well combined.

5. Taste and season with salt and pepper until you're happy (**see Jeff's Tip**). Serve immediately or cover with a lid or plastic wrap and chill in the fridge for 2–3 hours. It will keep well in the fridge for up to 5–7 days.

Acknowledgments

Seeing your words go from a chaotic document to a stunning book is surreal. And doing it alone is impastable. Here's a few people who made it all pastable.

Richard: Quite simply put, you are one of the brightest lights in my life. You are a constant source of intellectual conversation and my most trusted confidant; you make me laugh and smile on the daily and constantly talk me off ledges; and you aren't afraid to get your hands dirty when I am. I couldn't possibly love you more and I am thankful for you every day.

Mom & Dad: No child could have asked for more supportive and loving parents. Dad, you are my most trusted advisor who has shown me a life of possibilities—especially when I didn't see it myself. Mom, you are as wonderful as you are loud. You have always been there for me and I will always be there for you and I always cherish our outings together. Although I may seem like a grouch at times, I am grateful to you both every day and love you very much.

Amanda, David, Levi, Stevie & Mack: Thank you for being the best sister, brother-in-law, nephews, and niece a brother and uncle could ask for. From our trips together (like eating ashy raclette in Amsterdam) to the chaos that is a family trip to Disney, I relish it all. And seeing as you're all pasta lovers, I hope this book helps you out at dinnertime. Love you all.

Aleksey: My FIVE-time collaborator and trusted photographer. By now, I don't need to tell you how integral you are to this process (no photos in a step-by-step cookbook doesn't make it very exciting), but I do feel it important to publicly state how proud you've made me with the strikingly beautiful photos you've captured (even if the massive softbox light deemed "Big Bertha" took over my living room). One person who does the work of a whole team, you are a wizard who requires no wand.

Andy: I'll admit, it was a bit nerve-wracking hiring a food stylist I had never worked with before for a four-week shoot, but boy am I glad I trusted my gut. You are a brilliant, creative genius. I am still in awe at how quickly you took the food I made (six or seven recipes a day) and styled each dish to make it look like a work of art on a plate, yet all of them still so varied and approachable to the reader's eye. Your super fun demeanor and can-do attitude light up the room and are exactly what everyone needs in their life. And I am appreciative of your taste-testing honesty! You're a gem.

Michael & Thea: Thank you for giving me a shot at writing a cookbook of a different color (literally). My mission has always been to help others put a quick, easy, and rockin' meal on the table and you're the reason this vision came to light. It's always a joy working with you.

Pat: In a way, you're like a human distillery as the book production process funnels through you from rough to smooth. From manuscript to copyedit to layout, you are the person I trust most when it comes to making sure the book becomes a clean, crisp, and stunningly colorful final product. Thank you for always being so on-point and never letting me fall in these five trips 'round the sun.

Anja, Deri & Suzanne: From Anja being the first to shape it, to Deri's sharp copyediting making me look like a pro (and correcting my brain farts), to Suzanne being the fine-tooth-comb proofreader, thank you all for your amazing and painstaking work in helping to shape my manuscript to be the best it can be.

Nyamekye: Thank you for overseeing the production run of show for the book's stages from photo processing to design layout and then making sure it prints beautifully.

Katherine, Lauren & Gia: Thanks for helping me spread the word to the world and getting people as excited about this book as I am.

Nicole: As being possibly one of your only clients who ever penned and published five books in five years, I am always appreciative of you for looking out for my best interests and for encouraging me to get another book made. I hope you feed your sweet little one a few things from it!

Laura: All hail the royal queen of design! What can I say other than you are the reason this book looks as fun, exciting, and accessible as it does. You are the best of the best, and I am so lucky to have had you work on all five of my "children" to date.

Banjo: Hey, Monkey! Thanks for keeping me sane and curling up against my feet as I write (even if you do whine and stomp your foot like a perpetual two-year-old every time I'm cooking in the kitchen). I ruv you to pieces.

To My Nearest & Dearest: Thank you for all your support, encouragement, and laughter. I know I'm an easy person to poke fun at and can sometimes be more exhausting than relaxing, but spending time with you inspires me in more ways than you may think and it also gives me a nice reprieve to just stop what I'm doing and enjoy life. And special thanks to Alex for being the Sarah to my Fanny.

To You, My Reader: Thank you for taking a chance on this new baby of mine and trusting me beyond the Instant Pot. I hope this book earns a place in your cookbook library and that you learn a thing or two about cooking pasta in the easiest, quickest, and most delicious way I know. I would be nothing without you and I will never forget it and am eternally thankful.

Index

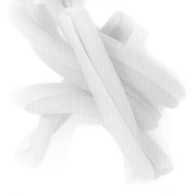

About the Author

JEFFREY EISNER is the #1 bestselling author of the Step-by-Step Instant Pot series of cookbooks. Featured on the Food Network, *Good Morning America*, and a frequent guest on Rachael Ray, he creates famously flavorful recipes in both the rural farmlands of northern New Jersey and in the bustling borough of Queens, New York. When not cooking, he enjoys traveling with his partner, Richard, and spoiling their dog, Banjo the Norwich terrier. He also loves pinball, Disney World, and theatre.

ISBN: 978-1523766826

Printed in the United States of America

The Day After th

End of the Worla

A tale of catastrophe and other g

Rebecca Long Howard